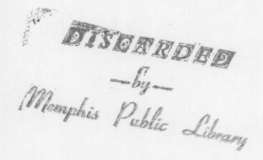

MOUNTAIN GEOGRAPHY

A Critique and Field Study

BY

RODERICK PEATTIE

PROFESSOR OF GEOGRAPHY, OHIO STATE UNIVERSITY

GREENWOOD PRESS, PUBLISHERS
NEW YORK

To

MARGARET RHODES PEATTIE

WHO SHARED WITH ME THE SACRIFICES NECESSARY TO CARRY
ON THE STUDY AS WELL AS THE PLEASURES
OF VOYAGING AND RESEARCH

PREFACE

A MAN may live a lifetime in a group of mountains and not complete the study of that single group. So much is there to know in geology, morphology, climate, plant ecology, and human responses and economies, that for one volume to treat of the geography of the mountains of the world may seem presumptuous. Also the writer's experience is, alas, more limited than he could wish. In America he has had experience or definite field work in the Laurentide and Nôtre Dame Mountains of Canada, and the Green and Taconic Mountains, the Blue Ridge, Ozarks, Rockies, and Sierra Nevadas of the United States. Most of his serious field study has been in Europe. There he has visited or studied the Sierra Nevada, the Sierra de Guadarrama, the Pyrenees, the French Alps in Provence, Dauphiné, and Savoy, and the Jura; in Switzerland the Valais, the Bernese Oberland, the St. Gotthard massif, Grisons, and Engadine; in Austria the Tirol, particularly the Stubaier Alps, the Salzburgkammer, the Tauren Alps, and the Karawankens of Carinthia; the Dalmatian Alps of Yugoslavia; the Trentino (Sud Tirol), the Apennines, and the Sicilian upland in Italy; the Bavarian Alps and the Black Forest. Many lesser ranges, as the Scottish Highlands, the Julian Alps, and the Albanian Mountains, he has seen sufficiently to judge their character.

This book is a personal field study and also a review of the present knowledge of mountains. The European studies in the field are many. Not only are mountains interesting to geographers because of the varied factors which present themselves within small areas, but love of mountains has called many scientists to highlands for vacation sojourns. With a few exceptions the European studies have a regional point of view. There is to date little in the way of a general critical summary.[1] The present is an attempt at this. The volume is, however, meant less for the use of Europeans than for that of Americans who have had little contact with the well populated mountains and who lack convenient access to much of the mountain literature.

The writer has spent time in the libraries of the Sorbonne,

---

[1] The recent study by Jules Blache, *L'homme et la montagne*, is a notable exception.

Heidelberg, and Munich. The University of Grenoble, where Raoul Blanchard maintains the Institut de Géographie Alpine, offered great assistance. A second institute of this type has recently been founded at the University of Innsbruck. The writer has had the advantage of reading and conferences at both these institutions. He has also visited the special library on mountain geography, the Bibliothèque Raymond at Bagnères-de-Bigorre. The library of the Geographical Society at Madrid gave access to the material on Spain. He had the advantage of conferences with courteous scientists at Montpellier, Zurich, and Florence. The assistance which was freely given to a stranger at each of these places has made possible this study and has demonstrated the universal brotherhood of men interested in science.

The writer would hesitate to weigh the mountain studies of others if he had not pursued at one time or another many of the type problems which have been investigated. He began his physiographic studies in mountains as a student with W. W. Atwood in the San Juan Range in 1911. His first climatic study of mountains was made under the late Robert DeCourcy Ward at Harvard University in 1916. In 1927–28 and 1931–32 he made a number of personal field studies in Sicily, Spain, France, Switzerland, and Austria. It is presumed that the reader is not without an appreciation of the theory of environmentalism and that certain technical aspects of the character of environmental conditions are understood. Where those technical aspects are peculiar to mountains, as in the case of temperature inversions and Foehn winds, they are explained herein. Moreover, not all technicalities of mountain environments are included. The physiography and climatology here discussed are geographical physiography and geographical climatology. In other words, only those facts from physical geography are selected which are pertinent to a knowledge of human relations.

This volume is also a bibliographical study. The bibliographies are inserted at the close of the several chapters, in order that they may be in intimate connection with the discussions which the references elaborate. Only occasionally is a title repeated, although some volumes are so comprehensive in scope as to deserve a place in several of the reference lists. Ordinarily the title is placed in the list which it serves best. Some titles of relatively slight consequence are included, usually in order to show authority for some item of the text. The references lists are *selected* study lists; selected for variety of points of view or of location. Not all books studied have been listed; not all books listed have been thoroughly studied. Generally I have indicated where the data are from my personal experience. The rest are gathered and coördinated from a wide field. Acknowledgments for every fact would be so numerous as to annoy the reader. Annotations in the bibliographical notes indicate the more important sources of data.

Lastly, acknowledgment should be made to my colleagues for helpful criticisms and to Ohio State University for financial assistance and leave of absence.

RODERICK PEATTIE

CONTENTS

ILLUSTRATIONS

MOUNTAIN GEOGRAPHY

INTRODUCTION

WHAT IS A MOUNTAIN?

A MOUNTAIN, strictly speaking, is a conspicuous elevation of small summit area. A plateau is a similar elevation of larger summit area with at least one sheer side. An essential and yet indefinite element in the definition of a mountain is the conspicuity. Conspicuity, like height, is a relative matter, and depends upon the personal evaluation or the standard by which it is measured. Many eminences but a few hundred feet high are termed mountains by dwellers on flat plains. One writer arbitrarily states that a mountain must be a quarter of a mile high. If this relief be measured from the surrounding country rather than from sea level, then certainly one would have a mountain. Seldom is relief as great as on the coast of Formosa, where there is a precipitous cliff of 4270 meters.[1] The Great Plains of the Western United States are a mile high. A slight eminence upon these plains would hardly be termed a mountain. Pikes Peak is, in truth, a mountain not because it rises more than 4270 meters but because its relief over the surrounding country is so great (2440 meters). Also it has steep sides. Its conspicuity is great. For days, in the era of traveling by ox cart, its white summit was a guide to the early settlers, who bore upon their covered wagons the slogan "Pike's Peak or Bust." It was a symbol, a goal, and it played a great part in the imagination of the plodding, hopeful travelers. Mountains should be impressive; they should enter into the imagination of the people who live within their shadows. Unfortunately it is next to impossible to include such intangibles in a definition. Mountains have bulk; mountains have also individuality.

The element of 'individuality' is not a far-fetched phrase. Fujiyama and Mount Etna are mountains of the same type, and yet they have individual characters. They are isolated volcanic cones, steep near the summit, with gentler curves in their lower reaches. Both are snow-capped. Both are majestic watchers of the human activity which mills about their bases like the con-

[1] For conversions to and from the metric system see Appendix A.

fusion of ant hills. Alike geologically and topographically they
have different psychological reactions in the minds of people who
daily regard them. Fuji is benign. Its serenity gives it a place in
Japanese philosophy. It is sacred and it is the most common
motive of Japanese art. Etna, if one is a dualist, is a devil rather
than a divinity. It is a force for evil, whose boiling arms of lava
reach out fiendishly towards the villages.

Attitudes Towards Mountains

To a large extent, then, a mountain is a mountain because of
the part it plays in popular imagination. It may be hardly more
than a hill; but if it has distinct individuality, or plays a more or
less symbolic rôle to the people, it is likely to be rated a mountain
by those who live about its base. In the days of the Greeks,
mountains such as Parnassus (2458 meters) and Olympus (2972
meters) were mysterious regions where dwelt the gods, and in
whose surrounding glens roamed satyrs and oreads. Possibly
because of their detached splendor, mountains were sacred in
early days, and the tradition is carried over into modern times.
Among the sacred mountains are Ararat in Armenia and Leb-
anon in Syria. China has at least five sacred peaks. One of
these, Omei, a peak in Szechuen, rising to a height of 3098
meters, has fifty-six pagodas and thirty-five monasteries and
temples for those faithful to Buddha. It was from a mountain
that Buddha ascended into heaven. It was on Mount Sinai that
Moses received the laws. David decided upon Mount Zion as
a site for his capital; Abraham took Isaac to a mountain in the
land of Moriah to sacrifice him to Jehovah; and throughout the
songs of the Israelites there runs a current of veneration for
mountains.

In the Middle Ages a certain dread of mountains was evident.
Dante makes mountains the guardians of the gates of Hell. The
Scandinavians peopled them with gnomes who were vassals of
the Ice Queen. On Walpurgis Night all the witches of the earth
and air danced in the Harz Mountains of Germany. In mountains were supposed to dwell those mystic folk, myrmidons,
pygmies, fingerlings, fairies, and specters. So great was the fear
inspired by mountains and wild gorges that in 1401, when Adam
of Usk went on a pilgrimage to Rome, he was carried blindfolded
over the St. Gotthard Pass in order that he might not rest his

eyes upon the fearfulness of the scene. Many an overlord passing through the mountains secured himself by a large military escort. Such was the fear inspired by the rugged heights that travelers wrote back in report upon the passage to say that they were safe in body and in soul.

In 1511, on the other hand, Luther on pilgrimage to Rome spoke of the pleasant life "of Switzerland," and said that the miles of that country were the "shortest miles." Yet Benvenuto Cellini looked in 1537 upon the Alps as full of dangers. In making the passage he was accompanied by a cavalcade and wore a shirt of mail. It was in the eighteenth century that the mountains came to be loved for themselves. A scientist and poet of Zurich, Albrecht von Haller, in 1732 wrote a long poem, *Die Alpen*, which did much to make known the beauty of the mountain regions. It is said to have been Swiss out-of-door literature that incited Rousseau passionately to preach his return to nature. Horace Bénédicte de Saussure, the first great Swiss Alpinist and an admirer of Rousseau, attempted the ascent of Mont Blanc four times between 1760 and 1787. This was a stupendous task in terms of the times. Saussure was so little acquainted with the problems of the first ascent that he took with him a sunshade and smelling salts. Veils were worn against snow-blindness. A Jacques Balmat was the first to reach the summit. For this feat he received the title 'Mont Blanc' from the king of Sardinia. Saussure in 1787 was the first to follow him.

It was then that the English discovered the Alps. They were the first tourists in numbers to visit the out-of-the-way valleys and climb the peaks. True, the Tillis in 1791, the Jungfrau in 1811, the Finsteraarhorn in 1812, and the Schreckhorn in 1842 were conquered by Swiss. That Hudson, Hadlow, and Lord Douglas lost their lives on Mont Cervin (Matterhorn) in 1865 was sufficient to challenge the English. From then on they literally flooded the remote valleys of Switzerland. The Swiss scientific interest gave way to the English sense of sport. The Alps became a subject for prose and poetry. One should not fail to mention the public imagination as reflected in two great poems. Schiller's poem, *Wilhelm Tell*, did for Central Switzerland what Byron's *Childe Harold* did for French Switzerland.

There are two attitudes which men today hold towards mountains. One is the attitude of the mountain climber and the other is that of the scientific man, whether he be geologist, geographer, or climatologist. Nor indeed are the two attitudes always distinct.

THE CULT OF MOUNTAINS

There has grown up among travelers and sportsmen a cult of mountains which is a modern and more conscious phase of the old worship of mountains. Particularly have the English, Germans, Austrians, Swiss, Italians, and French evidenced this. Each nation has its important Alpine club and journal. The journals, concerning themselves in part with the technique of mountain climbing and routes of ascent, also are devoted to praise of mountains. The best of the writings of Englishmen on mountains has been collected by Arnold Lunn in one volume, from which the following quotations are taken.

Shelley in his *History of a Six Weeks' Tour* expresses himself on Mont Blanc thus:

Mont Blanc was before us — the Alps, with their innumerable glaciers on high all around, closing in the complicated windings of the single vale — forests inexpressibly beautiful, but majestic in their beauty — intermingled beech and pine, and oak, overshadowed our road, or receded, whilst lawns of such verdure as I have never seen before occupied these openings, and gradually became darker in their recesses. Mont Blanc was before us, but it was covered with cloud; its base, furrowed with dreadful gaps, was seen above. Pinnacles of snow intolerably bright, part of the chain connected with Mont Blanc, shone through the clouds at intervals on high. I never knew — I never imagined what mountains were before.

Edward Whymper, famous among Alpinists, in his *Scrambles among the Alps in the Years 1860–1869*, describes the view from a lonely bivouac on the Matterhorn:

I returned to the view. The sun was setting, and its rosy rays, blending with the snowy blue, had thrown a pale, pure violet far as the eye could see; the valleys were drowned in purple gloom, whilst the summits shone with unnatural brightness; and as I sat in the door of the tent, and watched the twilight change to darkness, the earth seemed to become less earthy and almost sublime; the world seemed dead, and I, its sole inhabitant.

Douglas Freshfield, another famous Alpinist, in *The Italian Alps*, finds hardly sufficient adjectives to express the beauty about him.

The full midday glow of a July sun was falling from the dark va-
pourless vault overhead on to the topmost crags of Monte Rosa. A
delicate breeze, or rather air-ripple, lapping softly round the mountain-
crest, scarcely tempered the scorching force with which the rays fell
through the thin atmosphere. Round us on three sides the thousand-
crested Alps swept in a vast semicircle of snow and ice, clustering in
bright companies or ranging their snowy heads in sun-tipped lines
against the horizon.

F. W. Bourdillon in the *Alpine Journal* (vol. xxiv) speaks of the
love of mountains.

I suppose this ideal love of mountains — this love that we may almost
call a platonic love, since it seeks no selfish gain — really exists in most
or all of us; and is at the root of the instinct certainly of the climber, possibly even of the tourist. We have all of us had our 'moments,' either
on the mountains, or perhaps in some distant view of them, when life
and joy have assumed new meanings, and the world's horizons suddenly broken down and shown us realms of dream beyond and yet beyond. Sometimes it is on the top of some lonely peak, when the world
seems at our feet, and the blue dome of space an appreciable thing;
sometimes it is among the hush of snow-fields and glacier-walls, with
icy peaks above and moonlit mists below us; sometimes it is from some
lower height, where suddenly a panorama of silver tops breaks on us,
or we see the far-distant snow peaks mirrored in sunny lake waters.

Other than the visitor to mountains there is the dweller among
the peaks who, familiar with the masses about him to the point
of almost personal friendship, finds in the majesty of alpine pinnacles or the dearness of lesser hills, their ever-changing aspect in
light and shade, calm and storm.

Hardly less strong is the scientific interest in the multi-fold
phases of mountains and mountain life. A bibliography of the
scientific works on mountains would be overwhelming. The
store of knowledge which has resulted from the studies would
itself be of mountainous proportions. It is a brief of this many-
sided research that this book proposes to undertake. Incom-
plete as it must be, to be contained within the covers of a single
volume, it is hoped that it will yet present in résumé sufficient
material to enable the reader to understand the general factors
in the human geography of mountains.

BIBLIOGRAPHICAL NOTES

Human Attitudes Towards Mountains

Coolidge, W. A. B. *Alpine Studies*. London, 1912.
Coolidge, W. A. B. *The Alps in Nature and History*. New York, 1908.
De Beer, G. R. *Alps and Men*. London, 1932.
Engel, Claire E., and Vallot, Charles. *Les écrivains à la montagne: "Ces monts affreux" (1650–1810)*. Paris, 1934.
Fay, C. E. "The Mountain as an Influence in Modern Life," in *Appalachia*, xi (1905), pp. 27–40.
Godley, A. D. "Mountains and the Public," in *Alpine Journal*, xxxvii (1925), pp. 107–117.
Hamerton, P. G. *Landscape*. London, 1885.
Hedin, Sven. *Southern Tibet*. Stockholm, 1916–22. 9 vols. Vol. vii, pp. 9–10.
Hyde, W. W. "The Ancient Appreciation of Mountain Scenery," in *Classical Journal*, xi (1915–16), pp. 70–84.
Hyde, W. W. "The Development of the Appreciation of Mountain Scenery in Modern Times," in *Geographical Review*, iii (1917), pp. 107–118. These two articles by Hyde are very valuable.
Lunn, Arnold. *The Englishman in the Alps*, 2d ed. London, 1927. A delightful compendium of literary extracts.
Perry, T. S. "Mountains in Literature," in *Atlantic Monthly*, xliv (1879), pp. 302–311.
Reclus, Élisée. *The History of a Mountain*, tr. from the French by Bertha Ness and John Lillie. London, 1881. Chaps. xvii, xix, xx, xxi, xxii.
Stutfield, H. E. M. "Mountaineering as a Religion," in *The Alpine Journal*, xxxii (1918), pp. 241–247.
Tozer, H. F. *A History of Ancient Geography*. Cambridge, England, 1897. Chap. xv.
Van Dyke, J. C. *The Mountain*. New York, 1916.

CHAPTER I

MOUNTAIN TEMPERATURES

AIR PRESSURES

THE climate of any mountain region is, as with lowlands, primarily determined by latitude, prevailing winds, and continentality. But mountains have, as definite factors in their climates, the matters of altitude and exposure.

Altitude modifies:

> Air pressures.
> Air composition.
> Insolation.
> Air temperatures.
> Temperature ranges.
> Soil temperatures.
> Winds.
> Evaporation.
> Humidity.
> Clouds.
> Precipitation.
> Snow percentages.

Exposure, by its contrasts, exaggerates or modifies the quantity of the altitudinal modifications. These contrasts are:

> Sunny slopes and shady slopes.
> Wet slopes and dry slopes.
> Windy slopes and protected slopes.

How greatly these modifications are influential in the lives and economies of men it is hoped this volume will point out. Of necessity the following discussion treats the various factors and conditions separately. It is their interrelation, of course, that makes up the component whole. A warning is then made not to forget that it is the total character of the climate which is the significant concern. We are not here concerned to present a complete discussion of climatology. Only those aspects which are of human importance are discussed, and the treatment is thus truly geographic.

One introductory matter which must be thoroughly understood is the altitudinal decrease of pressure. If the pressure of the air at sea level at 20 degrees centigrade is normally 762 millimeters, the following decrease, other things being equal, will exist:

PRESSURE AND ALTITUDE

Altitude in meters	Mean pressure in millimeters	Change in altitude in meters for each mm. of pressure change
0	762	10.5
500	719	11.1
1000	678	11.8
1500	639	12.5
2000	601	13.4
2500	566	14.2
3000	532	15.1
3500	501	16.1
4000	470	17.2
5000	415	19.6
6000	364	22.5

Pressure in millimeters represents dead weight. Millibars represent energy. To convert the weight symbol to the energy symbol multiply by 1.35.

It will be seen that the rate of decrease of pressure with altitude is not regular. Following is a formula for computing the rate of decrease. If pressure at sea level is 1003 kilograms for one cubic centimeter, or 762 millimeters, the decrease with altitude is at first 1 millimeter for every ten meters, but at higher levels the rate of decrease is 1.9 millimeters. For further pressure reduction formulae, one should consult Knoch's edition of Hann. The above table is general, but serves the purpose of all save the most exacting. A rule of thumb is that one-tenth of 1 millimeter of pressure decrease approximates 10.5 meters of altitude change. One inch of pressure equals about 90 meters. This rule is not accurate above 900 meters or 3000 feet. Moreover, the pressure decrease varies with weather, latitude, and variation of vertical temperature gradients. Yet the decrease of pressure with altitude is the most regular of all mountain climatological phenomena.[1]

[1] A good aneroid barometer with a movable disc to indicate altitudes for climbers and surveyors is properly graduated to compensate for this differing rate of decrease. An altimeter is merely an aneroid barometer so equipped with a movable scale that as decrease of pressure is brought about by ascent the same needle indicates the increase in elevation. Interestingly enough, an early test of the barometer was accomplished by scaling a mountain. Blaise Pascal in 1648, five years after the invention of the barometer, persuaded his brother to climb Puy-de-Dôme in the Massif Central of France. Simultaneous observations were made at the base and the top of the mountain. The aneroid barometer was invented by Vidi in 1848.

Following are some mean pressures of high level stations.

PRESSURE FOR HIGH METEOROLOGICAL STATIONS AND
OBSERVATION POINTS

Station	Latitude	Height	Average pressure
Quito	0° 14′ S	2850 m.	547.5 mm.
Bogotá, Colombia	4° 35′ N	2660	558.4
Mexico	19° 26′	2278	586.3
Etna, Sicily	37° 44′	2950	534.4
Pic du Midi, France	42° 57′	2859	539.5
Mont Blanc, France	45° 50′	4359	447.0
Sonnblick, Switzerland	47° 3′	3105	519.7
Kloster Hanle, Tibet	22° 40′	4610	435.4

Decreasing pressures have significance in many aspects of climatology. They determine the inherent or dynamic heat of gases, they affect the dew point, and, of great human concern, they have distinct physiological effects upon the body. Appreciating, then, the decrease of air densities with altitude, we are prepared to take up the matter of insolation, that is, the action or effect of the sun's rays on a body exposed to them, and the consequent temperatures.

INSOLATION

There are three conditions affecting insolation received by mountains, which are purely results of local topographic modifications.[1]

Altitude.
Angle of exposed slope.
Position in the local relief.   (Figures 1 and 2.)

The percentage of insolation received by the earth increases with altitude. This has two causes.

One cause is the density of air. On lower levels smaller amounts of insolation are received because the subtraction of radiant energy by the absorbent air is great. At 2450 meters one is above one-fourth of the atmosphere by weight, and at 5800 meters above one-half the atmosphere by weight.

[1] Too late for incorporation in this work is the extremely interesting and thoroughly scientific discussion of insolation by Alice Garnett, "Insolation, Topography, and Settlement in the Alps," in *The Geographical Review*, xxv (1935), pp. 601–617. This is well worth the reader's attention. It represents an advance in the graphic representation of insolation data.

The lower layers of the atmosphere have high absorbent qualities, not only because of actual mass of material but also because of the quality of the material. Water vapor, carbon dioxide, and dust all absorb greater quantities of heat than other elements of the atmosphere. All are chiefly found near the earth. At 2450 meters one is above one-half the atmospheric moisture and more than one-half the suspended dust. The heavy carbon dioxide in calm air clings to the earth. Above 900 meters liquid and solid impurities have slight influence on the amount of insolation received. An exception is found in the humidity present during temperature inversions. This freedom of the atmosphere from impurities at high levels is indicated by the brilliancy of sunlight as well as the actual sighting of stars after sunrise. Thus Orion has been seen after sunrise from the Jungfraujoch in the Bernese Oberland of Switzerland, at an elevation of 3454 meters.

On clear days a rock surface at sea level receives 50 per cent of the possible insolation. At 1800 meters altitude some 75 per cent of the possible insolation reaches the rock.

PERCENTAGE OF INSOLATION RECEIVED AT CERTAIN ALTITUDES

Station	Altitude	Per cent of Insolation
Mont Blanc	4807 m.	94
Grands-Mulets	3050	80
Bossom glacier	1200	79
Grenoble	215	71

At Leh (3500 meters in the Himalayas) water was boiled by the sun when it was exposed in a blackened dish set in a transparent bottle. The difference between temperature in a black bulb thermometer in a vacuum and an ordinary thermometer increases with increasing altitude.

Not only is there more insolation at high levels but also a different quality. The ultra-violet rays are there more active and the chemical action of sunlight increases with altitude. The difference between the normal air temperature and the actinic temperatures accounts for the high sensible temperatures of high altitude. In formula, the sensible temperature equals 12 xl, where l equals the sun's rays in gram-calories per cubic centimeter per minute. The multiplier may be increased to 20 when the snow serves as a reflector. At Davos l has equaled 1.46 gram-calories.

$$12 \ (1.46) = 17.5 \text{ degrees Centigrade.}$$
$$20 \ (1.46) = 29.2 \text{ degrees Centigrade.}$$

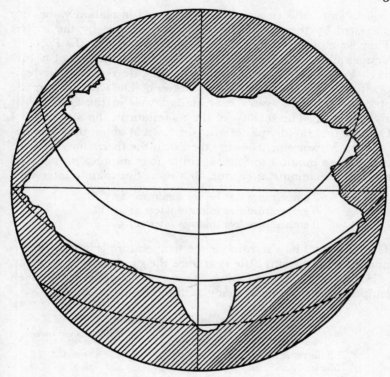

FIG. 1. SUNLIGHT CIRCLE

The point of observation is the center of the circle. The top and bottom arcs represent, each, the summer and winter solstice. The middle arc is the path of the sun at the equinoxes. The shaded portion is the horizon of surrounding mountains as seen from the point of observation, which in this case is a station in the valley of the Vénéon, French Alps. (*After Allix.*)

Comfort has been found above a snow cover at Davos when air temperatures were as low as −10 degrees. As if by way of compensation, high valleys suffer less from low air temperatures because of high insolation values. The high insolation means that where direct sunshine is found there are high soil temperatures and high plant temperatures. Therefore an increase of altitude is not exactly coincident with a decrease in economic possibilities. Plant zones are higher on mountain slopes than would be imagined from considering air temperatures. Heat in high altitudes is a response to insolation rather than to air temperature.

Relations between air temperatures and insolation values are suggested by the following measurements made by the writer. They were observed in a cirque (2250 meters) near the Porte de Vennasque, Central Pyrenees, at ten in the morning of a July day. Whereas the actinometer read 46.5 degrees, the air temperature in the shade was but 13 degrees. The writer also made observations of the sun's heat at Langweis in the Grisons [1] at 1383 meters. The shadow of the mountain in the afternoon of October first rapidly passes over the town at about nine minutes to four. Measurements were taken with the thermometer in the sun at nine minutes to four, again at four minutes to four and lastly at one minute after four, that is, at five minute intervals.

Temperature just before sundown: 27.5° C.
Temperature five minutes later: 21.25° C.
Temperature five minutes later: 17.5° C.

This illustrates how in rare air the temperature is largely insolation. The air retains little heat once the sun is down.

Hann (ed. by Knoch) shows the increasing difference between temperatures in sun and shade with increasing altitude.

TEMPERATURES IN SUN AND SHADE

Place	Elevation	Difference of temperatures in sun and shade
Riffelberg	2570 m.	21.0° C.
Hörnle	2890 m.	28.0°
Gornergrat	3140 m.	32.8°

AIR TEMPERATURES AND ALTITUDE

Generally speaking, air temperatures decrease with altitude. Exceptions to this generality exist and will be discussed later. The rate of decrease depends upon the composition of the air, the degree and character of the slope, the direction of the exposure, the mass of the elevation, the vegetal covering, and the existing wind currents. The fundamental reasons for decrease are:

Increasing rarity of air with increased altitude signifies actually less molecular material to receive and hold the heat. The table showing air pressures is a measure of this rarity.

[1] Grisons is the French and English, Graubünden the German name of the largest and easternmost canton of Switzerland. I have used the two names indiscriminately.

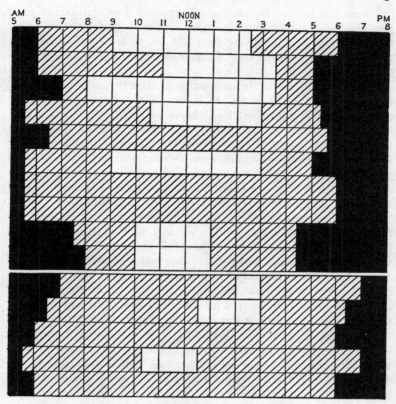

FIG. 2. HOURS OF SUNLIGHT AT VALLEY STATIONS

For ten stations on the sunny slope and five stations on the shady slope in the Valgaudemar, French Alps. The hours between the black areas represent the length of sunlight on the longest day of the year and the unshaded areas the hours on the shortest day. (Courtesy of the *Geographical Review*, published by the American Geographical Society of New York.)

A decrease with altitude of two principal heat-absorbing gases which are common 'impurities' of low air levels. These are carbon dioxide and water vapor.

Increasing rarity of air means less dynamic molecular heat. This decrease of dynamic heat is the adiabatic cooling.

The rate of adiabatic cooling is 1 degree centigrade for every 100 meters, or 1.6 degrees Fahrenheit for every 300 feet. Decreasing the pressure of a gas is the equivalent of permitting fewer molecules to occupy a given space. The number of impacts of molecules within the space will then be fewer and consequently the heat resulting from the impacts of the molecules will be less. We shall speak of this molecular heat of a gas as the inherent heat.

The lower levels of the atmosphere absorb much more heat than do the equivalent upper layers of the atmosphere. The amount of heat absorbed by a layer of air depends upon the molecular density and the composition. The chief elements, or, better, impurities of the composition important in this connection are dust, carbon dioxide, and water vapor. The air is not so constituted as to absorb easily the short wave length radiation of the sun. Air temperatures are raised much more largely by the long wave lengths of earth radiation and by conduction.

The actual rate at which temperature at any instant may be found to decrease aloft is the vertical temperature gradient. This gradient of actual temperature is different from the adiabatic decrease, since a number of other factors enter into the matter. The first measurement of the vertical temperature gradient in a mountainous region was made in 1788 by Saussure in the Alps. He found 1.6 degrees for 88.76 meters. The mean for 17 extra-tropical mountains has been computed as 0.57 degrees for 100 meters. Pikes Peak, Colorado, in a dry atmosphere gave 0.63 degrees for 100 meters. Shreve in the Santa Catalina Mountains, Arizona, has found the gradient as high as 0.76 degrees for 102 meters. Früh in a recent work states that the gradient for a mean of 169 Swiss stations is 0.52 degrees. Hann in his maps used 1 degree for every 200 meters. Bartholomew in his classic *Atlas of Meteorology* used the scale of 1 degree for every 150 meters. Thus they both reduced temperatures of the world to sea level temperatures. The advantage of such a map is that, confusing details being eliminated, one is able to see the general controls of climate. The mountain geographer wishes to have actual temperatures of the high stations. He may obtain these by dividing the height of the station in meters by 150, or 200 as the case may be, and subtracting the result from the surface temperature.

Alfred de Quervain has written upon methods of studying the vertical temperature gradient. He shows the influence of such factors as mass of mountain, cloudiness, exposure, and season. A. J. Henry has five articles of significance not only in presenting

FIG. 3. PIC DU MIDI DE BIGORRE, FRENCH PYRENEES

This isolated peak has the highest permanently inhabited house in Europe. It is a meteorological station with all-year observations. The foreground is a typical summer pasture for cattle. The higher slopes are available for sheep.

FIG. 4. A VILLAGE IN THE SUN, FRENCH ALPS

This village and its fields lie entirely on the sunny slope of a valley. The stream marks the edge of the forest on the shady slope. The scene is taken in one of the hanging valleys of the Tarentaise. (Courtesy of Ginn and Company, *New College Geography*.)

rado, which is not far from the latitude of Mount Etna, has an elevation of the mean annual zero degree isotherm of 3200 meters, as compared with 2950 meters for the Sicilian station.

MASS OF MOUNTAIN

The influence of mass of mountain (*Massenerhebung*) is indicated by the extraordinary fact that in the Himalayas at 4000 meters it is seldom below freezing from the end of May to the middle of October. Yet among the peaks at 5000 meters, where the mass is considerably less, it seldom is above that point even in summer. Other things being equal, the more massive the bulk of a mountain the greater the mean temperature at a given elevation. More significant is the fact that the greater the mass, normally the longer is the growing season. The most casual traveler among mountains cannot fail to notice the higher limits of agriculture on plateaus than on peaked mountains. Thus rye culture is notably higher on the plateau of the Cerdagne in the French Pyrenees than on the flanks of the mountains of the neighboring Conflent. Topography and accessibility might be thought to be hindrances to rye growing in the latter region, were it not that rye is grown in tiny fields in almost inaccessible spots. Forest limits are higher in the massive Alps than in the Fore-Alps of France. Imhof points out the same relationship for Swiss forests. Marek puts this fact in map form. Mass of mountain can be worked out quantitatively. Anfossi gives a formula for its computation.

Culture lines, or lines of human occupation and use, are higher on mountains of great mass because of a number of other reasons. Greater mass means ordinarily gentler slope. Roads mount such slopes easily. Fields and villages are thus found at higher levels. Mass generally increases the cultural heights in the Rhaetian Highland and the Central Alps of the Tirol in distinction to the limits in the less massive Eastern Alps. Because of greater snowfall, the character of the soil (mountains of great mass are commonly crystallines), and the degree of slope, there may be excessive ground water which forces the cereal lines valleyward. Cereal lines are therefore not in every case higher on plateau slopes than on the flanks of peaks.

The actual rate of decrease of temperatures on a given mountain range depends upon the adiabatic rate of decrease, the mass of the successive zones, the angle of slope, and the exposure, as well as other details of topography, vegetation, and winds. An actual example of decreasing temperatures with altitude is the following from the Carpathian Mountains:

TEMPERATURE AND ALTITUDE IN THE CARPATHIAN MOUNTAINS

Place	Height in meters	Jan.	Apr.	July	Oct.	Year
Crakow	220	−3.4	8.0	19.0	8.3	7.9
Turka	580	−5.8	6.2	16.7	7.3	5.9
Poronin	742	−5.6	5.0	15.3	6.1	4.9
Jablonica	900	−8.4	4.8	14.7	6.4	4.2
Zakopana	1000	−5.4	4.3	14.3	5.5	4.3
Jawarzyna	1019	−6.8	3.1	13.8	3.9	3.4

For the sake of geographic variety let us take certain data from Hettner's study of Colombia. The table is generalized.

TEMPERATURES AND ALTITUDES IN THE TROPICS

Altitude	Mean annual temperature	
400 meters	27.4	
600	26.2	Tierra caliente
800	25.0	
1000	23.8	
1200	22.6	
1400	21.3	
1600	20.2	Tierra templada
1800	19.0	
2000	18.0	
2200	17.1	
2400	16.1	
2600	15.1	Tierra fria
2800	13.9	
3000	12.7	
3200	11.5	
3400	10.3	
3600	9.1	Páramo
3800	8.0	
4000	7.0	

INVERSIONS OF TEMPERATURE

It is not always true that temperatures decrease with altitude. For a distance up temperatures may temporarily increase. This is known as an inversion of temperature. Thus an inversion of temperature exists when, upon ascent, a plus rather than a minus temperature gradient of air temperatures is experienced. Above this zone the temperature will decline. These warmer zones are known as thermal belts.

Examples of this phenomenon are many. In America the best known and well studied observation is on the front of the Blue Ridge Mountains of North Carolina. Here over a four-year period minimum temperatures averaged lower on the valley floors than in the thermal belts. On one slope, where there was 527 meters difference in elevation between the lowest and highest thermograph, the average minimum temperature was 1.84 degrees C. higher on the summit than at the base. The greatest inversion observed in this region was a plus gradient of 31 degrees F. in 1000 feet (17.2 degrees C. in 305 meters). The best known European inversion occurs in the Klagenfurt basin in Carinthia. Here it is at times necessary to mount 1000 meters to find again a temperature as low as that of the valley floor. In the following table the underlined figures represent the limit of the inversion according to Machatschek.

TEMPERATURE INVERSION IN THE KLAGENFURT BASIN

Station	Altitude	Jan. temperatures	Winter average
Klagenfurt	440 m.	−6.2	−4.6
Ebenstein	570	−4.2	−3.3
Huttenberg	780	−3.1	−2.3
Lolling Tal	840	−2.5	−1.6
Lolling Berghaus	1100	−1.9	−1.3
Stelzing	1410	−3.7	−3.2

The Engadine and the Upper Drave Valley have well known inversions. Sils in the Engadine at 1811 meters has a January temperature of −0.8 degrees, whereas St. Bernhard at 2478 meters is 8.3 degrees. Bevers, 75 meters below the summit of the Rigi, is 4.6 degrees colder. It is a general rule that isolated peaks in winter are warmer than high side valleys. This is demonstrated by figures from the Klagenfurt region given by Supan.

HIGH VALLEYS AND PEAKS IN THE KLAGENFURT BASIN

Station	Altitude, meters	January	Year
Klagenfurt	440	−6.2	7.2
Kappel	560	−5.2	6.6
Fellach	805	−4.0	6.0
Unterschäffler Alps	1063	−3.6	5.5
Obir I	1230	−4.3	4.7
Obir II	1612	−5.1	3.7
Hoch-Obir	2047	−6.8	0.6

A high valley at even greater altitude than an isolated peak may demonstrate this relationship. This is perhaps a demonstration of mass of mountain as well as inversion of temperature. Comparative temperatures between a valley station, Sils-Maria, and a peak, Rigi, follow.

TEMPERATURE ON SILS-MARIA AND ON THE SUMMIT OF RIGI

	Jan.	Feb.	Mar.	Apr.	May	June	July	Aug.	Sept.	Oct.	Nov.	Year
Rigi	−3.9	−4.5	−3.9	−0.2	3.0	7.5	9.9	9.4	7.5	2.7	−0.8	2.0
Sils	−6.8	−8.0	−4.0	−0.6	5.1	9.1	11.3	10.4	7.4	2.4	−2.4	1.5
Difference	−2.9	−3.5	−0.6	−0.4	2.1	1.4	1.4	1.0	−0.1	−0.3	−1.6	−0.5

Though inversions are a well known phenomenon of free air, inversions in mountain valleys differ because they are much intensified and stabilized. There have been many students of inversions, both observers and theorists. Bénévent is particularly lucid in his explanations. Früh has the best descriptions. Attention is called to the excellent and complete presentations of theories of inversion offered by Napier Shaw. The presentation in this present volume is generalized. Geographers are more concerned with the fact of inversion than the theories of origin.

The simplest type of inversion of temperature comes about from cold air drainage. There is commonly in mountain valleys a down-valley wind which sets in shortly after sundown on calm days. This wind varies in velocity from a drifting of air to a strong wind. It forces aloft the warm air of the valley, which hangs for a time in mid-height in the valley. These nocturnal inversions, due primarily to the drainage of cool air from peaks, are common in the western arid part of the United States. For them one should see the work of Shreve and other ecologists.

The inversion due to adiabatic heating of a descending air current is clearly described by Humphreys. This type could be best demonstrated by downward currents on a slope which is steep in the upper reaches but which flattens out on approach to the valley floor. Initially, when the temperature of the free air everywhere over the valley decreases with elevation, the speed of the surface air down, at least the steepest portions of the cooling walls, is quite certain to be sufficient to make its dynamic gain in heat exceed its conduction loss, and therefore to cause its temperature to increase with descent. As the bottom of the valley is approached, however, the rate of vertical descent and the consequent dynamic heating become less and less, and so finally cease altogether except in so far as there is drainage along the valley. At and near the bottom, then, where the dynamic heating is absent or small, the temperature of the surface and the adjacent air necessarily decrease more or less rapidly. In a short while, therefore, the valley basin begins to fill with a river of cold air.

If outside the mountain region there exists, perhaps for some days, a high pressure area of baric maximum, air currents are said to descend the barometric surfaces and then to experience an adiabatic heating as they meet and are compressed against the pool of cold, stagnant air of well enclosed valleys. Früh has recently given us not only the data of such inversions but vivid descriptions of them.

According to the meteorological description of such an inversion by Robert Billwiller, the heart of a Central-European maximum hovered with 780 mm. over the Bohemian Forest. From December 16th to 28th the following daily averages resulted:

EXAMPLE OF A TEMPERATURE INVERSION

Station	Altitude	Temperature
Geneva	408	− 7.2
Vitznau	445	− 4.9
Glarus	471	−11.8
Altsätten	478	−12.0
Neuchâtel	488	−10.6
Trogen	892	− 5.4
Elm	980	− 4.7
Chaumont	1128	1.3
Beatenberg	1150	5.0
Gäbris	1250	2.7
Rigi	1790	0.7
Great St. Bernhard	2478	− 4.9

(Great St. Bernhard is obviously above the thermal belt.)

That irradiation in itself is not the cause of the apparition is shown by the fact that during the night it is also warmer above, that the aforestated temperatures in the morning occur before sunrise, that, for instance, the village of Elm was without sun from September 30th until March 12th, and yet from December 16th to 28th, 1879, had a daily mean higher by 7.1 than that of deeper located Glarus. Brightness and heat above the fog are the result of the descending air, the dynamic warming up.[1]

A work on inversion which will always stand as a classic is

[1] Früh.

H. J. Cox's study of North Carolina temperature. The thermal belts or verdant zones of North Carolina are the most striking with which the writer has personal experience. They occur in the Eastern Appalachian Mountains, in basins at the margin of the Asheville Plateau and, strangely enough, on the open exposed eastern flank of the mountains. Here the inversions are all nocturnal inversions, accompanied frequently by an early morning fog. The vegetal response to this local prevention of frost is most striking. The writer has seen the valley at Tryon, North Carolina, brown with the dormant vegetation of winter. The mountain tops were white with snow, for here the mountains reach to some 1350 meters above the sea. Along the side of the mountains between the brown and the white was a strip of green, the verdant zone, the result of inversion. Grapes of a hardy variety are grown in the valley, but at a great hazard from frost. In the verdant zone there is a more successful *vignoble*,[1] and here the sensitive Isabella grape has been grown for thirty years without danger from frost.

GROWING SEASONS AND ALTITUDE

The decreasing length of the growing season with increasing altitude is critical to plant zones. The following is a generalized table of the relation of growing season and altitude in Colorado: [2]

GROWING SEASON AND ALTITUDE

Zone elevation	Length in days
Below 5000 feet (1525 m.)	146 days
5000–6000 " (1525–1830 m.)	138 "
6000–7000 " (1830–2135 m.)	113 "
7000–8000 " (2135–2440 m.)	90 "
8000–9000 " (2440–2745 m.)	56 "

So generalized a table is not accurate for detail. A pronounced difference in length of growing season may occur between stations of approximately the same altitude. It is such exceptions to the generalization which devitalizes to a large extent the conception of true vegetation zones on mountains. The value of the conception of the zone is discussed in Chapter IV. Below are five Colorado stations whose variations in days between average frosts are disproportionally great as compared with their slight

---

[1] A French term for vine culture worthy of our adoption.
[2] Robbins.

differences in altitude. In the table above, it will be noted that there is on the average an increase of a day of growing season for every 44 feet in elevation. In the following table we note that the difference in elevation between Castle Rock and Cedaredge is 55 feet, whereas the difference in length of the growing season is 39 days.

VARIATIONS IN GROWING SEASON OF STATIONS OF
APPROXIMATE ALTITUDE

Station	Elevation	Length in Days
Castle Rock	6200 feet (1897 m.)	98 days
Cedaredge	6175 " (1883 m.)	127 "
Conejos	7880 " (2303 m.)	128 "
Westcliffe	7864 " (2399 m.)	100 "
Pagosa Springs	7100 " (2166 m.)	85 "

Despite this table, there is some value in the conception of the general decrease of the growing season with altitude. The following table of well known Colorado farming communities illustrates a greater consistency of decrease of growing season. Lake City is the only exception to the comparative regularity of decrease.

REGULARITY OF DECREASE OF GROWING SEASON

Station	Elevation	Length in days
Las Animas	3899 feet (1189 m.)	161 days
Fort Collins	4985 " (1520 m.)	144 "
Glenwood Springs	5823 " (1776 m.)	112 "
Manos	6960 " (2123 m.)	106 "
Garnett	7576 " (2310 m.)	95 "
Lake City	8686 " (2649 m.)	99 "
Lake Moraine	10265 " (3138 m.)	78 "

This regularity is the more remarkable because these stations are not at increasing elevations upon a single slope but are widely scattered with a variety of exposures.

We have also data upon growing season differences in our arid Southwest. The growing season at 8000 feet (2440 meters) in the Santa Catalina Mountains of Arizona is about half of that of the city of Tucson at 2360 feet (720 meters) at a distance of only 20 miles (32 kilometers).

Angot found, in the case of French observations, that if the dates of harvest were reduced to sea level the harvest was retarded a day for every 25 meters of elevation. Bénévent discovered the harvest isochrones in the French Alps to be oriented west-southwest and east-northeast. In the Pyrenees the writer has seen at the same time rye ready for harvest and green rye higher up the slope. Elsewhere in the same range a 600 meters' difference in elevation meant 15 days' difference in harvest dates. This is at the rate of a day for every 40 meters.

The variation between Angot's general estimate and the writer's particular estimate is not surprising when one considers the variations in climate other than altitude which should be considered. Not the least important of the contributing factors is mass of mountain. Levainville, comparing the growing seasons of stations in the valley of Barcelonnette in the French Alps with stations of comparable altitude, but embedded in greater mass, demonstrated that greater mass of mountain lengthens growing season.

Temperature Ranges

It would appear from the low mean annual temperatures of mountain heights that we have there an essentially polar climate.

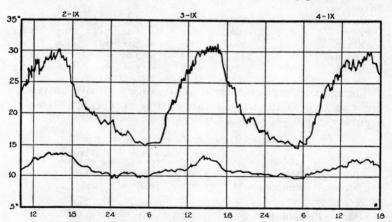

FIG. 5. DAILY RANGES OF TEMPERATURE AND ALTITUDE

Daily temperature records at Zurich (493 m.) and Säntis (2500 m.) September 2–5, 1895. (*After Früh.*)

Such is not the case. True, the Meije, a peak in Savoy of 3990 meters, has a mean annual temperature of − 10 degrees while the Siberian towns of Irkutsk and Verkoyansk have temperatures of − 11 and − 17 degrees respectively. The difference lies in the seasonal temperature ranges. Verkoyansk, for example, has a highly continental mean annual range, whereas mountain peaks have ranges much more typical of marine climates, even to the retardation. We do not, then, in climbing a tropical mountain from jungle to eternal snow pass through climates equivalent to those from equator to pole.

A still further difference from the polar climate is the intense insolation experienced in mountain climates. This intensity is a matter of great consequence to plant growth. The top of the Faulhorn in Switzerland, owing presumably to insolation, has on 415 hectares 131 species of plants, while in the archipelago of Spitzbergen there are but 93.

Both annual and diurnal ranges decrease with altitude. The following table illustrates the decreasing mean annual range: [1]

MEAN ANNUAL RANGES IN THE EASTERN ALPS

Place	Height in meters	Year in degrees	Jan.	July	Range
Bozen (Italy	290	11.7	0.0	22.5	22.5
Brixen (Austria)	580	8.7	− 2.5	19.4	21.9
Innsbruck (Austria)	600	7.9	− 3.3	17.8	21.1
Sterzing	1000	6.2	− 4.4	16.3	20.7
Schafberg	1780	1.6	− 5.1–Feb.	9.5	14.6
St. Bernard	2470	−1.8	− 9.0	6.2	15.2
Sönnblick	3105	−6.6	−13.3–Feb.	0.9	14.2

Though the decrease of the diurnal range with altitude is not as great as that of the annual range, it is appreciable [2] (see also Figure 5):

DECREASE OF DIURNAL RANGE WITH ALTITUDE

Place	Altitude in meters	Amplitude of range in degrees	Difference
Burlington, Vermont	70	27.9 ⎫	
Mount Washington, N. H.	1916	22.9 ⎭	5.0
Catania, Sicily	30	16.2 ⎫	
Mount Etna, Sicily	2947	10.8 ⎭	5.4
Toulouse, France	190	16.4 ⎫	
Pic du Midi, French Pyrenees	2877	14.1 ⎭	2.3

These mountain stations are all relatively isolated peaks. The range at a given altitude is in part the function of the mass of mountain. Plateaus do not have the marked decrease of range

[1] Machatschek.
[2] Martonne.

characteristics of isolated peaks. High valleys frequently have considerable range, particularly diurnal range, because of daytime heating through reflection and conduction of heat from enclosing valley walls and coldness at night due to cold air drainage. Indeed high valleys may have greater range than lowland stations: [1]

TEMPERATURES IN A HIGH VALLEY

Station	Altitude	Diurnal Range
Geneva	407 m.	11.6 degrees C.
Chamonix (a high valley)	1034	14.2
Mont Blanc	4810	3.5

Values for gradients on concave and convex slopes are given by Früh. Concave slopes are known as hatching ovens, *fourneaux*, by day, and cold holes by night. The concave slope concentrates heat waves, while the convex slope scatters them. Indeed, the topographic situation of a station is so great an influence in the range value that not every set of stations of increasing altitude shows decreasing ranges.

IRREGULARITY OF MEAN ANNUAL RANGE DUE TO SITUATION

Valley stations	Altitude in meters	Mean annual temperature C.	Range
Reichenhall	473	7.6	20.0
Traunstein	597	6.7	20.1
Pertenkirchen	715	6.5	18.9
Tegernsee	742	7.1	17.4
Obsertdork	820	5.8	19.2
Mittenwald	910	6.0	17.1
Peaks			
Wendelstein	1727	1.9	14.8
Zugspitze	2964	−5.2	13.2

SOIL TEMPERATURES

It follows that if the upper levels of the atmosphere absorb little of the sun's radiant heat, rock exposures and soils at high levels consequently receive a proportionally large amount of heat energy. The rarity of the air likewise permits rapid radiation of heat from rocks. Simply stated, rocks and soil at high levels become excessively hot in daytime and cold at night. As air temperatures are low, though rock in the sun may be hot, rock in the shade is of much lower temperature than differences

[1] Vallot.

of soil temperature in sun and shade at low levels would indicate.

This rapid heating and cooling accounts for the major part of weathering on mountain tops. Cracking and exfoliation are responsible for the angular blocks of summit rocks, as for example the rocks of the much-photographed summit of Pikes Peak, Colorado. The effect of this rapid heating was well appreciated when the writer stood some distance from the sheer rock cliff known as the Royal Arches of Yosemite Park, California, as the morning's sun first struck the cliff. Pieces of rock were flaked from the surface and whirled through the air until they sounded like bullets.

The soil temperatures of a sunny slope may be higher than soil temperatures of a valley station, for not uncommonly the high slope makes a greater angle of incidence with the sun's rays than does the valley floor. Though soil heat is derived largely from insolation rather than from air heat, yet, because radiation is so active in the rarer air levels, the average temperature of the soil decreases with altitude. As the vertical soil temperature gradient is less than that of the air the difference between the two is progressively greater as one ascends: [1]

DIFFERENCE IN SOIL AND AIR TEMPERATURES WITH ALTITUDE

Altitude in meters	Difference of soil and air temperatures in degrees C.
600	0.5
900	1.0
1200	1.3
1500	1.7
1800	2.0
2100	2.3
2400	2.5
2700	2.7
3000	2.9

The mean difference between the soil and air temperatures as observed in the Tirol is 1.5 degrees at 1000 meters, 1.7 degrees at 1300 meters, and 2.4 degrees at 1600 meters. The difference varies, however, with exposure, water content of the soil, slope, and latitude. In the National Park of Switzerland at 2200 meters the soil temperature has been observed to be 3.6 times that of the air. The following table illustrates the differences between the

[1] Jenny.

mean and maximum soil temperatures at Bagnères-de-Bigorre and the Pic du Midi in the French Pyrenees:

MAXIMUM AND MINIMUM SOIL TEMPERATURES

	Bagnères 511 meters	Pic du Midi 2877 meters	Difference
Mean air temperature	22.3	10.1	−12.2
Mean soil temperature	36.1	33.8	− 2.3
Maximum air temperature	27.1	13.2	−13.9
Maximum soil temperature	50.3	52.3	2.0

The temperature of the soil, dependent as it is on insolation, varies with exposure. The following observations on soil were made at the depth of 80 centimeters in Austria:

SOIL TEMPERATURES AND EXPOSURES

Exposure	Inn valley (600 meters)	Gschnitz valley (1340 m.)
N	9.5	5.1
NE	10.6	5.5
E	11.3	5.9
SE	12.6	7.5
S	12.6	7.8
SW	12.7	7.4
W	12.2	7.4
NW	10.2	9.5
Mean	11.5	6.7
Range	3.2	2.7

The migration of the maximum soil temperature from southwest in winter to southeast in summer is probably due to the diurnal variation in cloudiness.

The significance of soil temperatures at high levels is even more outstanding than at low levels. This is brought out by Shreve. It makes possible the promotion of root growth at levels where air temperatures would be prohibitive to the germination of seeds. Radiation strongly affects air temperatures near the ground, which accounts, in part, for the low branching of bush and tree growth. Moreover, the local warming of the air causes minor convection currents. The rate of evaporation on the sunny slope is less favorable for plants than that of the shady slope. Soil temperatures influence the length of the growing season and the duration of snow cover. All this Shreve supports with instrumental observations. One should also consult the work by Jenny.

BIBLIOGRAPHICAL NOTES

General References on Mountain Climate

The great book on this subject is Hann, revised by Knoch. It is a complete treatise in subject matter, taken, unfortunately, almost entirely from German source material. The Bibliographical Note on regional works at the end of Chapter VII should also be consulted.

Bach, Hugo. *Das Klima von Davos.* Zurich, 1907. A high climate fully treated.

Bénévent, Ernest. *Le climat des Alpes françaises; Memorial de l'Office National Météorologique de France.* Paris, 1926. A regional treatise of general application.

Blanchard, Raoul. "Le contraste climatique entre Vércors et Diois," in *Recueil des travaux de l'Institut de géographie alpine*, vi (1918), pp. 427–446. Involves fundamental principles.

Davis, W. M. "A Speculation in Topographical Climatology," in *American Meteorological Journal*, xii (1896), pp. 372–381. An early American article.

Davis, W. M. "Mountain Meteorology," in *Appalachia*, iv (1885), pp. 225–244, 327–350.

Dorno, Carl. "Klimatologie des Hochgebirges," in *Verhandlungen der Klimatologischen Tagung in Davos*, 1925, pp. 130–140. Medical climatology.

Exner, Franz. "Klima der Alpen," in *Die österreichischen alpen*, ed. by Hans Leitmeier. Leipzig and Vienna, 1928, pp. 165–175. General.

Ficker, Heinz von. *Klimatographie von Tirol und Vorarlberg.* Vienna, 1909.

Hann, Julius. *Handbuch der Klimatologie*, 4. Aufl. by Karl Knoch. Vol. i. Stuttgart, 1932. The great book on the subject.

Hann, Julius. *Handbook of Climatology*, part i, trans. by R. DeC. Ward. New York, 1903.

Huber, Anton. *Das Klima des bayerischen Alpenanteiles und seines Vorlandes.* Munich, 1929. (*Veröffentlichungen der Gesellschaft für bayerische Landeskunde*, 5.)

Humphreys, W. J. *Physics of the Air*, 2d ed. New York, 1929. A book of prime importance for the theorist.

Kendrew, W. G. *Climate.* Oxford, 1930.

Knoch, Karl. *Klimakunde von Südamerika.* Berlin, 1930. (*Handbuch der Klimatologie*, ed. by Wladimir Köppen and Rudolf Geiger, vol. ii.) Contains all the text and references needed for South American studies.

Martonne, Emmanuel de. *Traité de géographie physique*, 4ᵉ ed. Vol. i (Paris, 1925), pp. 307–331.

Maurer, Julius, Billwiller, Robert, and Hess, Clemens. *Das Klima der Schweiz.* Frauenfeld, 1909–10. 2 vols.

Miller, A. A. *Climatology.* London, 1931. Immethodical but readable material.

Peattie, Roderick. "Les apports de l'Amérique à la climatologie de montagne," in *Mélanges géographiques offerts à Raoul Blanchard* (Grenoble, 1932), pp. 467–479. Also in *Revue de géographie alpine,* xx (1932), pp. 253–266.

Rotch, A. L. "Mountain Meteorology," in *American Meteorological Journal,* viii (1891), pp. 145–158, 193–211. Of historical importance only.

Schlagintweit, Hermann and Adolph von. *Untersuchungen über die physicalische Geographie der Alpen.* Leipzig, 1850. An early treatise.

Shaw, Sir Napier. *Manual of Meteorology.* Vol. iii, Cambridge, England, 1930.

Shreve, Forrest. *The Vegetation of a Desert Mountain Range as Conditioned by Climatic Factors.* Washington, 1915. (Carnegie Institution of Washington, *Publications,* 217.) Excellent for mountains in an arid region.

Stone, R. G. "The History of Mountain Meteorology, in the United States and the Mount Washington Observatory," in *Transactions of the American Geophysical Union,* 15th Annual Meeting, 1934, pp. 124–133. With an excellent bibliography. Or see "Die Entwicklung der amerikanischen Bergobservatorien und das derzeitige Netz von Bergstationen in der Vereinigten Staaten von Amerika," in *Jahresbericht* of the Sonnblick-Verein, xliii (1934), pp. 11–30.

Supan, Alexander. *Grundzüge der physischen Erdkunde,* 7. Aufl. by Erich Obst. Berlin, 1927. 2 vols.

Ward, R. DeC. *Climate, Considered especially in Relation to Man.* New York, 1908. 2d ed., revised, 1918.

Ward, R. DeC. *The Climates of the United States.* Boston, 1925.

Ward, R. DeC. "A Visit to the Highest Meteorological Station in the World," in *Monthly Weather Review,* xxvi (1898), pp. 150–152.

Wegener, Alfred. *Thermodynamik der Atmosphäre.* Leipzig, 1911.

Insolation

One should consult the general references of the previous bibliographical note.

Ångström, Anders. "On the Atmospheric Transmission of Sun Radiation," in *Geografiska Annaler,* xi (1929), pp. 156–166; xii (1930), pp. 130–159. Has a good bibliography.

Church, J. E. "Summit Temperatures in Winter in the Sierra Nevada," in *Appalachia,* xi (1905–08), pp. 239–248.

Garnett, Alice, "Insolation, Topography, and Settlement in the Alps," in *Geographical Review*, xxv (1935), pp. 601–617.

Geiger, Rudolf. *Das Klima der bodennahen Luftschicht*. Braunschweig, 1927.

Harshberger, J. W. "Alpine Fell-Fields of Eastern North America," in *Geographical Review*, vii (1919), pp. 233–255.

Harshberger, J. W. "Slope Exposure and the Distribution of Plants in Eastern Pennsylvania," in *Bulletin of the Geographical Society of Philadelphia*, xvii (1919), pp. 53–61.

Kendrew, W. G. *Climate*. Oxford, 1930. Chap. xxxviii.

Kimball, H. H. "Observations on the Increase of Insolation with Elevation," in *Bulletin of the Mount Weather Observatory*, vi (1913–14), pp. 107–110.

Kolhörster, W., and Salis, G. von. "Variation of Penetrating Radiation on the Jungfrau," in *Nature* (London), cxviii (1926), p. 518.

Okada, T., and Yosida, Y. "Pyrheliometric Observations at the Summit and at the Base of Mount Fuji," in *Bulletin of the Central Meteorological Observatory of Japan*, no. 3. Tokyo, 1910.

Bibliographies in *Monthly Weather Review*, lv (1927), pp. 163–166, 168–169.

Temperature and Altitude

Ahlmann, H. W., and Eythorsson, J. "Introductory Survey of the Temperature Conditions in the Horung Massif during the Summers of 1923–1926," in *Geografiska Annaler*, ix (1927), pp. 13–21.

Anfossi, G. "Volumétrie de la Corse," in *Recueil des travaux de l'Institut de géographie alpine*, vi (1918), pp. 27–69. The measurement of mass of mountain.

Anfossi, G. "Volumetria della Sardagna," in *Memorie Geografiche, supplemento alla Rivista Geografica Italiana*, ix (1915), pp. 181–235. The measurement of mass of mountain.

Angot, Alfred. "La température de la France," in *Annales de géographie*, xiv (1905), pp. 296–309.

Angot, Alfred. "Sur la décroissance de la température dans l'air avec la hauteur," in *Comptes rendus hebdomaires des séances de l'Académie de Sciences*. Paris, cxv (1892), pp. 1270–1273.

Bäckman, Allan. "L'influence de l'altitude et de la position géographique sur la température de l'air dans la région sud-ouest de la Suède," in *Geografiska Annaler*, ix (1927), pp. 133–141.

Büdel, Anton. "Die Zugspitzbahn," in *Deutsches Meteorologischen Jahrbuch*, 1929, pp. E 1–30, and 1930, pp. E 1–5.

Hann, Julius. "Die Mittlere Wärmevertheilung in den Ostalpen," in *Zeitschrift des Deutschen und Österreichischen Alpenvereins*, xvii (1886), pp. 22–94. A classic.

Hann, Julius. "Die Temperaturverhältnisse der österreichischen

Alpenländer," in *Sitzungsberichte* of the Vienna Academy, math.-nat. Klasse, xc, 2 (1884), pp. 585–683; xci, 2 (1885), pp. 403–453; xcii, 2 (1885), pp. 33–198.

Hann, Julius. "Zur Meteorologie des Sonnblickgipfels," in *Zeitschrift des Deutschen und Österreichischen Alpenvereins*, xx (1889), pp. 71–93.

Henry, A. J. "Daily Changes in Temperature up to 4,000 Meters," in *Bulletin of the Mount Weather Observatory*, v (1912–13), pp. 1–18.

Henry, A. J. "Variations of Temperature and Pressure at Summit and Base Stations in the Rocky Mountain Region," in *Bulletin of the Mount Weather Observatory*, iii (1910–11), pp. 201–225.

Henry, A. J. "Variations of Temperature at Summit and Base Stations in the Central Rocky Mountain Region," in *Bulletin of the Mount Weather Observatory*, iv (1911–12), pp. 103–114.

Henry, A. J. "The Temperature at Mount Weather and Adjacent Valley Stations," in *Bulletin of the Mount Weather Observatory*, iv (1911–12), pp. 310–341.

Henry, A. J. "Vertical Temperature Gradients between Mount Weather, Va., and Valley Stations," in *Bulletin of the Mount Weather Observatory*, vi (1913–14), pp. 35–37.

Hettner, Alfred. *Die Kordillere von Bogotá*. Gotha, 1892. (*Petermanns Mitteilungen*, Ergänzungsheft Nr. 104.)

Huber, Anton. "Das Klima der Zugspitze," in *Beobachtungen der Meteorologischen Stationen im Königreich Bayern*, xxxv (1913), pp. L 3–L 62.

Imhof, Eduard. "Die Waldgrenze in der Schweiz," in *Beiträge zur Geophysik*, iv (1900), pp. 241–330. Forests and mass of mountain.

Jegerlehner, J. "Die Schneegrenze in den Gletschergebieten der Schweiz," in *Beiträge zur Geophysik*, v (1903), pp. 486–568. Snow and mass of mountain.

Liez, H. "Die Verteilung der mittleren Höhe in der Schweiz," in *Jahresbericht der Geographischen Gesellschaft von Bern*, xviii (1900–02), pp. 1–38.

Marek, Richard. "Beiträge zur Klimatographie der oberen Waldgrenze in den Ostalpen," in *Petermanns Mitteilungen*, lvi, 1 (1910), pp. 63–69.

Quervain, Alfred de. "Die Hebung der atmosphärischen Isothermen in den Schweizer Alpen und ihre Beziehung zu den Höhengrenzen," in *Beiträge zur Geophysik*, vi (1904), pp. 481–533.

Schalgintweit, Hermann and Adolph von. *Neue Untersuchungen über die physicalische Geographie und die Geologie der Alpen*. Leipzig, 1854.

Shreve, Forrest. "Conditions indirectly Affecting Vertical Distribution on Desert Mountains," in *Ecology*, iii (1922), pp. 269–274.

Somervell, T. H., and Whipple, F. J. W. "The Meteorological Results of the Mount Everest Expedition," in *Quarterly Journal of the Royal Meteorological Society*, lii (1926), pp. 131–143.

Vallot, J. "Variation de la température, de la pression, et de la vapeur d'eau au Mont Blanc et aux stations inférieures, d'après les observations de 1887," in *Annales de l'Observatoire du Mont Blanc*, i (1893), pp. 25–45.

Inversions of Temperature

For theory one should turn to the handbooks of Hann, Shaw, and Humphreys. For description, see the work on Switzerland by Früh.

Abbe, Cleveland. "Thermal Belts, Frostless Belts, or Verdant Zones," in *Monthly Weather Review*, xxi (1893), p. 365.

André, Charles. *Influence de l'altitude sur la température*. Lyons, 1888.

Blache, Jules. *Les massifs de la Grande Chartreuse et du Vercors*. Grenoble, 1931. 2 vols. Vol. i, pp. 415–419.

Blache, Jules. "Notes sur les conditions de l'inversion de température dans la région du Villard-de-Lans," in *Revue de géographie alpine*, xx (1932), pp. 361–370.

Brown, W. P. "Winter Temperatures on Mountain Heights," in *Quarterly Journal of the Royal Meteorological Society*, xxxvi (1910), pp. 17–19.

Chickering, J. W. "Thermal Belts," in *American Meteorological Journal*, i (1884–85), pp. 213–218.

Church, J. E. "Summit Temperatures in Winter in the Sierra Nevada," in *Appalachia*, xi (1905–08), pp. 239–248.

Clarke, W. T. "Peaches and Climate," *Monthly Weather Review*, xxxviii (1910), p. 1740.

Cox, H. J. "Weather Conditions and Thermal Belts in the North Carolina Mountain Region and their Relation to Fruit Growing," in *Annals of the Association of American Geographers*, x (1920), pp. 57–68.

Cox, H. J. "Thermal Belts and Fruit Growing in North Carolina," in *Monthly Weather Review*, supplement no. 19 (1922), pp. 1–98.

Dauzère, Camille. "Sur les inversions de la température," in *Comptes rendus hebdomadaires des séances de l'Académie des Sciences*, Paris, clxxxii (1926), pp. 978–980.

Davis, W. M. "Types of New England Weather," in *Annals of the Astronomical Observatory of Harvard College*, xxi, 2 (1889), pp. 116–137.

Früh, Jacob. *Geographie der Schweiz*. St. Gallen, 1929–33. 2 vols. Vol. i.

Henry, A. J. "Temperature Inversions at the Mount Weather Observatory," in *Bulletin of the Mount Weather Observatory*, i (1908), pp. 143–160.

Hutt, W. N. "Thermal Belts from the Horticultural View-Point," in *Monthly Weather Review*, supplement no. 19 (1922), pp. 99–106.

Kerner, A. "Die Entstehung relativ hoher Lufttemperaturen in der Mittelhöhe der Thalbecken der Alpen im Spätherbste und Winter," in *Zeitschrift der Österreichischen Gesellschaft für Meteorologie*, xi (1876), pp. 1–13.

MacDougal, D. T. "Influence of Inversions of Temperature, Ascending and Descending Currents of Air, upon Distribution," in *Biological Lectures from the Marine Biological Laboratory of Woods Hole, 1899* (Boston, 1900).

Soil Temperatures

Buhler, A. "Einfluss der Exposition und des Neigungswinkels auf die Temperatur des Bodens," in *Mitteilungen der Schweizerischen Zentralanstalt für das forstliche Versuchswesen*, iv (1895).

Jenny, Hans. "Hochgebirgsböden," in *Handbuch der Bodenlehre*, ed. by Edwin Blanck, iii (Berlin, 1930), pp. 96–118. Excellent bibliography.

Kerner, A. "Über Wanderungen des Maximums der Bodentemperatur," in *Zeitschrift der Österreichischen Gesellschaft für Meteorologie*, vi (1871), pp. 65–71.

Kerner von Marilaun, Fritz. "Die Änderung der Bodentemperatur mit der Exposition," in *Sitzungsberichte* of the Vienna Academy, math.-nat. Klasse, c, 2a (1891), pp. 704–729.

Shreve, Forrest. "Soil Temperature as Influenced by Altitude and Slope Exposure," in *Ecology*, v (1924), pp. 128–136.

CHAPTER II

HUMIDITY AND PRECIPITATION

HUMIDITY AND EVAPORATION

THE decrease of absolute humidity with altitude is more rapid than the diminishing of other atmospheric elements here considered. The following table illustrates the theoretical relative decrease of vapor tension and atmospheric pressure with increasing altitude: [1]

DECREASE OF VAPOR TENSION AND AIR PRESSURE WITH ALTITUDE

Altitude in meters	Vapor tension	Air pressure
0	1.00	1.00
1000	0.73	0.88
2000	0.49	0.78
3000	0.35	0.69
4000	0.24	0.61
5000	0.17	0.54
6000	0.12	0.47

This table is merely a slide rule by which vapor tensions may be generalized. Thus, if the vapor tension at 10 millimeters is found at sea level, the tension at 4000 meters would be 2.4 millimeters.

The actual absolute humidity found at elevations in mountains varies to such a degree as to defy generalization. It is, of course, a matter of weather and such permanent influences as exposure, angle of slope, character of soil, condition of ground water, and mass of mountain. It has its diurnal and seasonal altitudinal distribution. In the mornings the humidity of the air is great in the valleys as compared with the upper reaches. By afternoon convection currents have distributed this moisture in part to upper levels. The low absolute humidity of a high level station augments the intensity of insolation there and reduces the heat absorbing quality of the air.

Relative humidity and increasing altitude have no consistent relationship. Relative humidity is the ratio between the abso-

[1] Hann.

lute humidity of the moment and the saturation point at the existing temperature, and is therefore dependent upon the absolute humidity and the temperature. The irregularity of the vertical temperature gradient is more or less to be counted upon. The irregularity of the absolute humidity gradient has just been referred to. Relative humidity is the result, then, of two variables and cannot be generalized or reduced to a formula.

Evaporation and its significance are particularly difficult to treat because so little is known of the subject in high altitudes in its quantitative sense. In most high areas the potential evaporation is actually greater than precipitation. The effectiveness of humidity depends upon the potential rate of evaporation, which, in turn, depends upon the barometric pressure, the amount of vapor already in the air, the temperature of the soil, the temperature of the air, the velocity of the wind, and the character of the soil and vegetal covering. The less the barometric pressure and the less the water vapor content of the air, the more rapid the evaporation. All air constituents, and especially water vapor tension, constitute a hindrance to the release of gas molecules from water, the process which we know as evaporation.

The temperature of the air at high elevation is low, except in the shallow zone in immediate contact with the rock. On the other hand, the temperature of the soil is primarily a question of its physical character, its water content, its exposure, angle of slope, and vegetal covering. The physical character of the soil obviously influences soil temperatures. The scarcity of Alpine vegetation, though it decreases transpiration, increases evaporation of ground water because of the greater exposure of barren ground to the sun. The importance of soil temperatures is illustrated photographically and with text by R. R. Platt in Johnson's *Peru from the Air* (1930). On page 33 the legend of an illustration runs: "There is abundant rainfall here, but so intense is the heat of the afternoon sun that the northern and western slopes of the hills that border the valley do not retain sufficient moisture to support tree growth. Only in the gullies and on the spurs that are shaded from the afternoon sun is there forest." In the writer's *New College Geography*, page 465, appears a picture from the collection of E. M. Spieker. This shows a forested slope facing a barren slope. The legend reads: "This scene is taken on the Wasatch Plateau at an elevation of 8000 feet (2440 meters) in the valleys to 9000 feet (2745 meters) at the summits. The barren slope faces south. Here the sun's rays are hot enough to cause evaporation to an extent which prevents tree growth."

The velocity of the wind is critical in evaporation. The increased speed of wind with altitude is shown by the following table of averages for three stations:

RELATIVE AVERAGE WIND VELOCITIES

	Altitude	Relative speed
Kremsmunster	390 m.	3.5
Saentis	2500 m.	7.5
Sonnblick	3100 m.	9.3

The effect upon the Alpine plants is to eliminate all but those of a xerophytic nature. Is not the Edelweiss, famed flower of the heights, of this type? Strength of evaporation can be measured by the climber through the rapidity of the drying of perspiration and the great thirst which are experienced on mounting. Among high peaks dead animals are found mummified. Air-dried meat is a provincial dish in the high Engadine. Great and rapid evaporation is one of the most characteristic climatic conditions of high elevations.

PRECIPITATION

A primary concern in any discussion of precipitation at high altitudes is the paucity and inaccuracy of observations. In the nature of things, a rain gauge is not as automatic or accurate as a thermograph. In any case, year round records of high level precipitations are few. The writer is convinced that recorded totals of mountain rainfalls are frequently short of the true total. In spite of counter devices, wind-driven rain is not recorded as completely by the gauge as where there is relative calm. A high wind during a rain storm in mountains is common. But still greater inaccuracy exists in the failure of the rain gauge to record precipitation such as occurs on rocks and plants from fog or cloud driven against the cold mountain side. A support of this doubt lies in the fact that relatively small drainage basins in high mountains produce streams disproportionately large as compared with streams of similar drainage area on lowlands.

Generally speaking, mountains have higher precipitation values than surrounding plains. This is due to the uplift and cooling of winds. Even winds of slight relative humidity will reach a saturation point if sufficiently cooled. This uplift of the wind may involve a considerable zone of the air. The depth may be so great that the flexing of the zone may cause uplift of air even over a piedmont area of no great relative elevation. Mountain piedmonts are more rainy than adjacent plains. Thus the depth of the monsoon wind is considerable, with a resulting heavy rainfall on the piedmont of the Himalayas disproportionate to the slightly greater elevation of the piedmont over the plains.[1]

INFLUENCE OF PROXIMITY OF MOUNTAINS ON PRECIPITATION OF PIEDMONT STATIONS

Station	Dacca	Bogra	Mymensing	Silhet
Distance from Himalayas in kilometers ..	161	96	48	32
Rainfall in centimeters	191	231	274	380

The increase of precipitation with altitude is characteristic only of the windward slope. The converse is true of the lee slope. On the lee side the wind is descending and therefore warming. As the descending wind warms, rather than permitting condensation of moisture, it is constantly acquiring a greater and greater capacity for absorbing moisture. There is on the lee

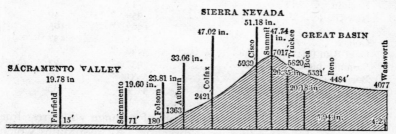

FIG. 6. TOPOGRAPHY AND PRECIPITATION, AMERICAN SIERRA NEVADA
Note that the summit station is above the zone of maximum precipitation. Reno lies in the 'rain shadow.'

slope a region drier than the more general weather controls of that part of the world would justify. This region is said to be in the 'rain shadow' of the mountains. It should be noted that the lee slope of the summit may have considerable rain as a carry-over from the rain on the windward slope.

The factors involved in the increase of precipitation with altitude are the amount of moisture in the air in terms of absolute and relative humidity, the angle of the mountain slope, the

[1] de Martonne.

height of the range, and the vertical temperature gradient. What actual precipitation occurs on a mountain range depends upon climatic location, orientation of the mountain crest, relative height of the range above the plain, and the angle of the slope of the mountain. The rate of precipitation from sea level to a zone of maximum precipitation has been computed by formulae by a number of scientists. McAdie has worked out an elaborate formula for his California study. De Martonne quotes Huber, who has devised a formula that includes altitude and angle of slope. Precipitation increases with altitude until the zone of maximum precipitation is reached. The following table, from California, illustrates the increase rate, the zone of maximum rainfall, and the rain shadow:

PRECIPITATION IN CALIFORNIA AND THE SIERRA NEVADA
(See also Figure 6)

Station	Elevation	Relative amounts
Oakland (on San Francisco Bay)	36 feet	100
Sacramento (in California Valley)	71 "	80
Rocklin	249 "	121
New Castle	956 "	140
Auburn	1363 "	165
Colfax	2421 "	237 (max.)
Gold Run (maximum zone)	3222 "	226
Summit (highest elevation)	7037 "	223
Boca (rain shadow)	5531 "	83
Reno, Nevada (rain shadow)	4484 "	35

The Sierra Nevada is an example of a range with crest line normal to the prevailing wind direction. All mountains which are barriers to wind progress show similar precipitation condition. Mountain ranges whose crest lines are parallel to the wind direction show little or no increase of precipitation with altitude. Below is a table to illustrate the relationship of altitude and precipitation in the French Alps. Examples from three slopes are given on the opposite page.[1]

Hann gives formulae for the relations of rainfall and altitude. Blache analyzes the inaccuracy of records. Shreve discusses the irregularity of decrease on desert ranges of Arizona. The irregularities are those of observation, always found on mountains, and the irregularities due to slope and exposure.

[1] Blache.

RAINFALL AND ALTITUDE IN THE CHARTREUSE AND VERCORS

Station elevation	Precipitation
215 m.	1153 mm.
275	1282
1025	1328
1200	1446
....	....
410	1707
643	1947
....	....
270	1146
1000	1500

The zone of maximum precipitation is of prime significance in consideration of mountains and their human relations. There are some authorities who argue that forest limits are controlled to a greater or less degree by this upper limit of the zone of maximum precipitation. Certainly decrease of moisture is one factor in the upper limit of tree distribution. How important it is depends in part upon the comparative aridity of the region. Not enough measurements have been made to determine properly the zone of maximum precipitation. Hann has stated that such a zone in the Alps approximates 2000 meters in elevation. Bénévent, dividing the northern section of the French Alps into the Fore-Alps, Central Alps, and Intra-Alpine Zone, places the maximum precipitation at 2000 meters, 2500 meters, and 2500 to 3000 meters respectively. Joseph Vallot, who established the observatory on Mont Blanc, makes the assertion that the summit of Mont Blanc has less precipitation than Montpellier, a town on the dry Mediterranean coast of France. The maximum height of the zone in the Pyrenees is not definitely ascertained, and one authority believes it to be higher than the usually accepted figure of 2000 meters. The writer's observation in Andorra, in the heart of the range, is that the summit plateau at 2000 to 2600 meters is relatively dry as compared with the slopes. The relative aridity is a definite barrier to beech trees and rye at these higher levels. There is danger, however, in judging rainfall of higher altitudes by the character of plant cover, since high winds and strong insolation there counteract the effectiveness of precipitation to a high degree. It must be noted, nevertheless, that the shepherds in the Tian Shan and the Pamirs actually drive their flocks to higher levels in winter than in summer in order to avoid the zone of maximum winter snowfall.

Mass of mountain once again deserves consideration. It is a matter of common observation that the greater the mass the higher the level of the clouds. The cloud zone on Mont Blanc is said to be 3000 meters, and in the Fore-Alps 2000 meters. The greater the cloudiness of a zone the less the evaporation and the more effective the rainfall.

One looks to the lowering of cloud zones in winter as the reason for slight winter precipitation in high altitudes. At Davos, at 1560 meters, January is the driest month (45.7 mm.) and July and August the wettest months (127.7 mm.). This is a range of 82 mm. amplitude. It must be remembered that this is true in spite of the fact that the rainy season of Switzerland is in winter. Bach, who has demonstrated the above fact, finds the same anomaly in the case of other high level stations. It must not be assumed, however, that the annual average decrease of rainfall with altitude would show the same curve. The low winter level of maximum precipitation is of short duration.

The most common cause for the difference in rainfall totals of two near stations of like altitude is the matter of exposure. The following table is a rainfall cross-section of the Vosges Mountains of France. Nancy on the windward side and Colmar on the leeward slope have the same altitude: [1]

PRECIPITATION OF TWO FLANKS OF THE VOSGES

	West (windward)			East (leeward)		
	Nancy	Mirecourt	Epinal	Le Syndicat	Wesserling	Thaun	Colmar
Altitude (m.)	200	279	339	620	437	238	200
Precipitation (mm.) ...	786	881	950	1374	1208	932	479

One of the most extraordinary examples of exposure is on a mountain on an island in the north of the Hawaiian group. Here the rainfall on the windward side has been measured to more than 450 inches in a year, whereas seventeen miles to the leeward the rainfall is but twenty-two inches.

The influence of exposure is well illustrated by the French Alps. The driest section of this group is the Briançonnais, which owes its significant aridity to protection. Of the French Alps, the Savoian section is in the belt of westerly winds. The Provençal section is in the Mediterranean zone. High crests mark the division between the two sets of valleys. Savoy is decidedly moist as compared with Provence. The following table emphasizes

[1] de Martonne.

this contrast, showing that the Provençal station, though at a
lesser altitude than the Savoian station, has the greater rainfall.

EXPOSURE AND PRECIPITATION IN THE FRENCH ALPS

	Monts du Vercors (Savoy) Lente	Alpes-Maritimes (Provence) Thorene
Altitude	1080 m.	1250 m.
Total Precipitation	1639 mm.	1171 mm.

Exposure to wind is so important in rainfall totals that in a
sense the word wind is often equivalent to weather. *Le vent* is the
same as *Regenluft*, and *Regentwer* is the weather wind. South of
the *Wetterhorn* (Bernese Oberland) is the *Wetterlueche* or the gap
through which the rain wind comes. The location of a station in
line with prevailing winds coming through a gap or pass accounts for many local variations of rainfall within a small area.

Mountain barriers cause comparative aridity in their lee. Such
leeward stations, relatively dry for their altitude, are known as
dry holes. A well known example is the region of Sion in the
Upper Rhone Valley. Tremendous barriers there keep out
weather winds and rain. On the other hand, a comparatively
slight topographic difference will account for paucity of rain.
The towns of Prades and Villefranche, in the valley of the Tet,
Eastern French Pyrenees, are dry holes, yet the barriers against
rain weather are merely of foothill proportions. Exposure, causing contrasts of precipitation, is one of the most decisive of climate
controls in mountains.

DRY HOLES IN THE EASTERN FRENCH PYRENEES

Station	Altitude in meters	Rainfall in millimeters
Perpignan	31	554
Vinca	259	612
Prades	354	500
Villefranche	889	465
Olette	1133	560
Theres	1137	597
Mont Louis	1586	827

SNOW

Snow on mountains must be considered from the point of view
of quantity and frequency of fall and duration of mantle. The
factors which control these considerations are total precipitation,
altitude, slope, exposure, and evaporation. Precipitation varies

greatly with the exposure. The percentage of the precipitation which is snow is more or less directly in relation to the altitude and latitude. For two stations of the same latitude and same general climatic situation, the greater the altitude the greater the snowfall, until the zone of maximum snowfall is reached.

NUMBER OF DAYS OF SNOWFALL AT DIFFERENT ALTITUDES IN BAVARIA
(The Roman numerals indicate months)

Station	Alt.	Begin.	1888–89 End	Days	Begin.	1890–91 End	Days
München	526	21 II	10 III	18	25 XI	22 II	90
Rosenheim	449	3 II	24 III	50	25 XI	5 III	101
Mieabach ...;...	717	3 II	12 IV	69	25 XI	10 III	106
Onsersdorf	842	3 II	20 IV	77	24 XI	22 IV	150
Peissenberg	994	3 II	21 IV	78	25 XI	17 III	113
Wendelstein	1730	3 II	22 IV	79	17 X	8 V	204

There are differences in factors influencing the date of the first day of snow cover and the last day. The first appearance of snow on all but the higher reaches is frequently the result of general weather conditions of the area. Therefore altitudes of a considerable range of elevation will experience snow on the same day. The duration of snow in the spring time is, however, the result more largely of weather factors. Most of these local climatic conditions have direct relation to altitude. Therefore the disappearance of snow begins at lower levels and gradually mounts higher. The exceptions are largely those of exposure. A shady slope, especially if forested, may hold snow far out of season. A well insolated mountain slope may lose its snow before a valley bottom. Nevertheless the number of days of snow cover is, up to the zone of maximum snowfall, a rough measure of altitude.

The variation of total days of snow cover in the two years presented in the above table is characteristic of mountain snowfall in a belt of westerly winds. The variation of snowfall should be greater than the variability of total precipitation, because in the case of the former there are two variables, storminess and the critical temperature for snow formation. An example of the extreme variation which may be found is recorded at Lente in Savoy. This station had 1.81 meters of snow in 1921 and 6.03 meters in 1922. A generalized table of the relation of snow duration and altitude is that of the Harz Mountains of Central Germany.

SNOW DURATION IN THE HARZ MOUNTAINS

Altitude in meters	240	400	550	700	850	1000	1150
Duration in days	60	82	104	122	136	162	180

The depth of snow cover as increasing with altitude is demonstrated by this Swiss table: [1]

AVERAGE ANNUAL DEPTH OF SNOW IN SWITZERLAND (1896–1905)

Station	Altitude in meters	Depth of snow in centimeters
Elm	963	416
Engleberg	1018	437
Davos	1561	519
Sils-Maria	1814	408
Berhardin	2073	955
St. Bernhard (1874–83)	2476	1050

In the valley of the Inn at 2500 meters there are but 8 weeks free from snow on shady slopes. Permanent snow is found at 3000 meters. In the Vallée de Conches at 1370 meters snow will reach the depth of three and more meters. In 1496 drifting snow covered the church at Münster. At 1700 meters the depth has been 7 meters. Tall poles must be set to guide travelers.

One of the most decisive elements of mountain climatology is the snow line. By the snow line is meant the lower limit of snow. There are two types of snow lines. The *climatic snow line* is the highest of the lower limits of the snow, that which is seen in mid-summer. Though the general meteorological elements enter into this limitation, it may well be also the limit of *névé* or hardened snow. The second type of snow line is the *orographic snow line*. This is the lowest of the lower limits of snow, that of mid-winter. Snow lines as limits to human cultures should be considered by months. Perhaps the snow lines of April, May, and June are more critical than those of other months. Obviously, and especially considering the preceding table of snow duration in Bavaria, the snow line of spring is more significant than that of autumn. (Figure 10.)

Fritzsch gives the following numerical relations between climate and orographic snow lines. The regularity of the differences is worthy of note:

[1] Maurer.

SNOW LINES IN THE ORTLER ALPS

	North	East	South	West	Average
Climatic snow line	2870 m.	2940 m.	3060 m.	2990 m.	2965 m.
Orographic snow line ..	2540	2640	2750	2630	2640
Difference	330	300	310	360	325

The elevation of the snow line is the result of balance between supply and wastage. What is perhaps the highest climatic snow line in the world is in the Himalayas at 6100 meters, as reported by Strachey in the *Encyclopaedia Britannica*. Here is illustrated the question of supply and wastage. The extreme elevation is due to meager supply. The climatic snow line in the Alps varies locally

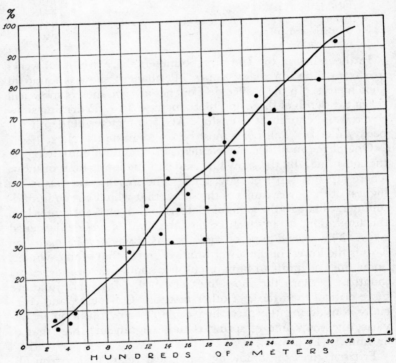

FIG. 7. PERCENTAGE OF TOTAL PRECIPITATION IN SNOW, SWISS ALPS
(*After Maurer.*)

The dots represent the stations of observation. The line, an average, shows a consistent increase of snow percentage with increasing altitude.

between 2700 and 3100 meters according to latitude, exposure, cloudiness (which affects evaporation), and mass of mountain. Where precipitation is slight and annual range of temperature is small the snow line will be low, that is, below the level of the mean annual isotherm of o degrees. The relation of the snow line to isotherm levels is discussed in another section.

The height of the orographic snow line in Switzerland is indicated by the following very general table (see also Figure 11):

DURATION OF SNOW COVER ACCORDING TO ALTITUDE IN SWITZERLAND

Altitude in meters	Number of days
650	77
1300	200
1950	245

If the snow line, in a general way, has a mean annual temperature of o degrees there should be a decrease of elevation with increasing latitude. The failure of precipitation in the trade wind belts in continental stations causes a break in the curve. The following table was compiled by the late Robert DeCourcy Ward:

CLIMATIC SNOW LINE IN NORTHERN HEMISPHERE HIGH LATITUDES

Latitudes	Locality	Alt. in meters
82° N	Franz Joseph's Land	100–300
77	Spitzbergen	460
73–74	Nova Zembla	600
70–71	Norway: coast	700–800
	inland	1000
70	Greenland: inland	700–800
64–65	Iceland: north side	300
	south side	600
60	Mt. Saint Elias: west slope	1600
	east slope	1800
55	Kamchatka	1600
50	Vancouver Island	1600–1800
49	Cascade Mountains	2000
47	Tyrolean Alps	2820
45	Mt. Hood	2250
43	Pyrenees: north side	2790
	south side	2400
42	Mt. Shasta	2400

There is no climatic snow line for the northern tropical regions, though isolated patches of snow remain upon the mountains. The one exception to the increasing elevation in the table is the low record of Mount Hood, where the supply of snow is excessive. In the Arctic the climatic snow line is not known on land surfaces, but in the Antarctic it does reach sea level. Much geography may be read into the foregoing table. Latitude, marine influences, continentality, and exposure are indicated. Mass of mountain is hardly less important than the other factors. Snow lines are generally 600 meters lower in the central massifs of Switzerland than in the border ranges. In this respect mass of mountain can be thought of as influencing temperature.

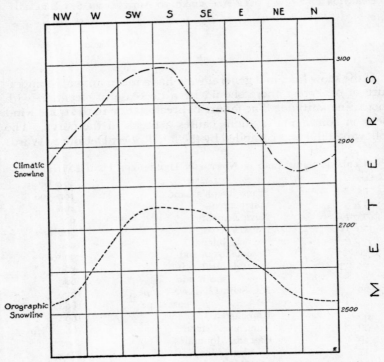

FIG. 10. SNOW LIMITS IN THE ORTLER ALPS, AUSTRIA. (*After Fritsch.*)

An obvious element in the distribution of snow is the degree of slope. A steep slope will not hold snow. Such steep eminences as K² and Nangi Parbet in the Himalayas shed snow in avalanches to such a degree that glaciers do not originate at the peaks but far below at a break in slope.

FIG. 8. SNOW COLLECTING FIELDS OF THE ALETSCH GLACIER, BERNESE OBERLAND

FIG. 9. TUNNEL IN AN AVALANCHE, SWISS ALPS

A scene in June. It is frequently cheaper to drive a tunnel through an avalanche deposit than to clear a passage. This deposit is from an annually recurrent slide.

The best example of the influence of precipitation upon the snow line is found in transverse valleys in mountains sufficiently high to be true climatic barriers. The Himalayas are not everywhere exposed to the moisture bearing winds. At Leh in Western Tibet a snow cover of 3 centimeters would be normal and in the high passes at 5100 to 5800 meters snow cover is frequently not more than 6 centimeters. Yet eastward, where the ranges are struck by monsoon winds, the passes are blocked from September to mid-June.

Of the two controls, precipitation and solar heat, we may do well to regard precipitation as the greater in determining snow lines. Again referring to the Himalayas, between 27 and 34 degrees North latitude we find that on the Indian or wet side average climatic snow line is 4900 meters, while on the Tibetan or dry side the line is 5600 meters. Supply here negatives the influence of exposure to sun. Moisture and aridity seasons often counteract the temperature seasons. In the mountains along the Upper Mekong the winter snow line is 5180 meters, while in summer it is only 4270 to 4570 meters. This is because of the excessive aridity of the monsoon winter. As latitude increases, the matter of exposure to sun becomes relatively more important. This is illustrated by the south and north exposures in the Inntal of Austria.

EXPOSURE AND SNOW IN THE INNTAL

	South slope	North slope
March	960	720
April	1270	1110
May	1700	1540
June	2190	2030
July	2680	2470
August	3130	2930
September	3210	2760
October	2150	1890
November	1300	1010
December	740	680

The Caucasus illustrates at once the factors of precipitation and temperature.

MEAN CLIMATIC SNOW LINES OF THE CAUCASUS

	Latitude	North slope	South slope
Western ranges	47.7–43.5 N	3400	2920
Central ranges	41.5–42.7	3300	3230
Eastern ranges	40.5–41.5	3600	3720

As the Peruvian Andes are north-south ranges in low latitudes the question of temperature exposure is largely eliminated and precipitation exposure is demonstrated. Near Quito on the snowy exposure the line has a mean altitude of 4560 meters while the dry side has an altitude of 4740 meters.

Human Responses to Snow

Though the human responses of climate are for the most part assigned to later chapters, it is convenient to consider here the importance of snow and the importance of avalanches. Snow has four types of influences on human affairs:

1. Direct influence of snow cover.
2. Influence of snow on temperature.
3. As a source of water supply and floods.
4. As avalanches.

One of the best studies of the influence of snow upon the life of mountain folk is that of Aimée Bigallet, a school teacher in the hamlet of Etages, in the commune of Saint-Christophe-en-Oisans. In the winter recorded, that of 1921–22, the hamlet of Etages had 160 centimeters of snow in January alone. The mountain torrent roared under a roof of ice. Wind shook the houses until the furniture trembled. February saw 69 centimeters of snow, and even March had 14 days of snowfall. Yet the altitude was great enough to permit a degree of insolation, so that in spite of low air temperatures the school children ate out of doors on March 17th, and the men gathered for gossip on the only level spot in the hamlet, the bridge across the stream. Communications were broken; the telephone was down on November 18th and repaired in June. The post got through only between storms and when there was not too great danger of avalanches. There was no beast travel. All movement outside the village was on skis. A child fell ill in March; the father was not able to get down the valley for a physician's advice and remedies until April 12th; the child itself could not be taken to the doctor until a month later. A dead body was retained five days in February before a party of men on skis could be gathered to remove it. Dead bodies in some valleys are frozen and kept for months.

Descriptions of the influence of isolation due to snow upon cottage industry are numerous. Men who would otherwise be idle have time to carve wooden toys, to construct clocks and watches carefully, to manufacture optical glass and scientific instruments. The women make lace and do weaving and embroidery work. Though water-power or labor supply has centralized these industries in such places as Geneva and Neuchâtel, the delights of summer life on a Swiss farm will always keep from the city many people who in winter will turn to the cottage industry.

In winter the Swiss live in substantial and often ornate houses of wood and stone, since both materials are at hand. Because the buildings are low, they are more easily heated. Where there is much snow, the roofs are usually high-pitched so that the snow may be easily shed. However, in the Alps there are places where the winds are so strong that, to withstand them better, the roof is low and the slabs or shingles are weighted down with stones. The period of indoor living is long, since the snow may lie upon the ground for seven or eight months of the year. During this period poor ventilation and lack of exercise or mental stimulus have a decided ill effect upon health. This condition, plus the hard struggle for existence, may be a reason for the large number of insane in the more remote districts. The tavern life of the little villages is another unfortunate result of the indoor confinement. Certainly the rigor of winter life is among the causes of the large seasonal migration.

The long duration of the snow cover limits the growing season. No matter how high are the temperatures of air and soil on cleared areas, the regions given over to snow are more or less dormant. Even trees are limited in their upward expansion by snow, as in the Tirol at 2400 meters, where the duration of snow is nine and one-half months. On the other hand, a moderate duration and depth of snow cover is beneficial to both trees and grain, because it protects against severe cold. To quicken melting in spring, earth is at times scattered over the snow.

Snow greatly facilitates transportation. This is true of valley roads where there is flattish land and not too great danger from avalanches. Little trails on steep slopes are difficult under snow. Logging on slopes is greatly facilitated by winter. The common custom in European mountain meadows of building the hay barn in the center of the meadow instead of near the stable, indeed, it may be, several miles from the stable, is explained by the fact that hay is more easily transported in winter over the

snow than over summer roads. More often than not, the barn is
up the mountain from the stable. The hay is brought down in
winter on sleds, when the difficulty is not so much in moving the
hay as in controlling the speed at which it descends to the valley.
Clear cold days and nights may witness an almost constant procession of sleds coming to the village. So isolated are many of the
meadows that without snow transportation the hay could be
brought down only with the greatest difficulty. In mountains
where snow is scanty, hay may be brought from the meadows by
aerial cables.

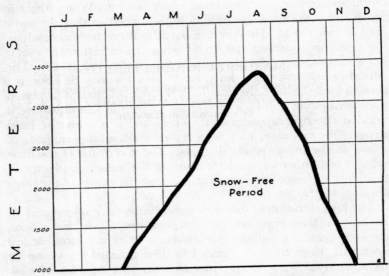

FIG. 11. SNOW FREE PERIOD IN THE OISANS ACCORDING TO ALTITUDE
(*After Blache.*)

The relation between snow and temperature readily suggests
itself. By reducing mountain temperatures to sea level one has
evidence of the influence of snow on temperature. Bénévent has
done this for the French Alps. He finds Ventoux in the Southern
Alps a cold island in winter because of snow. The degree to
which snow cools air may be suggested by the differences in snow
and air temperatures.

A characteristic of high lands in spring is that the season will be
well advanced before the snow disappears. Once the snow is

gone the soil, easily dried because of its slope position, warms quickly. The rapidity of budding and flower growth is one of the delights of spring at high altitudes. Because the snow remains in patches well into the warm season, flowers push up through the snow. During the period when snow has disappeared from the valleys but not from the uplands there is, naturally, an increase of the vertical temperature gradient over the normal.

AIR AND SNOW TEMPERATURES AT DAVOS
(1560 meters alt.)
7 A.M.

Days of Observation			Air	Snow	Difference	Amt. of cloud
1891	February	28	−12.0°	−16.7°	4.7°	2.2
	March	31	− 5.3	− 7.0	1.7	6.6
	December [1]	12	− 9.3	−13.9	4.6	4.5
1892	January	31	− 9.7	−11.9	2.2	6.2
	February [1]	20	− 6.0	− 7.5	1.5	6.6
		122	Mean − 8.5	−11.4	2.9	

2 P.M.

Days of Observation			Air	Snow	Difference	Amt. of cloud
1891	February	28	1.9°	− 7.2°	9.1°	1.8
	March	31	2.9	− 1.1	4.0	0.4
	December [1]	12	−3.1	−10.1	7.0	4.0
1892	January	31	−1.7	− 6.0	4.3	5.6
	February [1]	20	1.2	− 3.2	4.4	6.6
		122	Mean 0.2	− 5.5	5.7	

The snow of high elevations melts slowly. It is warm air temperature rather than direct insolation that is effective in melting snow. Snow reflects solar heat some ten times more than does soil. This is true because of the lack of color and the crystal surface of snow. Therefore insolation values during the snow cover are increased by the amount of reflected light and heat.

The most recent development of mountain studies is that of snow surveying. All work along this line is of the present century and most of it of the last decades. The object of such studies is to ascertain the amount of snow stored on the heights, in order to forecast the possibilities of irrigation and water supply for the summer, and, secondarily, to indicate the probability of floods. Snow storage depends upon not only the amount of precipita-

[1] Records not complete.

tion and the extent and slope of terrain but also the weather conditions during the storage period. Moreover, depth of snow is not necessarily a measure of the water content of a field. Snow has compressibility. The difficulties of judging the water content have been more nearly overcome by American students than by the Europeans. The article of J. E. Church on "Snow Surveying" meets the need of students in that subject. His article goes into conservation of snow, forecasting of run-off, floods, and certain matters not discussed in this volume. Some generalities and statements from Church's article are given here:

The higher the mountains the longer the period of snow storage.

The evaporation of snow on mountain heights is great. On the summit of Mt. Rose (10,800 feet) in 69 hours an evaporation of 2.32 inches, water content, was recorded.

Evaporation will occur at night and below freezing temperatures. A 31-mile wind created an evaporation of snow of .08 to .10 inches in a single night.

The efficiency of mountain forests as snow gatherers and conservation is shown by contrasts between measurements on the summit of Mt. Rose and forest stations in April, 1910:

On summit:

Sheltered by Observatory	52.5 inches
Wind-swept slope	8.1 "
Protected slope	78.1 "
Average of unforested talus slope	40.8 "
Average forest station	88.6 "

Talus slopes are less efficient conservers of snow than forest slopes. Dense forests hold snow on trees and increase evaporation.

The depth and character of the cover is a basis of forecasting available water for irrigation. So accurate are the methods that farmers have changed their crop plans because of the forecast.

A. J. Henry has studied the relations between snow and floods. He lays stress on the unimportance of insolation as a factor in snow melting and as a cause of floods. Flood waters from snows come only at a time of high *night* temperature. Fresh snow melts more rapidly than old, packed snow. The decreasing depth of snow is not always a measure of the melting. Depth of snow may decrease by (1) settling, (2) packing by wind, (3) absorption by ground when not frozen, (4) evaporation.

Lastly, snow as a source of water may pass through the ice

stage. Glaciers melt slowly. Curiously, several of the large American cities depend on water which originates with glacial streams. As the glaciers are becoming seriously reduced in size, there is genuine concern as to the water supply of the future.

SNOW SLIDES

The varied forms derived from the Latin word for slide, *labina*, suggest the ubiquity of slides in mountain regions. We have for snow slides the terms *lavina, lavigna, avalanga, levina, avalanche,* and *valanga.* The significance of the place names Lavanchy, Lavancher, Lanch, Lanchettes, and Lakne is apparent.

An obvious factor in the retention of snow on steep slopes is the character of the surface upon which the snow lies. Is the terrain a continuously downward slope, or is it rough and uneven in its grade? Are there rocks, ledges, or fences to hold the snow? Is there a bush or forest covering? The slope necessary for slides depends upon weather conditions, the quality of the snow, and the topography. A very general set of slope limits for snow without slides is:

22 degrees slope and 40 to 50 centimeters of snow
30 " " " 15 " " "
50 " " " 5 " " "

Allix is our chief student of the avalanche. He divides snowslides into two classes: the cold avalanche and the warm avalanche. The cold avalanche involves the movement of dry snow. It takes place in mid-winter at the time of greatest cold and often after a drop in temperature. Though the snow involved in a slide may lie directly upon the ground, movement is more likely if the snow lies upon an icy surface developed in the autumn and subsequently covered with the dry snow. A chief danger of the cold avalanche is the impacting of the snow as it strikes its resting place. This type of avalanche is perhaps the equivalent of the *Staublawine* of the Germans. This is a dust-snow avalanche attended by a whirlwind. This cold snow dust may also slide in a less catastrophic manner. In a ravine dry snow may descend as a powder 'waterfall' for days. The dust avalanche which commences upon high alps and gains the oversteep slope of the lower valley may roar toward the valley way at 100 to 200 kilometers an hour.

The warm avalanche (warm is here a relative term) is of damp snow. Such avalanches are water-soaked, heavy, and tend to act as a single mass. Their destructiveness can be easily imagined. The descent may be as a cascade, bringing destruction unwarned to a village. More often the descent is as a landslip, a relatively slow movement but one of force to be feared. Such a snow slip will have a velocity of from a few to 50 miles per hour. This warm avalanche is the possible equivalent of the German *Schlaglawine*. In the period including the winters of 1900–01 and 1913–14 in Savoy, of 586 avalanches, 421 were warm avalanches, 31 were cold avalanches, and two were glacial.

Protective works can be divided into two classes, preventive and curative.

(1) Preventive methods aim at precluding the formation of the avalanche by retaining the snow on the high slopes. This has been done in many cases by the construction of wooden or stone fences. There should be reforestation of high slopes wherever feasible. Avalanches may start from above or below the tree line. About two-thirds of the ground avalanches and about half of the other avalanches start below tree line. This indicates the importance of reforestation. Stone walls of a meter or more in height and a few meters long are scattered over steep hillsides. Slat fences are used in the same manner. In the Lower Engadine ditches one meter broad, of similar depth, and six to nine meters long, were built as protection against avalanches. Today protection against the avalanche is so common a feature of Alpine valleys as to excite little curiosity in the traveler. (See Figures 12 and 13.)

(2) Curative methods consist in devices to restrict the destructive power of avalanches and include the building of strong masonry walls in the shape of plowshares. In Switzerland artificial channels in stonework have been built to carry off the torrent of snow. Roads and railroads which are forced to cross the path of avalanches may have a stone shed built over the road with a slanting roof. The slide then passes over the roadway. When roads are not so protected and the snow blocks the road, a tunnel may be driven through the snow. The tunnel may last far into the summer. (Figure 9.)

There is little possibility of forecasting the precise moment of release of an avalanche. The only observers qualified to speak on this matter have all been impressed by the suddenness of the

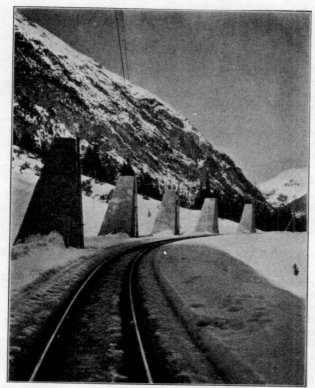

FIG. 12. PIERS TO PROTECT POLES AGAINST AVALANCHES, ENGADINE
(Courtesy of the Rhaetischebahn.)

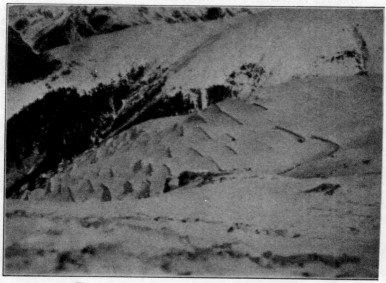

FIG. 13. FENCES USED TO PREVENT AVALANCHES
(Courtesy of the Rhaetischebahn.)

occurrence. One's best guide in escaping the dangers of avalanches is prudence. Trifling causes such as the following may start an avalanche: the passage of a party of persons; a slight shaking of the ground; the sounding of a distant train; or bells of the flocks. There is reported to be a local regulation against the Swiss national habit of yodeling, lest snow slides be started. There are critical periods during which avalanches are particularly to be feared. At such times the snow is in a position of unstable equilibrium.

In the prediction of avalanches the most one can hope to obtain is the determination of this state of unstable equilibrium, indicating the liability to accidents at critical periods. The only practical method, outside of native intelligence, is the preparation of meteorological probability charts. For this it would be necessary to determine for a number of years, by means of daily observations taken in the high mountain regions, the meteorological characteristics of the periods that precede the starting of avalanches. This would include pressure, winds, temperature, and precipitation. In addition, one should know the density and temperature of the snow and the condition of the surface upon which the snow rests. As has been said, an icy surface developed in the autumn will increase the probability of avalanches through the winter. A marked rise in temperature, an accumulation of soft snow, or a wind striking the inclined snow fields are conditions which indicate probability of an avalanche.

In high mountains whose slopes have been oversteepened by glaciation avalanches are the rule rather than the exception. It is difficult for a plainsman to appreciate the extent of the danger. In Switzerland there are 9368 avalanche corridors, of which 5294 see service many times a year. There are, in addition, many avalanches which occur occasionally but do not develop regular corridors. A limited region in the French Alps, the Tarentaise, is known to have 46 important slide corridors which are greatly feared for their recurrent avalanches.

The erosive effect of the avalanche on the mountain surface, aside from the damage done in the zone of habitation, is a matter of no small moment. It is true that the work of an avalanche is over in a moment, but during this moment it can move more earth than the stream in the ravine during the entire year. Mougin measured the amount of material dropped by avalanches in the inhabited valleys of Savoy from 1908 to 1912; the total volume of earthy material thus carried amounted to 44,000 cubic meters. If we assume that a large ground avalanche descends through 2000 meters with a speed of 10 meters a second and a mass of 200,000 cubic meters, its energy is approximately 20,000,000 horse power.

A second danger is the destruction of forests. The ravines scoured each year by avalanches are denuded of trees and new tree growth there is impossible. Moreover, there is a pushed wind which precedes the avalanche. The writer has seen a tree two feet in diameter which was broken off 20 feet from the ground by such a wind in the Yosemite Valley. This blast may create havoc with a forest before the snow actually strikes. The blast not infrequently is forced upon a forest of an opposite slope so as to destroy forests beyond the reach of the snow. An example of this is to be found in a valley above Pralognan, French Alps. Reports state that avalanche winds are felt kilometers away from the snow slide.

Some minor results of avalanches are the favorable deposition of soil in valleys, the early removal of snow from high level fields, the provision of wood for fuel at the base of the slide, the storage of water in the compact and slowly melting snow deposit of the valley. There is also a local lowering of temperatures from the accumulation in the valley.

Avalanches in certain valleys prevent winter travel. So frequent are they that they form a constant danger to the traveler. It is the slides rather than the depth of snow cover which isolate certain villages. This is particularly true because, while sometimes they follow known tracks, at other times they are as capricious as lightning. In addition to the element of danger, the slides often obstruct roads. Travel may temporarily go over the deposit, roads may be dug out, or, as previously mentioned, tunnels may be constructed. Telephone and telegraph lines, of course, suffer. The villagers of St.-Maurice and St.-Jacques in the French Alps are held virtually prisoners for months by the fear of avalanches. The Rhone Valley of Switzerland has numerous crosses marking the place of death of winter travelers.

In 1879, along the 5-kilometer route from Toesch to Zermatt, there was no space of 50 meters free from avalanche deposit. In the same year in the Saas and Binnen valleys it was dangerous to venture from the houses. In 1917 one valley in Switzerland counted 30 avalanches. That year there was great loss of life, houses, barns, and cattle throughout the Alps. A railway train at Wolfgang near Davos was destroyed with the loss of ten lives. The country gave 192,000 francs for relief in the devastated areas. Swiss history is indeed full of snow slide catastrophes. On January 16th and 17th of the year 1594, slides tore down at Bedretto in Switzerland a church, a rectory, houses, and barns. On January 22nd, 1634, the priest's house was destroyed and the priest himself buried. In 1695 the snow measured there 3.6 meters and slides came from all sides. The church, houses, and barns were destroyed.

In the valley of St. Antonien in Grisons from 1608 to 1876 there were destroyed 38 houses, 200 barns, 4 saw mills, 43 persons, and 130 head of cattle. In 1618 at Henkerbad 61 persons were killed. An avalanche in Valais in 1719 wiped out a town, killing 60 persons; that of Obergestelen in 1720 destroyed 120 houses and killed 80 persons and 400 head of cattle; that of Saas in Grisons in 1689 wiped out the village and all the inhabitants.

On the 20th of February, 1720, the Swiss village of Obergestelen was destroyed and 84 of its 200 inhabitants were killed by an avalanche which leaped an intervening forest and wrecked one-third of the village. In a dairy country the loss of a cow is a calamity, and at that time six hundred head of cattle were destroyed. The snow from the avalanche blocked the river Rhone, which quickly cut through it and then flooded a portion of the settlement. The remainder of the town was laid in ruins by a fire. The indomitable villagers rebuilt their town, only to have it subsequently destroyed by an avalanche from the other side of the valley.

BIBLIOGRAPHICAL NOTES

Evaporation

Camp, W. H. "The Grass Balds of the Great Smoky Mountains of Tennessee and North Carolina," in *Ohio Journal of Science*, xxxi (1931), pp. 157–164.

Chodat, Fernand. "Résultats d'une enquête atmométrique au jardin alpin 'La Linnaea,'" in *Archives des sciences physiques et naturelles*, 5me période, ix (1927), supplément, pp. 126–127. Evaporation rates of Alpine habitats.

Gates, F. C. "Evaporation in Vegetation at Different Heights," in *American Journal of Botany*, xiii (1926), pp. 167–178. Also, in part, in *Monthly Weather Review*, liv (1926), p. 61.

Harshberger, J. W. "Alpine Fell-Fields of Eastern North America," in *Geographical Review*, vii (1919), pp. 233–255.

Livingston, B. E. "Evaporation and Plant Habitats," in *The Plant World*, xi (1908), pp. 1–9.

Lüdi, Werner. "Die Ergebnisse von Verdunstungsmessungen in Lauterbrunnental und in Bern in den Jahren 1917 bis 1920," in *Festschrift Carl Schröter* (Zurich, 1925), pp. 185–204. Good.

Maurer, J. "Verdunstungsmessungen an Freien Wasserflächen in Hochgebirge," in *Verhandlungen der Klimatologischen Tagung in Davos*, 1925, pp. 119–126.

Precipitation

Ahlmann, H. W. "Precipitation Conditions in the Horung Massif," in *Geografiska Annaler*, ix (1927), pp. 21–35.

Bénévent, Ernest. "La pluviosité de la France du Sud-Est," in *Recueil des travaux de l'Institut de géographie alpine*, i (1913), pp. 323–442.

Bénévent, Ernest. "Du rôle des montagnes dans la formation de la pluie," in *Revue de géographie alpine*, xii (1924), pp. 173–187.

Blanchard, Raoul. "Énormes précipitations dans le massif de la Chartreuse," in *Recueil des travaux l'Institut de géographie alpine*, vii (1919), pp. 717–720.

Brockmann-Jerosch, Heinrich. *Die Niederschlagsverhältnisse der Schweiz*. Zurich, 1925.

Brooks, C. F. "Orographic Rainfall," in *Geographical Review*, xv (1925), p. 311. A review of Bénévent's article of 1924.

Goodnough, X. H. "Rainfall in New England," in *Journal of the New England Water Works Association*, xxix (1915), pp. 237–438.

Hann, Julius. "Der Regenfall auf den Hawaii-Inseln," in *Meteorologische Zeitschrift*, xii (1895), pp. 1–14.

Hellmann, Gustav, and others. *Klima-Atlas von Deutschland*. Berlin, 1921.

Henry, A. J. "Increase of Precipitation with Altitude," in *Monthly Weather Review*, xlvii (1919), pp. 33–41.

Huber, Rudolf. *Die Niederschläge in Kanton Basel in ihrer Beziehung zu den orographischen Verhältnissen*. Zurich, 1894.

Jefferson, Mark. "The Rainfall of Java," in *Geographical Review*, v (1918), pp. 492–495.

Knoch, Karl, and Reichel, Eberhard. *Verteilung und Jahrlicher Gang der Niederschläge in den Alpen*. Berlin, 1930. (*Veröffentlichungen des Preussischen Meteorologischen Instituts*, Nr. 375.) Important.

Lee, C. H. "Precipitation and Altitude in the Sierra," in *Monthly Weather Review*, xxxix (1911), pp. 1092–1099.

Lee, W. T. "The Raton Mesas of New Mexico and Coiorado," in *Geographical Review*, xi (1921), pp. 384–397. Human significance.

Lütschg, Otto. *Über Niederschlag und Abfluss im Hochgebirge.* Zurich, 1926. (Schweizerischer Wasserwirtschaftsverband, Nr. 14.)

McAdie, A. G. "The Rainfall of California," in *University of California Publications in Geography*, i (1914), pp. 127–240. Excellent.

Varney, B. M. "Monthly Variations of the Precipitation-Altitude Relation in the Central Sierra Nevada of California," in *Monthly Weather Review*, xlviii (1920), pp. 648–650.

Wells, E. L. "Precipitation in Oregon," in *Monthly Weather Review*, l (1922), pp. 405–411.

Snow

Allix, André. "Neiges d'été en 1922 et leur 'limite instantanée,'" in *Revue de géographie alpine*, x (1922), pp. 649–664.

Bénévent, Ernest. "La neige dans les Alpes françaises," in *Recueil des travaux de l'Institut de géographie alpine*, v (1917), pp. 403–498.

Bigallet, Aimée. "La vie d'hiver dans le Haut-Vénéon," in *Revue de géographie alpine*, x (1922), pp. 625–634. Excellent.

Brooks, C. F. "New England Snowfall," in *Monthly Weather Review*, xlv (1917), pp. 271–285. Heavy snow on low mountains.

Brückner, Eduard. "Die Eiszeiten in den Alpen," in *Geographische Zeitschrift*, x (1904), pp. 569–578.

Brückner, Eduard. "Über den Einfluss der Schneedecke auf das Klima der Alpen," in *Zeitschrift des Deutschen und Österreichischen Alpenvereins*, xxiv (1893), pp. 21–51.

Church, J. E. "The Conservation of Snow: Its Dependence on Forests and Mountains," in *Scientific American Supplement*, lxxiv (1912), pp. 152–155, and, in German translation, in *Meteorologische Zeitschrift*, xxx (1913), pp. 1–10.

Church, J. E. "Snow Surveying," in *Geographical Review*, xxiii (1933), pp. 529–563. An important article.

Dainelli, Giotto. "Il limite delle nevi nel bacino superiore dell' Indo (Caracorùm e Himàlaia occidentale)," in *Recueil de travaux offert à M. Jovan Cvijić* (Belgrade, 1924), pp. 1–10.

Dansey, R. P. "The Glacial Snow of Ben Nevis," in *Symons's Meteorological Magazine*, xl (1905), pp. 29, 32.

Ficker, H. von. "Der Einfluss orographischer Verhältnisse auf die Niederschläge in Tirol und Vorarlberg," in *Meteorologische Zeitschrift*, xxvi (1909), pp. 311–315.

Fisher, L. C. "Snowfall on Mount Rainier," in *Monthly Weather Review*, xlvi (1918), pp. 327–330.

Henry, A. J. "The Disappearance of Snow in the High Sierra Nevada of California," in *Monthly Weather Review*, xliv (1916), pp. 150–153.

Hofmeier, Walter. "Die Hochalpen im Winter," in *Zeitschrift des Deutschen und Österreichischen Alpenvereins*, lv (1924), pp. 246–268.

Huber, Rudolf. *Die Niederschläge in Kanton Basel in ihrer Beziehung zu den orographischen Verhältnissen.* Zurich, 1894.

Jegerlehner, J. "Die Schneegrenze in den Gletschergebieten der Schweiz," in *Beiträge zur geophysik,* v (1903), pp. 486–568. A factual article.

Knoch, Karl, and Reichel, Eberhard. *Verteilung und jährlicher Gang der Niederschläge in den Alpen.* Berlin, 1930. (*Veröffentlichungen des Preussischen Meteorologischen Instituts, Nr.* 375.)

Köppen, Wladimir. "Die Lufttemperatur an der Schneegrenze," in *Petermanns Mitteilungen,* lxvi (1920), pp. 78–80.

LeConte, J. N. "Snowfall in the Sierra Nevada," in *Sierra Club Bulletin,* vi (1907–08), pp. 310–314. A famous American student of mountains.

Maige-Lefournier, Mathilde. "La vie traditionnelle hivernale à Bonneval-sur-Arc (1846 m.)," in *La montagne,* xiii (1917), pp. 1–16. Good description.

Maurer, J. "Temporäre Schneegrenze und mittlere Schmelzwasserhöhen im schweizerischen Alpengebiet nach neueren Erhebungen," in *Meteorologische Zeitschrift,* xxvi (1909), pp. 539–546.

Palmer, A. H. "The Region of Greatest Snowfall in the United States," in *Monthly Weather Review,* xliii (1915), pp. 217–221.

Ratzel, Friedrich. "Die Schneedecke, besonders in deutschen Gebirgen," in *Forschungen zur deutschen Landes- und Volkskunde,* iv (1890), pp. 107–277.

Sherier, J. M. "Mountain Snowfall and Flood Crests in the Colorado," in *Monthly Weather Review,* li (1923), pp. 639–641.

Avalanches

See especially Bénévent under *General References on Climate.*

Allix, André. "Avalanches," in *Geographical Review,* xiv (1924), pp. 519–560. Repeated, with slight modifications, in the next item.

Allix, André. "Les avalanches," in *Revue de géographie alpine,* xiii (1925), pp. 359–423. With a large bibliography.

Alter, J. C. "Avalanche at Bingham, Utah," in *Monthly Weather Review,* liv (1926), pp. 60–61.

Coaz, Johannes. *Statistik und Verbau der Lawinen in den Schweizeralpen.* Bern, 1910.

Frech, Fritz. "Über die Lawinen der Alpen," in *Petermanns Mitteilungen,* lviii, 1 (1912), pp. 126–128.

Lunn, Arnold. "Mountaineering on Ski," in *Mountain Craft,* ed. by C. W. Young (London, 1920), pp. 397–470.

Pollack, Vincenz. *Über die Lawinen Österreichs und der Schweiz und deren Verbauungen.* Vienna, 1891.

Pollack, Vincenz. *Über Erfahrungen im Lawinenverbau in Österreich.* Vienna, 1906.

Zdarsky, Matthias. *Beiträge zur Lawinenkunde.* Vienna, 1930.

CHAPTER III

WINDS, CLOUDS, AND SUN

Mountains and Winds

MOUNTAIN areas, like plains, are subjected to prevailing winds. There are, however, a number of wind conditions which are characteristic of mountains.

Mountains thrust their peaks into upper reaches where wind velocities are greater.

Mountains form wind shelters.

Mountains deflect winds and cause special local prevailing wind directions.

Local valley relief may increase velocities.

Out of physical conditions inherent to the mountain area there originate special winds.

Exposure to prevailing winds means greater precipitation, or greater evaporation, or greater warmth or greater cold, as the case may be. These matters need no explanation. But reference must be made to the potency of these conditions. Even low mountain peaks suffer excessive evaporation from high wind velocities, more so apparently than equal altitudes on a flank of a large mountain.

Wind velocity in free air increases with altitude. Unless broken relief of high areas is of such a nature as to offer considerable friction, wind velocities increase with altitude among mountains. The rate at which winds increase in velocity with altitude is suggested by de Martonne in the following table:

Wind Velocity and Altitude

Mountain	Altitude	Relative velocity
Krememunster	390 m.	3.5
Säntis	2500	7.5
Sonnblick	3100	9.3

Indeed, wind velocities may be greater near and about a peak than in free air at the same altitude. The reason for this is the same as that which causes stream currents to become stronger around an impeding boulder than in free channels. A wind of

164 miles per hour (262 kilometers per hour) has been measured in the winter of 1933–34 at the observatory on the summit of Mount Washington, New Hampshire.

Sheltered valleys may be relatively calm, as tourists in the Swiss area can testify. Many of the winds there experienced are indraft or reverse winds which are of slight velocity as compared with the prevailing winds. Peaks, on the other hand, are seldom calm. In a year's observations valley stations as Allsalten in the Rhine Valley had 859 calms, Lugano 949, and Locarno 1001. The summit of Säntis had but 72 calms and the Great St. Bernard but one calm.

Even on plains lower winds do not always have the same direction as that of the prevailing winds over the area at the moment. If a mountain range forms an angle with the prevailing wind direction there will be local deflections of surface winds as compared with the wind directions among and above the peaks. (Figure 14.) An excellent example of valley deflection of wind in the Davos valley, Switzerland, is given by Hugo Bach, *Das Klima von Davos* (Zurich, 1907), p. 86.

Valleys transverse to the wind directions may have relative calm. Generally an obstacle mountain range protects a plane level for a length 16 times its height. This will vary slightly according to the wind velocity and the slope of the mountain. Such is, however, a theoretical rather than an actual protection. Winds may descend sharply on leeward sides of mountains. Mentone on the Riviera is protected from a strong north wind (the Mistral) by the Provençal Alps. But this Mistral may abruptly strike the sea a kilometer from shore.

When a wind has a dominant trend coinciding with a valley axis, the velocity of the wind is intensified along the valley. So intense does the wind become in the valley of the Grand-Buech in the French Alps that it prevents progress in walking. At such times wind velocity in free air may not be intense and the side valleys may have comparative calm.

Throughout the French Alps there is an Italian wind known as La Lombarde which has great force. The explanation is that when a cyclone lies over Southern France and anti-cyclonic conditions prevail over Italy there is difficulty in adjustment of pressures because of the mountain barrier. The wind pouring over the crest is particularly severe. In the Haute Tarentaise it is known as the 'Petit St. Bernard.' In 1882 La Lombarde destroyed 52,000 trees near Chamonix and in 1904 it destroyed 2600 cubic meters of wood (700 cords) in a forest on the French slope. At Séez large stones are needed to weigh down roofs. If the valleys of the French Alps were longitudinal this wind would evolve into a Foehn wind. The Foehn wind is described later in this chapter.

Clouds in Mountains

In addition to the irregularity of clouds according to the variations of current weather, mountains impose upon prevailing winds certain special conditions and create special clouds. The result is that no weather element has greater irregularity than cloudiness.

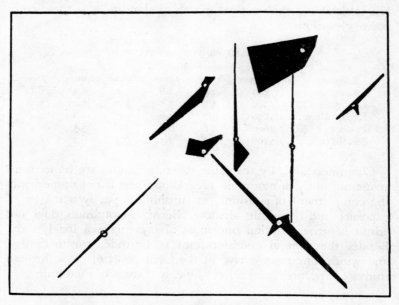

Fig. 14. Wind Roses for Switzerland

Topographic controls are clearly indicated. The massive wind rose in the northeast corner is for the isolated peak of Säntis and so represents winds of the free air. (*After Früh.*)

There cannot even be declared a relationship between altitude and clouds. True, in summer the cold peaks condense moisture and so have hood clouds. The cloud zone of winter is lower than that of summer. Hence the valleys, already deprived of much direct sunlight, are furthermore cloud-enshrouded, whereas the higher elevations are in sunlight. Also the nebulosity of valleys in winter is increased by local fogs. If one were to attempt a generalization as to the relation between altitude and cloudiness, the statement might read in this fashion: Cloudiness increases with altitude within limits. These limits are those of stratus clouds and vary with season, latitude, exposure to wind, and degree of slope. It may be possible that the steeper the slope the greater the cloudiness.

Hann took five principal cities on the Swiss plain, two towns in low valleys in Tirol, three high valley stations, and four pass stations. These he compared with observations on Sonnblick. His table shows the seasonal march of cloudiness at these composite elevations:

SEASONAL CLOUDINESS AND ALTITUDE
(10 equals overcast)

Station	Alt. in meters	Winter	Spring	Summer	Autumn	Year
Swiss plain	420	7.3	5.8	5.2	6.2	6.1
Low valleys	1300	4.6	5.8	5.4	5.2	5.2
High valleys	1830	3.7	4.6	5.0	4.2	4.4
Passes	2600	4.6	6.1	5.6	5.5	5.4
Sonnblick	3100	5.2	7.1	7.3	6.2	6.5

Cloudiness and, by the same token, sunshine are basic in an economic study of mountain life. Cloudiness is not numerically the complement of sunshine, as sunshine is partly a matter of exposure and mountain shadow. Because cloudiness does not admit of generalization one must always make a local study. Besides the general considerations of latitude, continentality, and winds, one must arrive at the local point of view through study of exposure, local relief, slope, and mass of mountain.

LOCAL WINDS

The question of local winds, like the question of local clouds, so varies according to locality that generalizations are out of the question. The best that can be done is to describe some actual occurrences of typical winds.

On the windward side of a mountain barrier valleys may have winds of a direction reverse to the prevailing wind of the moment. The apparent explanation of a valley wind of a direction opposite to the prevailing wind of the unobstructed upper layers is that the lower edge of the wind is caught by the projecting mountain crest and forced down and backwards along the valley. This is much the same as a back eddy at the side of a river. Such a wind is illustrated in the valley of Bagnères-de-Bigorre in the central French Pyrenees. This town has an altitude of 550 meters. Seventeen kilometers up the valley is the Pic du Midi, whose summit is 2877 meters in elevation. Both town and peak have meteorological stations, and indeed the summit station is reputed to be the highest permanently inhabited house in Europe. The valley has a north-south trend. The range crest runs east-west and the Pic du Midi is an outlier separated from the crest.

From the records a sequence of 20 days was selected at random.

CONTRASTED WINDS OF VALLEY AND PEAK

March 1910	Pic du Midi	Bagnères
1	NW	NW
2	NE	S*
3	NE	S*
4	W	SE*
5	SW	S*
6	SSW	S*
7	NW	S*
8	ENE	S*
9	SW	SSE*
10	WSW	S*
11	SW	S*
12	SW	SE*
13	NE	NW*
14	NE	S*
15	NE	Calm
16	NW	Calm
17	NW	S*
18	W	S*
19	W	N
20	NE	NNW

From the table it will be seen that there are 18 days of wind in the valley. Of these, 15 (marked with asterisks) have the valley reverse wind.

On clear days, with a serene and deep blue sky, there is frequently to be seen a pennant-like cloud which stretches out from the leeward side of a peak. There are two theoretical explanations of the origin of these cloud banners commonly given in print. One is that the wind striking the face of the mountain increases locally the atmospheric pressure. On passing to the far side of the peak the wind enters a region of reduced pressure and condensation occurs. The second, and more common, explanation is that the face of the mountain chills the wind and the condensed moisture is blown to windward. If the first of the two explanations is true, why should the cloud occur only at the peak? There is the same differentiation of pressure to be found lower on the mountain flanks. As to the second explanation, alpinists know well that the rock temperatures of mountain peaks at midday are quite high as compared with the air temperatures.

The true explanation is that a wind will, upon passing a peak or a range, form an indraft of ascending air. At such times the valley wind will be exactly opposite in direction to the high-level prevailing wind of the day. This is a common occurrence. The ascending wind is not infrequently cloud-forming at the head of the valley. The same thing will happen at a peak. There will be, even though quite localized, an ascending current on the leeward side of the peak which forms clouds. The cloud upon coming within the influence of the prevailing wind will stream out from the peak as a banner. In figure 17 we have a situation which goes far towards explaining this type of cloud formation. This example was seen in the Tarentaise not far from the Petit Saint Bernard. The east wind coming from Italy not infrequently covers the Tarentaise and especially the Vanois with clouds. This is perhaps owing to the contrasted temperatures of warm Italy and somewhat cooler France. But the extent to which the indraft on the leeward sides of mountains contributes to this cloud formation may be guessed at from the diagram. Definite movements of the clouds showed the direction of the winds. The more steep the leeward side of the mountain the more definitely curved was the direction of the indraft. One is led to suspect that the steeper the leeward side the stronger the current of the indraft.

A well recognized example of this indraft is a common phenomenon at the observatory of the Pic du Midi in Bigorre. The usual summer wind over this peak is from the southwest. The west wind is commonly accompanied by a strong wind up from the northern valley and a cloud where this wind coming up

FIG. 15. CLOUDS IN THE COL DE TOURMALET, FRENCH PYRENEES

The clouds in the valley are a stage in the clearing of weather following a general storm derived from clouds of a higher level. This is sheep country. The material in the foreground represents road repairs. The trail leads to higher pastures.

FIG. 16. CLOUDS AFTER A SNOWFALL, HOHEN TAUREN, AUSTRIA

Typical of clearing weather in mountain valleys.

(*amont* [1]) meets the prevailing wind. Almost exactly half of the platform upon which the Observatoire is located is then in cloud, according to M. Camille Dauzère, the Director.

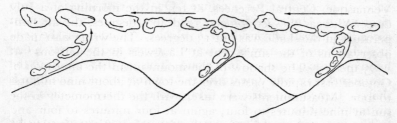

FIG. 17. INDRAFT WINDS IN THE TARENTAISE, FRENCH ALPS

Proof extraordinary comes from the volume *First over Everest* by P. F. M. Fellowes and others (London, 1933), the story of the airplane flight. The planes flew through the famous cloud banner of that peak. The observers reported the cloud to be a stream, several miles in length, of icy particles drawn up from the slope immediately below. It was not blown from the windward side like a 'smoking' sand dune. Indeed the windward side was bare of snow and ice.

The writer is familiar with winds and clouds in the region of the Conflent and Valespir, Pyrénées-Orientales. A remarkable indraft or contrary wind is experienced in the valleys of the Conflent under the influence of the southwest high-level wind which occurs with great regularity in summer. The normal valley wind under these conditions is an indraft wind from the north. This wind forms not infrequently a cloud at the headwaters of the Cadi, a north-flowing stream, and upon the summit land on the crest of the Pyrenees. The observations of the writer during a period in June, 1928, were typical of those weather conditions.

EXAMPLE OF AN INDRAFT WIND

Day	Prevailing high-level wind	Wind at Vernet-les-Bains
11	SW	NE
12	SW	NE
13	SW	NE
14	SW	NE
15	SW	NE

[1] The reader will do well to add to his geographical vocabulary the French words *amont*, meaning upstream, and *aval*, meaning downstream.

Under such conditions a cloud banner forms about the peak of Mount Canigou. The situation is much the same as at the Pic du Midi. Mount Canigou is a sharp peak with summit surface barely large enough for a refuge. On the east side is a steep cirque wall. Under the influence of a southwest wind there is an ascending indraft of considerable velocity. Standing on the peak at such a time one may be in warm sunlight and yet stretch one hand over the cirque and into cloud. This fog that rises from the cirque makes its way upward for some twenty meters, and then is sharply turned and carried off in a northeasterly direction as a distinct cloud banner.

The importance of these winds and resulting clouds may be great. The Valespir is a valley region which runs in the direction of the prevailing (southwest) wind of summer. It lies just south of Mount Canigou and runs from the Pla de Guilhem towards the Mediterranean Sea. The head of this valley and the Pla de Guilhem are famous for the amount of summer cloud which they experience. The tree line on the west, north, and east of Mount Canigou is consistently at 2200 meters, but on the south, or Valespir slope, is only 1600 to 1800 meters. The zone of the mountain pine is here missing. The only explanation for the lower tree line on this southern slope which seemed plausible to the writer was that cloudiness during the growing season was so great that it reduced temperatures and therefore the height limit of the tree. Ordinary cloudiness would be easily explained, as in the other cases, by the indraft condensing upon ascension at the valley head. The extraordinary cloudiness, especially in summer afternoons, called for another explanation. So heavy is this fog that foot paths across the Pla de Guilhem between the Conflent and the Valespir are marked with cairns only a few meters apart, and even then one is in danger of losing the way. A possible explanation lies in considering this indraft of air a continuation of an afternoon sea breeze from off the Mediterranean. Moist air from the sea is brought across the narrow plain of Roussillon and sucked up by the indraft or contrary wind, which, on coming in contact with the cool prevailing wind and experiencing adiabatic cooling, undergoes a dense condensation.

The Mistral and Bora are forms of fall wind. The Mistral is a cold wind which descends with force and lowering of temperature from the French Massif Central to the Mediterranean plain. The Bora is a similar wind coming from the Dalmatian highlands to the Adriatic, to the consternation of sailors. Both words indicate 'north,' but they are used regardless of direction for winds arising from similar topographic and weather conditions in other parts of the world. They are, it is usually thought, the result of barometric low pressure over the lowlands while the uplands are receiving cold air from an anticyclone. The normal adjustments between anticyclone and cyclone are impossible because of the plateau or upland area. The elevation of the upland intensifies the low temperatures. Though Mistral and Bora are heated by descent, nevertheless they arrive on the plains critically cold because of the low initial temperature. These winds result from an accumulated lack of equilibrium. A warm spell in the winter on the French Mediterranean littoral, if of several days' duration, might well intensify the Mistral when once a convectional overturn began and the cold, heavy air of the massif continued its descent.

The Mistral and the Bora are much feared. The lowering of temperature to people used to mild winters is most unpleasant, especially as the wind has great force. Stone walls and other windbreaks protect the fruit. It is said that one village on the southern slope of the Massif Central has been abandoned because of the force of the Mistral. The railway crossing the barren crest of the Dalmatian Alps and descending to Sušak (Fiume) is particularly exposed to the Bora. On the north side of curves of the track are heavy masonry walls some five meters high as a protection against this wind. Generally speaking, Mistral or Bora winds are of greater significance to peoples on plains or seas than to the mountaineers themselves.

Mountain and valley winds are phenomena of clear weather. The mountain wind blows down the valley between sunset and sunrise. The valley wind is a daytime phenomenon and blows up the valley, usually with much less velocity than the downvalley or mountain wind. The mountain wind may be zephyrlike, or it may attain the velocity of a gale. The wind becomes an 'aerial torrent' only when the valley is more or less free from forest, the valley floor is long and steep, and the upland and drainage area is relatively great. The rate of the descent of air and consequent introduction of low temperatures into the valley would be greater if it were not for adiabatic heating.

The mechanics of the origin of the mountain wind are these. On clear evenings the radiation of the heat from the rocks at high levels is more rapid than in the valleys, and the resultant cooling of air in contact with the rocks creates a relatively heavy stratum of air on the walls of the upper valley which then slips down the valley. In planning a camp in a canyon, the bedding roll should be spread on the up-canyon side of the fire to avoid the smoke.

The valley wind is somewhat less simple. The heating of the valley bottom and walls results in a decided increase in air temperature. There is expansion of air in the valley bottom and a blowing-up of the isobaric surface over the middle of the valley. Air slides down the curved isobaric surface and forces its way *up* the valley sides. For obvious reasons a sunny slope will have a stronger amount of breeze than a shady slope. There is no essential difference between a daytime valley wind and a convection current over a plain, except for the guiding influence of the valley wall.

Valley and mountain breezes are characteristic of valleys transverse to a range. They are ordinarily not phenomena of large corridor valleys. Mountain winds may exist in daytime because of glaciers or snow-covered surfaces. The same factors would increase the intensity of the night-time mountain wind.

So persistent and forceful are mountain winds in the valleys of the Tarentaise that the trees lean leeward. In Tibet and Kashgar these winds are said to make travel most difficult. On the other hand, they give pleasant ventilation to valleys on hot summer days, and they serve to lessen the contrast of day temperature between sunny and shady slopes.

The Foehn Wind

A Foehn [1] wind is a movement of air across the mountain during the passage of a cyclonic low on the lee side of the range. It has a strong development in the Alps during the passage of cyclones over the North Sea area.

The typical Foehn wind then approaches the Alps from the south. In ascending the mountain it gives out rain. The latent heat of condensation warms the air and counteracts in part the adiabatic loss of heat occasioned by the ascent. The wind arrives at the mountain crest without the complete loss of heat which is a measure of expansion at the summit elevation. There is no reason why the heat of descent should not be completely taken on by

[1] The American term is Chinook.

FIG. 18. EMERGING FROM THE CLOUDS, SPANISH SIERRA NEVADA
On this day the peaks resting in sunlight were invisible from valley stations.

FIG. 19. VALLEY CLOUDS IN WINTER, KARAWANKEN ALPS, AUSTRIA

the wind as it descends into the lee valley. A Foehn wind therefore arrives hot and dry on the north slope stations (Figures 21 and 22).[1]

Hann was among the first to state that the Foehn was not, as popular belief would have it, the hot breath of the Sahara, but appeared on the Italian slope as a rain wind. Ficker and Billwiller are the most searching students of the Foehn today.

The reality of the Foehn is easily discoverable by coincident observations on two sides of the Alps. The following table compares an Italian station at the same time as an Austrian station:

FOEHN WEATHERS ON OPPOSITE SLOPES OF THE ALPS

	Temperature	Relative humidity
Milan	3.2° C.	96%
Bludenz	11.1° C.	29%

At Bludenz on February 1, 1869, the temperature was found to be 19.3 degrees and the relative humidity 14 per cent. This temperature was 15.7 degrees above normal for that day, whereas the relative humidity was 58 per cent below normal. The succession of weathers during a Foehn at a single station is shown by the following data:

WEATHER DURING A FOEHN AT ZURICH

Nov. 28, 1897

	1 A.M.	3	5	7	11	1 P.M.	3	5
Press.	721.0	20.7	19.9	19.4	18.1	16.2	14.6	13.3
Temp.	0.4	1.6	0.3	−0.5	4.8	8.3	10.1	9.3
R. H.	75	62	76	74	44	29	20	16
Wind	N	NW	WNW	NW	WNW	WNW	SW	WSW

Nov. 29, 1897

	7	9	11	1 A.M.	3	5	7	9
Press.	11.3	9.3	8.0	6.0	4.3	1.9	99.9	2.8
Temp.	8.4	9.6	10.1	6.9	5.1	6.7	6.3	2.4
R. H.	12	5	18	62	84	78	82	85
Wind	WSW	WSW	W	WSW	WSW	SW	W	W

The importance of the influence of the Foehn depends greatly upon the details of exposure. One field will have vines while the

[1]
> "If the Foehn does not blow
> The good God and the warm sun
> Can do little with the snow."

"The Foehn can achieve more in two days than the sun in ten."
"Tonight the wolf is going to eat the snow."

next, deprived of the influence of the Foehn, will not have sufficient warmth for vines. This localization is demonstrated by the higher temperatures at Altdorf, which, though lower in elevation than Zurich, is better exposed to the Foehn. The difference in elevation is not sufficient to account for the difference in temperature.

IMPORTANCE OF EXPOSURE TO FOEHN

	Altitude	Winter	Spring	Summer	Fall	Year
Zurich	470 m.	−0.3	8.9	17.6	8.8	8.7
Altdorf	454	1.1	9.5	17.3	10.8	9.5

Of importance equal to the raising of temperatures is the drying effect of the wind. Under the Foehn influence the snow is quickly evaporated and the ground dried and 'sweetened' for early spring plant growth. The vine and maize are grown in certain localities of Grisons and Vorarlberg. Their culture is confined almost exclusively to the areas exposed to the Foehn. The

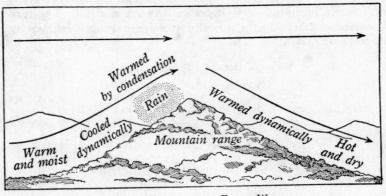

FIG. 20. FACTS OF THE FOEHN WIND
(Courtesy of Ginn and Company, *New College Geography*.)

same cause in part explains the grape culture which produces the *fondant de Sion*, the best Swiss wine.

The writer's personal experiences with Foehn winds have been numerous. Once on a train trip from Lausanne to Milan via the Simplon a rapid cross section of the Foehn was made. Going up the Rhone Valley the weather became hot and dry. The low relative humidity of the air was shown by the clarity of long distance vision. After leaving Sion in heat and dust, one discovered

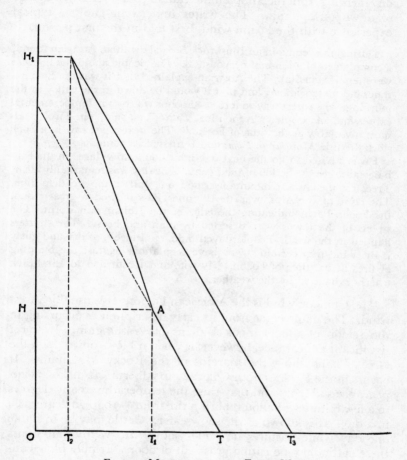

FIG. 21. MECHANICS OF THE FOEHN WIND

The altitude (H) equals elevation and the base (T) the temperature. As air rises to the level H adiabatic cooling decreases the temperature from T to T_1. At H precipitation takes place and the rate of cooling is reduced because of liberated heat of condensation (6°C per kilogram of water). This rate is the line AH. On descending the air has adiabatic heating at the same rate as indicated by TA. The air has then on arriving at the lee base of the mountain the Foehn temperature of T_3.

on emerging from the Simplon the Italian countryside in a deluge of downpouring rain. The writer underwent another typical experience with the Foehn wind, best told in the first person:

During an evening in an Innsbruck *Beerstube* with an Austrian friend, I complained of a sense of nervousness. The people about me likewise were temperamental. The Austrian explained that it was the Foehn a thousand meters above, and that it would be down in the valley in the morning. His surest way to forecast Foehns was by the temperamental expressions of people. "A political *Putsch*," he said, "in Tirol is almost invariably at the time of Foehn." The next day I saw in a book store the title *Menschen in Föhn*, and I guessed its contents.

I was advised to go the next day into mountain villages in the Stubaiertal to see the action of the Foehn. The day was remarkably clear. Trees on the distant mountains stood out with complete definition. The crest of the Alps over the Brenner Pass showed a great cloud, the Foehn bank, indicating the edge of the Italian rain storm. The streets of the towns were deserted by man and beast. The shutters flapped in the wind. People stayed indoors. Indeed, so dry and gusty is the wind that certain towns have regulations against the building of fires at the time of Foehn. My wife and I returned to Innsbruck utterly exhausted by the weather.

The Chinook wind is the American Foehn. It is usually a west wind. The name came from its early description as occurring in the region of the Chinook Indians of Washington. Its most significant appearance, however, is when it blows down upon the Great Plains along the margins of the Rocky Mountains. It occurs in the Rockies from Colorado to Alberta. It makes its appearance suddenly and may raise the temperature many degrees in a few minutes. Ballou reports a rise from −10 to 20 degrees C. in a day. It is known as the snow-eater. Cattle may be in stable one day while pastures lie under snow. In twenty-four hours these cattle may be eating grass out of doors. It may blow continuously for many days, during which special fire laws prevail because of the low relative humidity.

BIBLIOGRAPHICAL NOTES

Wind, Cloud, and Sun

One should consult the Note on *General References on Mountain Climate*, especially Hann, Humphreys, and Bénévent. Bénévent is particularly clear. Hann is the great classic, and has an exhaustive bibliography of

German references. Humphreys is theoretical. Most of the regional studies will be of value here.

Ballou, H. M. "The Chinook Wind," in *American Meteorological Journal*, ix (1892–93), pp. 541–547. With a bibliography.

Billwiller, Robert. "Über verschiedene Entstehungsarten und Erscheingungsformen des Föhns," in *Meteorologische Zeitschrift*, xvi (1899), pp. 204–215.

Blair, W. R., and Ross, L. C. "Stationary Clouds to the Leeward of Hill and Mountain Ranges," in *Bulletin of the Mount Weather Observatory*, ii (1909–10), pp. 75–77.

Burrows, A. T. "The Chinook Winds," in United States Department of Agriculture, *Yearbook*, 1901, pp. 555–566.

Davis, W. M. "The Foehn in the Andes," in *American Meteorological Journal*, iii (1886–87), pp. 507–516.

Defant, Albert. "Berg- und Talwinde in Südtirol," in *Sitzungsberichte* of the Vienna Academy, math.- nat. Klasse, cxviii, 2 (1909), pp. 553–604.

Defant, Albert. "Das Klima von Innsbruck mit besonderer Rücksicht auf den Föhn," in *Deutsche Rundschau für Geographie*, xxxiv (1912), pp. 405–410.

Dersch, Otto. "Über den Ursprung des Mistral," in *Zeitschrift der Österreichischen Gesellschaft für Meteorologie*, xvi (1881), pp. 52–57.

Douglas, C. K. M. "Some Alpine Cloud Forms," in *Quarterly Journal of the Royal Meteorological Society*, liv (1928), pp. 175–178.

Ficker, H. von. Ficker has written extensively on the Foehn, and is an authority. One should see *Denkschriften* of the Vienna Academy, math.-nat. Klasse, lxxviii (1906) and lxxxv (1910); *Meteorologische Zeitschrift*, 1905, 1910, and 1911; and *Zeitschrift des Deutschen und Österreichischen Alpenvereins*, xliii (1912), pp. 53–77, "Die Erforschung der Föhnerscheinungen in den Alpen."

Hales, W. B. "Canyon Winds of the Wasatch Mountains," in *Bulletin of the American Meteorological Society*, xiv (1933), pp. 194–196.

Hann, Julius. "Bewölkung und Sonnenschein auf dem Sonnwendstein (1470 m.) bei Wien," in *Meteorologische Zeitschrift*, xxxiii (1916), pp. 554–556.

Hann, Julius. "Über den Föhn in Bludenz," in *Sitzungsberichte* of the Vienna Academy, math.-nat. Klasse, lxxxv, 2 (1882), pp. 416–440.

Hann, Julius. "Zur Theorie der Berg- und Thalwinde," in *Zeitschrift der Österreichischen Gesellschaft für Meteorologie*, xiv (1879), pp. 444–448. Classical.

Huber, Anton. "Der Gang des Sonnscheins auf der Zugspitze und in Partenkirchen," in *Deutsches Meteorologischen Jahrbuch für Bayern*, 1930, pp. G 1–G 13.

Huber, Anton. "Sonnenschein an Niederschlagstagen," in *Beiträge zur Geophysik*, xxxiii (1931), pp. 118–124.

Loud, F. A. "The Diurnal Variation of Wind-Direction at Colorado Springs," in *American Meteorological Journal*, i (1884–85), pp. 347–354.

McCaul, C. C. "South Alberta and the Climatic Effects of the Chinook Wind," in *American Meteorological Journal*, v (1888–89), pp. 145–159, 362–369.

Martonne, Emmanuel de. "Note préliminaire sur le vent d'autan," in *Bulletin de la Société Languedocienne de géographie*, xxx (1907), pp. 100–114.

Peattie, Roderick. "Nuages en bannière: Petite étude des vents et des nuages de montagne," in *Revue de géographie alpine*, xvii (1929), pp. 329–335.

Peppler, W. "Zum Einfluss des Föhns auf die Mitteltemperatur im Alpenvorland," in *Meteorologische Zeitschrift*, xliii (1926), pp. 374–375.

Pernter, J. M. Über, die Häufigkeit, die Dauer, und die meteorologischen Eigenschaften des Föhns in Innsbruck," in *Sitzungsberichte* of the Vienna Academy, math.-nat. Klasse, civ, 2a (1895), pp. 427–461.

Stupart, R. F. "The Chinook in Southern Alberta and Temperature Inversions at Sulphur Mountain, Banff," in *Proceedings and Transactions of the Royal Society of Canada*, 3d ser., iv (1910), section 3, pp. 51–52.

CHAPTER IV

VEGETATION ZONES AND THE HEIGHT LIMITS OF FIELDS

MOUNTAIN ZONES

ONE of the most attractive concepts in the study of mountains is the conception of zones. Travelers among mountains delight in telling how their climb began amidst a splendor of tropical foliage. Then in succession they went from the evergreen broad-leafed zone to that of the deciduous trees, to the evergreen conifers, to an arctic heath, and so to eternal snow. The rapid contrasts of vegetation within so small a space challenge the imagination. (Figure 22.)

There are many ways of describing and defining zones. The most common type is the following: [1]

VEGETATION ZONES IN NORTHEASTERN COLORADO

1. Plains (grass-steppe or short grassland), up to 1830 meters.
2. Chaparral or brushland of chokecherry, thornapple, mountain mahogany, etc. A narrow, interrupted belt.
3. Yellow pine, Douglas fir zone, 1830–2440 meters.
4. Lodgepole pine zone, 2440–3050 meters.
5. Engelmann spruce, balsam fir zone, 3050–3500 meters.
6. Alpine zone. Above timber line.

SEASON ZONES IN ALPS
In meters

	500–600	650–1000	1000–1300	1300–1600
Awakening of vegetation ...	Mar. 17	Mar. 30	Apr. 10	Apr. 21
Cherries blossom	May 5	May 10	May 16	May 21
Hay harvest	June 15–20	June 24	June 25	June 27
Cherries ripen	June 25	July 18	Aug. 3	Aug. 20
Winter wheat ripe	July 18	July 31	Aug. 8	Aug. 18
Oats ripen...............	Aug. 14	Aug. 27	Sep. 5	Sep. 16
General snow cover	Dec. 10	Nov. 30	Nov. 20	Nov. 10

[1] Robbins.

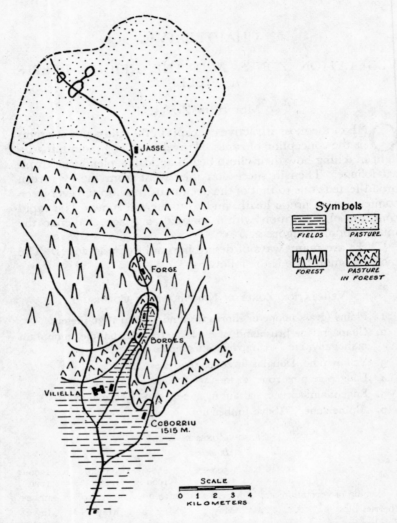

FIG. 22. SIMPLE ZONING IN THE VALLEY OF LLOSA, SPANISH PYRENEES
(*After Sorre.*)

SEASON ZONES IN ALPS (*continued*)

In meters

1600–2000	2000–2300	2300–2600
May 2	June 2	June 28
June 21	July 11	July 29
July 1	Aug. 3	———

Sep. 3 } Sep. 29 } 1690 meters		
Oct. 28	Oct. 15	Oct. 1

Here retardation in blossom time is 10 days for 300 meters and the retardation in fruit time is 12.5 for the same difference in elevation. Of the same type is the following data from Andorra. The chestnut and walnut are found only in the neighborhood of the lowest village, Sant Julia. The live oak occupies sunny slopes in the basin of Andorra la Vieja. The climate, always rigorous, increases in severity very quickly with altitude. Many valleys are entirely subalpine and alpine in character. In less than three hours of valley way one may pass from harvest rye to green rye. On the plain of Andorra (1000 meters) the grain is harvested from July first to the tenth. At Encamp (1600 meters) the harvest is nine days later. At Lo Serrat (1600 meters) harvest is not until the twentieth of August, when the peasants have already begun plowing some fields for the next season's crop.

DURATION OF THE DORMANT PERIOD OF VEGETATION IN ANDORRA

Vegetation	Locality	Beginning	End	Duration (months)
Broadleaf evergreens	{ Plain of Andorra (1029 m.)	Dec. 15	Jan. 15	1
Deciduous	{ La Massana (1252 m.)	Dec. 1	Feb. 15	2½
	{ Encamp (1266 m.)	Dec. 11	Feb. 15	2$\frac{1}{7}$
	{ Ordino (1304 m.)	Dec. 15	Feb. 30	2½
Coniferus subalpine	{ Soldeu (1825 m.)	Oct. 15	Apr. 15	6
	{ Cortals d'Encamp (1860 m.)	Oct. 15	Apr. 15	6
	Lo Serrat (1600 m.)	Oct. 1	Apr. 30	7
	{ Bordes d'Inclès (1825 m.)	Oct. 1	Apr. 30	7
Alpine	{ Port de Soldeu (2407 m.)	Sept. 25	June 1	8$\frac{1}{6}$
	{ Portella Blanca (2515 m.)	Sept. 25	June 15	8$\frac{2}{3}$

Zones at best illustrate an average condition. There are, nevertheless, in the broader sense, belts of vegetation along mountain sides, and there are, likewise, belts or zones of economic adjustment of mountain slopes to man's use. These we shall call culture zones. An example of culture zones among tropical mountains is given by Bowman:

HEIGHT LIMITS OF ZONES IN PERU

Snow	17,000 feet	5185 meters
Potatoes	14,000 "	4270 "
Barley	13,000 "	3965 "
Wheat	12,000 "	3660 "
Corn	10,000 "	3050 "
Sugar	8000 "	2440 "
Banana	6000 "	1830 "

This type of data demonstrates climatic limits but not climatic optima. Dainelli shows, in a study of an isolated Italian peak, that though the chestnut is found at 1250 meters, it is important only between 700 and 1000 meters. Alas, however, our data on culture limits are ordinarily on extremes rather than optima.

Fritsch in his work on the Ortler Alps gives the altitudes of the economic zones, indicating the exposure upon which the observation was made:

LIMIT ELEVATIONS IN THE ORTLER ALPS IN METERS

	Maximum	Minimum	Mean
Permanent habitations	1664 SW	1147 N	1377 m.
Grain limits	1642 "	1207 NW	1390
Mown fields	2108 "	1474 N	1767
Herdsmen's cottages	2154 "	1757 NE	1952
Forest line	2159 "	2023 NE	2118
Shepherds' huts	2342 "	2065 W	2189
Tree line	2323 NW	2166 NE	2253
Orographic snow line	2754 S	2533 N	2629
Climatic snow line	3089 S	2854 N	2964

Let us consider a series of zones on the flanks of Mount Canigou. Mount Canigou is a relatively isolated peak in the eastern French Pyrenees. Its peak, 2785 meters in elevation, is within sight of the Mediterranean. Sorre would have three climatic levels on the Mediterranean flank, each with characteristic vegetation. Up to 700 meters vegetation is conditioned by the need of conserving a limited supply of water. Winter cereals, the olive,

and the evergreen oak flourish. From 700 to 1700 meters there is
an abundance of well distributed rain and an increased rigor of
winter. Here are hay fields, rye, conifers, and the beech tree.
Above is a forest and pasture zone, inhabited only in summer,
where there are lower temperatures, greater precipitation, and
considerable snow cover. But only in a general sense does one
find zones on this peak.

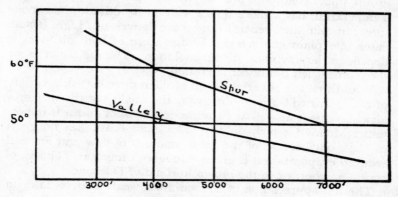

Fig. 23. Reversal of Vegetation Zones

The reversal of vegetation zones through interlocking of spur and valley. Thus if
50.6 degrees F. is a critical temperature for a plant, such temperature is found at
7000 feet on the spurs. By following the abscissal direction the same condition is
discovered in the valley at 4650 feet elevation. (*After Shreve.*)

Shreve, in his excellent study of the Santa Catalina Mountains
of Arizona, gives a description of zones well worth retelling. A
journey from the base to the summit of these mountains im-
presses upon one the constant changing of plant types. There is
no portion of the mountain slopes, at least below 7500 feet, where
a climb of 500 feet does not materially alter the physiognomy of
the vegetation. The cacti and desert shrubs give way to evergreen oaks, leaf succulents, schlerophyllons, shrubs, and plants.
The upper limits of the desert are 4000 feet on the north slope
and 4500 feet on the south. The lowest limit of the true forest is,
on the north slope, at about 5800 feet, while on the south slope it
is about 6300 feet. The mountains here are not high enough to
attain the climatic forest line. No native plant is able to adjust
itself to the range of conditions found within the 6000 feet. Most
plants here do not have altitude ranges of more than 1000 feet.

The climatic factors involved in the determination of a normal altitudinal gradient of vegetation are of three groups. They are moisture factors, temperature factors, and light factors. The moisture factors include not only zones of rainfall but duration and thickness of snow cover. Negatively they include evaporation, which is, of course, a function of wind, temperature, soil, and vegetation. The temperature factors, like the previous group, imply conditions of relief, as exposure and angle of slope. Temperature has a more direct relation to altitude than moisture, but even then generalizations are dangerous. Light factors enter into plant characters. Temperature at high altitudes is dependent largely upon direct insolation. The soil factor is for the moment left out of consideration.

With three sets of variables, all of them interrelated, a variety of conditions will arise. Moreover, the quality of the meteorological element as well as its numerical total or mean is important. Mount Carmel, on the Palestinian coast, has no great rainfall, but because of the great amounts of dew and fog and reduced evaporation it is green throughout the year. This is, of course, in contrast to the brown lowland of Palestine.

The full appreciation of the variables weakens one's faith in the idea of mountain zones. Krebs in his great study of the Eastern Alps finds it necessary to abandon the use of zones. Blache in a detailed study on the Pre-Alps of Savoy is cautious in speaking of zones because of their lack of sharp boundaries. He refers to them only in a general manner. Shreve says, "The occurrence in nature of irregularities of relief is responsible, however, for local departures from the ideal vertical gradients of climate and also from the ideal altitudinal distribution of vegetation which would be anticipated on a geometrically constructed mountain."

The value of the conception of zones in a study of mountain geography lies in the perspective we may obtain in the general relations between mountains and modifications of climate. Thus, for example, the importance of latitude as a factor in climate is brought out with a clearness which could not be obtained were we to break down the broader idea of zones by laying most stress upon details which mark exceptions. Zones on mountains lead us to such generalizations as may exist on the relationship between altitude and temperature. On the other hand, the further we proceed in details of the study of mountain vegetations and altitudinal arrangements of economies the less important does the zone conception become.

HEIGHT LIMITS OF FIELDS

The determination of the factors controlling height limits of cultures, particularly agriculture, is one of prime importance in the economic geography of mountains. It is difficult to generalize in the matter of elevation of field limits. Each field in mountainous terrain has its distinctive climate, soil, degree of accessibility, and economic history. Numerous field observations are here unrecorded because they have each a particular rather than a general value. We shall do well, however, to discuss what is meant by a height limit. Are we to take an extreme figure or an average figure? Ellsworth Huntington would probably favor the average height limit figure for fields or for a single crop as approximating an optimum. The discrepancy between the maximum field height and the average field height is ordinarily not greater than 200 meters. Otto Lehmann in his article on the heights of dwellings has two agricultural limits: *farm limits*, that is the limit of continuously enclosed agricultural regions, and *field limits*, which include tilled islands beyond the area of continuously enclosed agricultural regions.

Factors of slope, accessibility, distance from sources of manure, density of population, and local agricultural habits and economics also influence height limits of fields. Ratzel calls this altitudinal frontier of tillage the *Kampsaum*. The actual limit is determined by observation, but the factors are partly economic and partly climatic. More often the *type* of agriculture has a climatic limit rather than the agriculture itself. Thus in the Stubaier Alps the grains are confined to the valleys and lower slopes and the determining factors are climatic, yet potatoes and turnips are grown in fields far above the normal agricultural zone. Barley for grain is limited about Zermatt, Switzerland, by the 2100 meter contour. Barley for straw for cattle bedding is produced above that contour.

Though we are unable to discuss the generalized data of height limits of fields because of the variety of factors, we shall be able to analyze the character of the factors. Altitude *per se* has no important effects upon the cultivated plants, and though the climatic factors indirectly are of prime consequence we shall be able to ignore the direct importance of diminution of pressure. This chapter will consider in turn topography, exposure to the sun, and geology as factors in the height limits of fields. The special study on Andorra is of both topographical and climatological significance. The study of the Conflent stresses accessibility. The study of the Doron brings out topographic economic factors. The importance of the economic factor is tersely stated by Blache when he says that if an inhabitant of a particular valley wishes to content himself with a mediocre harvest he will cultivate the vine, wheat, maize, and fruit trees up to a considerable altitude. If, however, the commercial element becomes predominant, the marginal zone will be abandoned and the limit of cultivation will recede.

Topography affects cultivation limits in several manners. First, in the alternate distribution of valley and spur it creates an interlocking of contrasted climates. Secondly, the contrast of level land and slope so steep as to be prohibitive for field cultivation is a matter of great significance; but it is too obvious to need elaboration except in its climatic implications.

One of the chief irregularities in the general zonal conception of mountain plant distribution is due to this interlocking of spur and valley (Figure 23). Because of this there may occur an inversion of order of plant associations. Plants of a lower zone may be found at a higher elevation on the floor of a well warmed valley than plants of the upper zone on the exposed mountain spur. An observation on a plant elevation should be made always in the light of the topographic situation, the angle of slope, exposure, nature of slope, total elevation, and mass of mountain. Mayer in his excellent article on the physiographic basis of height limits says that field limits on slopes are usually expressive of *topographic* conditions. He would have us find the *climatic* limitation always along the valley bottom. Indeed, the two are interrelated, especially when we consider water tables. Certainly it is true that the height of fields in many mountain areas represents the height of valley bottoms. In this regard it must be remembered that the height of valley bottoms is a function of mass of mountain. Other considerations to be taken into account are that the steepness of the valley walls is commonly a measure of the severity of glacial erosion. The U-shaped corridor valley, other things being equal, will have lower slope tillage than the broad, gentle-sloped valley. In the Alps the pastures ordinarily stop short of the peaks because of the steep cliffs which mark the upper mountain reaches. On the other hand, the rounded domes of Central Sicily are farmed to the top because the slopes at the summit are gentle.

Not only do the main valleys alternate with the main spurs, but some valleys have interlocking of side valley and side spur. Again there may be inverted culture zones. An enclosed side valley may have flanking walls so close together because of a narrow valley bottom that there is a definite raising of temperature due to heat reflection. Moreover, side valleys are hotter because of the mass of mountain in which they are embedded. The color of rock also influences the amount of reflection.

Cultivation does not always prefer level land. Though the matter is discussed later, let us say here that a sunny slope may be more valuable than the level land because of the more direct angle of the sun's rays. Not only does a favorable slope receive greater warmth during the maturing season, but one which receives rays at a favorable angle in the spring will lose its snow and become warmed earlier. Soil temperatures are favorable for a longer time on a sunny slope than in a valley bottom. Moreover, the slope has the advantage of early draining. Valley bottoms in glaciated valleys may remain wet during the summer so as to preclude all but hay culture. This is due not merely to the irregularity of glacial deposits but also to torrential fans or cones which commonly block the stream course in over-steepened valleys. In addition to this, the drainage of cool air to the valley bottom may create frost pockets and the slope for this reason alone will have a longer growing season than the valley bottom. On the other hand, glaciated valleys frequently have slopes so steep that cultivation or forests cannot creep up the valley walls. This is a reason for the greater height limits of cultivation in valley courses than on valley sides.

The character of the crop likewise may be different from that on the valley floor. Grass thrives well in the moist, shady valley bottom. Vines are a dry-land crop, needing little or no irrigation and much sunlight. They grow well on slopes, and because of the character of cultivation fit in well on terraces. Mown crops are found on slopes because, unless the ground is too steep for a foothold, it is actually easier to mow with a scythe on a slope than on the level. Very steep slopes are devoted to grass, if the rainfall is of the proper type, for the roots prevent soil erosion. (Figure 48.)

The Sunlight Factor

The matter of sunlight is so important that each mountain speech or dialect has its special terms for the sunny and shady slopes.   Some of these are herewith given:

	SUN	SHADE
German:	Sonnenseite	Schattenseite
	Sonnenberg	Schattenberg
French:	Adret	Ubac
	Endroit	Envers
Catalan:	Sola	Bøga
	Solana	Ubach
	Soula	Ubago
Italian:	Indretto	Inverso
	Adritto	Opaco

Frequently villages straddle streams.   That portion of the village which is on the shady bank is less desirable for living quarters.   There are, for example, Envers Fontenille and Inverso Pinusca.   A farm which is famous as a rendezvous for epicures in the Provençal hills is known as 'le Ferme de l'Ubac Foron.' Granö calls the shady side of a mountain the *versant de la nuit*.   Because 'sunny slope' and 'shady slope' are tongue-twisters, the French terms *adret* and *ubac* will here be used in their stead.

In considering the land values of mountain fields, a concern of the first importance is exposure to the sun.   (Figures 4, 24, and 25.)   It is the field in the sunlight that brings a high price.   A Catalan saying distinguishes between the two slopes in the following manner: "A *solane* is a portion of a commune conceded to a *cuart* (a section of a commune) for pasture.   Anybody has a right to go to the *ubach*."   Indeed, in general, mountain people live in the sun.   In the east-west Tarentaise valley of the French Alps downstream from Bourg-Saint-Maurice 89.6 per cent of the population lives on the *adret*.

The examples of exposure contrasts in geographic literature are legion.   Let us turn to a description of the Val de Conches, which is a high valley in Valais.   The valley has been severely glaciated and has slopes of thirty degrees.   The contrast here between *adret* and *ubac* is great.   Fifty-seven per cent of the unproductive land and 61 per cent of the forest is found on the *ubac*.   The *adret* has 70 per cent of the grass land and 97 per cent of the total tilled land.

FIG. 24. SUNNY AND SHADY SLOPE IN THE TARENTAISE, FRENCH ALPS

FIG. 25. AGRICULTURAL LIMITS, GRISONS, SWITZERLAND
These highest tilled areas on the road to Arosa are scanty potato patches.

The 3 per cent of the cultivation on the *ubac* is really on secondary *adrets*. Flückiger states that in the Löetschen valley of Switzerland the southerly exposure is in pastures, fields, and settlements, while the *ubac*, the northerly exposure, is almost exclusively devoted to forests. Fritzsch gives us the following contrasts in the Ortler Alps:

EXPOSURE IN THE ORTLER ALPS

	Adret	*Ubac*
Alpine huts	2154 m.	1757 m.
Forests	2159	2023
Trees	2240	2166

An unusual study of hours of sunlight in a single valley is that of Levainville writing on the Barcelonnette Valley of the French Alps (Figure 26). He shows in this study a surprising fact, namely, that the *ubac* there actually has greater duration of sunlight than the valley bottom. Five stations on the *adret* had a possible mean daily insolation of 597 minutes. Five stations on the valley bottom gave an average of 449 minutes of sunlight. Yet an average of four stations on the *ubac* received sun for an average of 545 minutes. Duration of sunlight in a valley station is, then, not only a matter of latitude, height of barrier, and height of station, but also of detail of slope, trend of valley, and detail of barrier crest topography.

The economic aspects of sunlight should be thought of in terms of seasons. It is relation of sun to field in growing season that counts. *Adret* and *ubac* near Innsbruck have a growing season of 15 days difference in length.

The quantitative importance of an *adret* position rather than a site on a level valley bottom is indicated by the location of the most elevated fields in the drainage basin of the Doron, Tarentaise. They are found in the hamlet of Fontanette at 1680 meters. Some hundred meters below is the flat valley bottom of Pralognan. This land is devoted entirely to hay. At Fontanette there is, however, a small *adret* slope. Here on the lowest level of the alp there are potato fields (Figure 29).

The best resumé of the story of *adret* and *ubac* is that of Marcelle Vessereau. It is an excellent article laying stress upon sunlight as a factor in height limits to the exclusion of other factors which modify, and in some cases counteract, the effect of insolation. In her conclusion she says rightly, "The law of the *adret* and *ubac* is a general law." The exceptions, however, would seem to be so many that one should apply the law not generally but specifically, and then only after taking note of the local modifications and exceptions. An exception to the law of exposure is found in the existence of sunny slopes on an *ubac*. These slopes are the 'secondary *adrets*.'

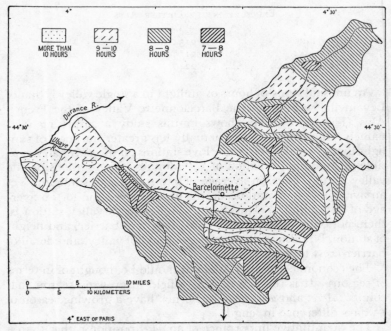

FIG. 26. SUNLIGHT HOURS IN THE VALLEY OF BARCELONNETTE, FRENCH ALPS

The irregularity is due to secondary adrets. (*After Levainville*.) (Courtesy of the *Geographical Review*, published by the American Geographical Society of New York.)

Is there a difference in the insolation values on an east and west slope? There is, but the difference is not great. The writer made a study in the valley of Allues, drained by a suspended stream which runs north to join the Doron at Brides-les-Bains in the French Alps. Its two valley walls are of the same declivity and the crest lines of the flanking mountains are approximately of the same altitude. Here may be studied the relative effects of morning and afternoon sunlight. Cultivation on the west-facing or afternoon slope is higher by one hundred meters than on the east-facing or morning slope. This is normal, as the morning sun is frequently weakened by haze. But the local inhabitant says that the discrepancy in culture lines to be noted at the head of the valley is distinctly a matter of inferior soil on the morning slope. Here is another case where one might easily draw hasty and erroneous conclusions.

Blumer gives us a study of a north-south range with all the contrasts of wind, precipitation, and evaporation that might be expected. But the range, according to that author, has an insolation difference for the two slopes. The east represents the *ubac* and the west the *adret*. The range considered is the Rincon Range of Arizona (2100 to 2400 meters). After describing the difference in vegetation on the two exposures he noted the following facts. Both sides have the same type of bed rock. The east is the steeper slope, but it has a better humus, and the geologic structure provides better ground water conditions. But, also, the east slope has a sunrise three hours before the west, and at a time when, in this desert climate, there is heavy dew. Moreover, the sun sets three hours earlier on the east than on the west slope. It sets shortly after the time of maximum temperature. On the west as the sun rises there is little dew on the ground. The afternoon sun shines on this slope during the hottest hours of the day. Insolation is greater on the west. Minimum temperatures are lower on the west. The summer diurnal range on the east approximates 8.3 to 8.8 degrees while on the west it may be as high as 18.3 degrees. The west slope has perhaps twice the summer precipitation of the east slope. The important winds are from the west with their attendant evaporation. On the summit the tips of the pine leaves all point east.

Normally we speak only of an *adret* or *ubac* of a valley. The terms also may well be applied to slopes of an isolated mountain range. The *adret* of a valley and of an isolated mountain range are, however, not completely analogous. In a valley the difference between the two slopes is lessened by reflected heat and by mixing of air by mountain and valley winds. Also the exposed mountain range more than the valley is open to the prevailing wind with its consequent precipitation or evaporation. The Sierra Nevada Mountains of Spain offer excellent opportunity for determination of the importance of insolation. Unfortunately, the writer saw them during stormy weather only. Many of his conclusions are based upon data presented by Boissier, who made a study nearly a century ago. But the relation of *adret* and *ubac* is probably the same as today.

The Sierra Nevada is an east-west range of schists and granitic rocks. The core is surrounded by loosely consolidated sedimentaries. The geology and topography of the two slopes are identical. Therefore these two factors can more or less be eliminated from our consideration. The southern slope is climatically open to African influences. The northern slope receives the brunt of the cyclonic storms and is exposed to cold winds from the Meseta Central. The north slope is the more moist. At the south piedmont there is the orange, and, not far distant, sugar cane is grown. The north piedmont is the famous Vega and does not support the orange. The vine, walnut, olive, fig, potato, and maize are all found at greater heights on the south slope than on the north, higher on the *adret* than on the *ubac*. Boissier would consider greater wind and its attendant evaporation the cause for the lower limits on the north. Few today would agree with him. Most would consider the matter one of insolation. Particularly this is true since on the north slope there is plentiful snow water for ground water and irrigation.

We have suggested that soil and topography may be eliminated from consideration. Here in the Sierra Nevada there is no question of balance of land utilization. No land is reserved for domestic animals at the expense of fields. Other than a few sheep in the cirques there is only the household goat. The matter of social characteristics of the farmers on the two sides of the range is here not of concern, for they are the same on both slopes. Manure is generally lacking and therefore does not influence the height of fields. Accessibility, a matter so important in the Pyrenees and Alps, does not control the height of fields. There are potato fields near the snow line, three and four hours' travel from the nearest village (Figure 61). The men, while tending these fields, live in miserable little *cortalos*. The distance to the village or any building is so great that seed potatoes are buried for the winter in pits near the fields. With so many factors eliminated or equal on the two slopes, the measurements which Boissier gave nevertheless show a great discrepancy. There is a difference of 215 meters in the height limit of the vine on the two slopes, 150 meters difference for the walnut, 520 meters for the olive, and 300 meters for the fig. Rye shows distinct dif-

FIG. 27. FIELD LIMITS IN THE VALLEE D'OUELL, FRENCH PYRENEES

The upper limit of the fields here is due to the lack of soil on the upper slopes. The limit is not climatic. (Courtesy of the *Geographical Review*, published by the American Geographical Society of New York.)

FIG. 28. HIGH FIELDS ON THE SUNNY SLOPES, VAL D'ISERE, FRENCH ALPS

ferences. If insolation is the sole factor, why should the figures of differences vary so greatly? The truth is that crops vary in sensitiveness to the climatic elements at different numerical points of intensity. It may not be insolation which is the determining factor of the limit of a particular crop, but the sum total of climatic aspects. Moreover, physical conditions are never uniform over any great area. Boissier himself notes that the high rye fields on the south side were in certain well protected nooks. One is led to suspect the importance of any figures denoting extreme limits of crops. It may be that to measure sunlight effect we shall be forced to disregard crop limits and crop characters, since so many other factors intrude themselves there, as, for example, geologic and soil factors.

THE GEOLOGIC FACTOR

Geology makes itself felt in influencing height limits not only as it influences the character of topography but also because it has consequences on the soil and influences the capacity of the soil for ground water. Sieger, in discussing alp huts, shows that their elevation is not so much a matter of exposure as of geology. The geology by its determination of soil character, mass of mountain, and ground water outweighs other physical factors. As the alp hut bears direct relation to the alp, the elevation of the hut is a climatic and topographic matter.

HEIGHT OF ALP HUTS IN AUSTRIA

Region	Exposure	Limit	Nature of Rocks
Imst, Zirl	*Adret*	1611 m.	Calcareous
	Ubac	1707	Crystalline
Gailtal	*Adret*	1509	Calcareous
	Ubac	1718	Schists
Haut-Pustertal	*Adret*	2006	Crystalline
	Ubac	1766	Calcareous
Haute-Drave	*Adret*	1966	Crystalline
	Ubac	1701	Calcareous

Crystalline massifs generally give gentler slopes, greater mass of mountain, and more abundant ground water than do calcareous mountains. In the preceding table it will be noted that the mean altitude limit on the *adret* is 1886 meters and on the *ubac* is 1720 meters. But let us arrange the table in another form. Then it will be seen that the *adret* calcareous stations are lower than the *ubac* crystalline stations.

Adret	*Ubac*
1611 crystalline	1707 crystalline
1509 calcareous	1718 schists
2006 crystalline	1766 calcareous
1966 crystalline	1701 calcareous

The matter of soil patently influences not only the height of agriculture but also its character. A calcareous soil is warm and dry. Crystalline rocks create infertile siliceous soils or fertile clays. In the Dolomites and Carnic Alps the beech finds its highest limits in limestone and its lowest limits in siliceous rocks, regardless of exposure.

The geologic factor influences slope. Great degree of slope, besides its more apparent influence on cultures, increases avalanches and landslips, which locally have more effect in lowering cultural lines than at first would be expected. Oversteep slopes have no soil. Such slopes commonly have alluvial fans or cones at the base. These deposits, though in places subject to torrential floods, may be loosely compacted and consequently well drained. If the gradient of the erosive portion of the stream's course on the fan is not too steep, the deposit may be fine enough for agriculture. (Figures 28 and 50.) Much depends also on the character of the rock suffering erosion. These cones of dejection are favorite sites for fields and villages. When on the *adret* they are better insolated than on the valley bottom. They are less exposed to cold air drainage than the valley, and less subject to floods.

There is perfect gradation from the alluvial fan to a sheet of soil lying on a slope. On a moderately steep slope soil formation may not be sufficiently rapid to cover the entire slope in opposition to soil slip and soil erosion. In such a case perhaps only the lower half of the slope will have soil suitable for agriculture. As one passes up a valley, both the stream profile and the crest of the flanking mountains increase in altitude. Likewise the limit of the fields rises. One immediately suspects that the field limit is higher because of greater mass in the interior of the range, but quite commonly the increasing field limit is a question of soil. The soil maintains its proportional cover of the slope regardless of the increasing elevation of the slope. Perhaps the most common error in studying height limits is to ascribe to climate a cessation of culture really due to thinning of soils.

An example of lack of soil on an upper slope was discovered in the Vallée d' Ouell near Bagnères-de-Luchon in the central French Pyrenees (Figure 27). This is a high side valley with a bottom of 1000 to 1400 meters elevation. The flanking mountain spurs had an elevation ranging from 1400 to 2100 meters. The slope of the valley walls was about 30 degrees. The limit of fields was 500 to 600 meters higher at the upper end of the valley than near the mouth. Seen from the high vantage point of Super-bagnères this upper limit appeared to be a matter of accessibility of fields from the villages, or an increase of tillage limits due to mass of mountain in the interior of the little massif. Closer examination showed that the upper half of the slope did not maintain a sufficiently thick apron of soil. This condition is a common one. The soil limit of agriculture undoubtedly has been frequently mistaken for a temperature limitation.

ZONES IN ANDORRA

Let us approach the question not from the consideration of the isolated factors but by means of regional studies, thus showing the interrelation of the factors. We shall consider two regions in the Pyrenees: Andorra and the Conflent. The agricultural products of Andorra are potatoes, garden vegetables, rye, barley, and tobacco (Figures 50 and 51). A few vines exist near Sant Julia, the lowest community. Vine culture (the grapes are used today for raisins) is now restricted because improved transportation makes possible the importation of wines from the Lérida region of Spain.

The cereals of Andorra are largely rye and barley. The people eat black bread. Where there are gentle breaks in the valley walls and tillable slopes extending up to the level of the summit plain, rye occupies the top fields. Elsewhere rye is grown on the shoulders of the canyon walls. These fields, the highest in Andorra, lie at 1850 meters, and not infrequently are an hour's tramp from the nearest house. The isolated position of these grain fields is the result of the eager search for sunlight. The deep gorges and their alluvial cones may have but a few hours of sun during the day. The high fields are invariably up out of the gorge on the sunny exposure of the valley.

The question of sunny slope and shady slope is here, naturally, of the utmost importance. Every inch of the *solana* (*adret*) is cultivated. True, the *umbaga* (*ubac*) is farmed, but the value of the harvest is much less than that of the *solana*, and the upper limit never so high. Because of the convex form of the slope, the greater the altitude on the *umbaga*, the more numerous the hours of sunlight. Also the shade of the mountain to the south may cover the lower slope of the *solana*. But the crops on the shady side are commonly so slight or even precarious as to have relative unimportance. It may be stated as a principle of mountain geography that though the shady slope may be farmed as extensively as the sunny side, the economy of the two vary greatly.

The writer did not feel that the climatic limit of agriculture of one sort or another had been reached by the Andorrans. Matters of accessibility, distance, difficulty of carrying manure to the fields and the crops to the granges, and unwillingness to encroach upon pasture lands, as well as unfavorable soils on the *plas* (plateaus), are factors which obviously all play a part. It would almost be easier to determine a lower climatic limit for grain in the gorges than to designate an upper limit. In the steep-sided valleys the duration of sunlight is so slight that the season necessary for the maturing of grain is lengthened. In places men may sow one grain crop in autumn before the grain of that year is harvested in an adjacent field. The land must then either lie fallow a year or be put into field crops.

Tobacco is the most distinctive crop of Andorra. It had its start when smuggling was a recognized profession. Climatically, the interesting thing in connection with tobacco is that the highest cultivated fields in the basins of Andorra are devoted to this plant. The highest field in the basin of Andorra lies in the side valley of the Entremesaigues. These canyon fields are 1455 meters in altitude, the duration of sunlight is short (on September 15th, with the tobacco still on the stalk, there were but eight hours of sunlight), the canyon is cooled by the icy stream and in the evenings it suffers with great regularity from cold mountain winds. The explanation of this ability of tobacco to grow at this extreme height is that these fields have the advantage of being close to summer pastures and therefore to manure.

In the Conflent

In the eastern French Pyrenees is a region known as the Conflent. Here is an opportunity to study the question of accessibility. Two examples may be cited from this region of receding culture lines due to difficulty of access and to changing economic and social conditions (Figures 46 and 47). The first is that of the abandoned Ferme de Randais. This farm is situated on the northern slope of the range on a level spot lying on a spur at 1700 meters. Generally the mountain flank has a 50 degree slope and is covered with forest growth, where, in occasional clearings, cattle graze in the summer. Vegetables and grains were in the past successfully grown on this farm. Because of steep slopes and the large amount of pasture land available, one suspects that the basis of the farm's economy was pastoral. The fact remains that at this altitude on a reverse or northern slope it was possible to raise crops successfully. The height limits of agriculture, as represented by the highest fields in the valleys, are then not a matter of decrease of temperature with altitude. Long before the climatic limit of tillage is attained, topography, accessibility, and water for irrigation control the height limits of cultivation. The abandoning of the Ferme de Randais was a question of accessibility. Accessibility in this case is more a social matter than a physical one. In terms of the current values of life in France today the farm is too remote.

The Ferme de Randais was an outlier of the agricultural zone. In the zone of continuous agriculture which lies in the level valley bottom, the finer details of the limits of fields are usually topographic, if we bear in mind that topography influences soil character, ground water, and the possibility of irrigation. The topography of the foothills which flank the lower valleys is such that gentler slopes (35 per cent) [1] are not incapable of agriculture. In two ways the per cent of slope influences tillage. Plow land is anything up to 40 per cent of slope, and mattock-tilled fields are to be seen on much steeper slopes. The critical incline, as found upon the foothills, is that which is too steep for good ground water conditions. A slope of given incline will have a greater probability of verdure if it is situated upon the higher portions of the foothills near the rain-forming mountains.

In this zone in the Conflent there are many abandoned vine terraces. Here is an example of changing economy rather than climate. The abandoned vine terraces were cultivated in days of meager economy, when there were more people and less money in the Conflent. Men could then be hired to work among the vines for a franc (pre-war) a day, women for seventy-five cen-

[1] A 100 per cent slope has a grade of 45 degrees.

times, where now the laborer asks twenty-five francs, if he can be hired at all. Men carried the manure up the slopes in great baskets fastened to the back. Likewise they carried the heavy grapes down the slope. The most arduous work the valley farmer had was on the steep slopes flanking the valley flat. Here the matter was not one of distance but of incline. He became unwilling to struggle up the hillsides, especially in view of the declining price of wine. Today with increasing wine prices the terraces are coming into use again. Economic pressure is inducing man to take the climb.

THE VALLEY OF THE DORON

In 1928 the writer made a study of the valley of the Doron in the Tarentaise (French Alps). The Doron is a stream made by ·two branches, the Doron de Champagny and the Doron de Pralognan, meeting at Le Villard, and is itself tributary to the Isère at Moûtiers. Between Le Villard and Brides-les-Bains the valley has for 12.5 kilometers a true east-west direction. At Bozel the La Rosière enters the main stream from the south, having a valley of another 12.5 kilometers. The Doron de Pralognan is 20 kilometers in length, not counting its Alpine tributaries, and has a north flow (see Figure 29).

Economically the valley is pastoral and agricultural. There is also an active tourist trade, some iron mining, and a large chemical industry. The agriculture on the *adret* is of vines, grains, and hay. On the *ubac* hay predominates and grains are less important. The vine there is totally lacking. Vegetables on both slopes are largely represented by the kitchen garden, except the potato which is a true field crop. There is a distinct agricultural zone, but above this are isolated cultivated fields. These fields which lie above the true agricultural zone are on the margins of the pasture zone. We shall call this margin the *mayen alp*; that is, the high pasture for May. On the *adret mayen* alp, grass predominates. The fields on the *ubac mayen* are scarce. One generally thinks of villages as lying on the *adret*. In the main valley of the Doron there are twelve villages on the *ubac* as against seven on the *adret*. It is difficult to determine the relative prosperity of the two slopes. It is a question whether insolation is the sole factor in either the quality or the limits of agriculture. Rye represents the grain of the *mayen*. The high rye fields are of excellent stand, not meager crops. One wonders if in reality this is the greatest altitude for the region at which rye can be successfully grown. It is true there is a well marked agricultural zone which

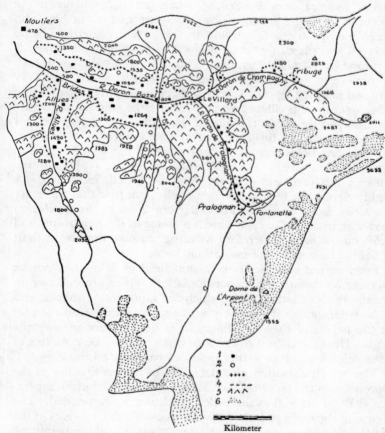

FIG. 29. LIMITS OF CULTURE IN THE VALLEY OF THE DORON, FRENCH ALPS

1. Permanent villages. 2. Temporary villages. 3. Limits of fields. 4. Limits of vine. 5. Forests. 6. Glaciers.

might be of climatic significance. But frequently limits of definite agricultural zones are to a large extent due to an attempt on the part of the farmer to balance the use of his land to the best economic purpose. In any alpine valley there is a certain percentage of land which is most advantageously devoted to tillage, to forests, and to pastures.

The fields about the alp villages of the Doron do not necessarily represent the climatic height of tillage. The *mayen* alp holds fields for several reasons. People remain in the alp villages in the Doron a fortnight in the spring to pasture cattle, cut hay, and plant a crop, another fortnight in the autumn to cut hay and harvest, and the cattle are again in these stables in the winter to consume the hay in the grange. Thus there is a valuable storage of manure in these villages. Many of the villages are essentially hay and manure depots. It is an important fact in the growing of crops near the alp villages that the greater the amount of manure spread upon the fields, the shorter the growing season needed for grain maturity. In this region every *adret* village had fields close by, and few fields were any distance from the villages. It is a burden to haul manure a great distance. True, at this altitude where air is rare and does not hold heat well, insolation is a highly significant factor. Certainly, also, is it true that there are few *mayen* fields upon the *ubac*. But one is led to the conclusion that manure as well as sunshine is a factor in the height limits of fields on the *adret*. Therefore we must not take the height limit of fields as a measure of insolation.

Even on the *ubac* the lesser height limit of fields may not be taken as a measure of the poor insolation. Grass grows better on the shady alps than on those which are sunburnt. Granting this to be true, though it may be possible to grow grains on the *ubac* at the height of the alp villages, it is better economy to grow grass. Hence the limit of fields on the *ubac* may be a matter of economic climatology rather than deterministic climatology.

The principal evidence of glaciation in the main valley of the Doron lies in the fact that the valleys of the two tributaries meeting at Bozel, as well as the valley of Allues, are suspended. The course of the main stream is now in a post-glacial gorge. On the *ubac* of this gorge there is forest and grass, the slope being too steep for fields. On the *adret*, where the slope is not precipitous, the gorge is devoted to vines; a direct case of the importance of insolation. But does the upper limit of the vine represent the limit climatically? Does the angle of slope of this gorge side represent the most favorable angle of exposure to the sun's rays? One is inclined to think not. The curious thing is that the upper limits of the vineyard plot are frequently determined by the more gentle slope. The more gentle slope above the gorge can be devoted to field crops and here vines cannot economically compete for area. Vines are maintained, generally speaking, only on land too steep for other crops. The distribution of the vine is, then, not purely a matter of insolation but of declivity also.

There is, then, a distribution of fields in the valley of the Doron according to insolation; but factors of economy as well enter into the question. Level bottom land is lacking because of a postglacial gorge. On the *adret*, in what would normally be the forest zone, there are fields wherever the slope is gentle enough. A complement of the fields is the upper pasture lands. In places the need for pasture restricts the advance of cultivation. Elsewhere fields invade the zone of pasture at a considerable altitude because large deposits of manure call for the cultivation of crops. The needs of the community and the details of topography are more important than climate in the distribution of fields. Too much has been written about the importance of a single factor in the distribution of tilled fields. In reality the control is not single but complicated.

BIBLIOGRAPHICAL NOTES

Zones and Factors in the Height Limit of Fields

Arènes, J. "Étude phytosociologique sur la chaîne de la Sainte-Baume et la Provence," in *Bulletin de la Société botanique de France*, lxxiii (1926), pp. 1016–1022; lxxiv (1927), pp. 65–85.

Ball, John. "The Distribution of Plants on the South Side of the Alps," in *Transactions of the Linnean Society of London*, v, pp. 119–227 (1896). This and the preceding article are examples of the huge literature of the botanical and ecological study of mountains.

Bates, C. G. *Forest Types in the Central Rocky Mountains as Affected by Climate and Soil*. Washington, 1924. (United States Department of Agriculture, bulletin 1233.) An example of modern ecology.

Bénévent, Ernest. "Le Manival: Etude de cône de déjection," in *Recueil des travaux de l'Institut de géographie alpine*, iii (1915), pp. 69–100. A detail of soil relations. The importance of local conditions is shown.

Blanchard, Raoul. "La limite septentrionale de l'olivier dans les Alpes françaises," in *La géographie*, xxii (1910), pp. 225–240, 301–324. A valuable study.

Boissier, Edmond. *Voyage botanique dans le Midi de l'Espagne pendant l'année 1837*. Paris, 1839–45. 2 vols. Referred to in the text.

Bonnier, Gaston. "Études sur la végétation de la vallée de Chamonix et de la chaîne du Mont Blanc," in *Revue générale de botanique*, i (1889), pp. 28–36, 79–84, 146–154, 204–211.

Brockmann-Jerosch, Heinrich. *Die Vegetation der Schweiz*. Zurich, 1925–29. 4 pts. A writer who always sees clearly the geographic factors.

Brown, W. H. *Vegetation of the Philippine Mountains: The Relation between the Environment and Physical Types at Different Altitudes*. Manila, 1919. (Manila Bureau of Science, Department of Agriculture and Natural Resources, Publication no. 19.)

Brückner, Eduard. "Höhengrenzen in der Schweiz," in *Naturwissenschaftliche Wochenschrift*, xx (1905), pp. 817–825.

Chardón, C. E. "Life Zones in the Andes of Venezuela," in *Bulletin of the Pan American Union*, lxvii (1933), pp. 620–633.

Christ, Hermann. *Das Pflanzenleben der Schweiz*. Zurich, 1882. Translated by E. Tièche as *La flore de la Suisse et ses origines*. Basel, 1883. Material on relief, degree of slope, and exposure.

Clements, F. E. *Plant Succession*. Washington, 1916. (Carnegie Institution, Publication no. 242.) An important American reference.

Dainelli, Giotto. "Le zone altimetriche del Monte Amiata," in *Memorie Geografiche, supplemento alla Rivista Geografica Italiana*, iv (1910), pp. 292–363. The Italians have been especially concerned with studies of altitude. This is a detailed study of an isolated peak 1734 meters high.

Evrard, F., and Chermezon, Henri. "La végétation de la Haute-Tarentaise," in *Bulletin de la Société botanique de France*, lxv (1918), pp. 153–209. This region is referred to frequently in the text.

Flahault, Charles. "Essai d'une carte botanique et forestière de la France (feuille de Perpignan)," in *Annales de géographie*, vi (1897), pp. 289–312, with a map. Excellent.

Flückiger, Otto. *Die obere Grenze der menschlichen Siedelungen in der Schweiz*. Bern, 1906. A classic.

Flückiger, Otto. "Pässe und Grenze," in *Mitteilungen der Geographisch-Ethographischen Gesellschaft in Zürich*, xxvii–xxviii (1926–28), pp. 36–65.

Fritzsch, Magnus. "Über Höhengrenzen in den Ortler-Alpen," in *Wissenschaftliche Veröffentlichungen des Vereins für Erdkunde zu Leipzig*, ii (1895), pp. 105–292. A classic article.

Gaussen, Henri. *Végétation de la moitié orientale des Pyrénées*. Paris, 1926. The work of a master ecologist.

Gaussen, Henri. "A View from Canigou: Nature and Man in the Eastern Pyrenees," in *Geographical Review*, xxvi (1936), pp. 190–204.

Haret, Michel. "Le paysage alpine carpatique," in *Revue de géographie alpine*, xiv (1926), pp. 617–657.

Herzog, Theodor. *Die Pflanzenwelt der bolivischen Anden und ihres östlichen Vorlandes.* Leipzig, 1923. (*Die Vegetation der Erde*, xv.)

Hupfer, Paul. "Die Regionen am Ätna," in *Wissenschaftliche Veröffentlichungen des Vereins für Erdkunde zu Leipzig*, ii (1895), pp. 293*–362.*

Kashyap, S. R. "The Vegetation of Western Himalaya and Western Tibet in Relation to their Climate," in *Journal of the Indian Botanical Society*, iv (1924–25), pp. 327–334.

Kerner, Anton von. "Studien über die oberen Grenzen der Holzpflanzen in den österreichischen Alpen," in *Der Wald und die Alpenwirtschaft in Österreich und Tirol.* Berlin, 1908. A classic.

Koegel, L. "Die Pflanzendecke in ihren Beziehungen zu den Formen des alpin Hochgebirges," in *Ostalpine Formenstudien*, pt. 1, no. 5 (1923), pp. 5–126. Topographic ecology.

Marinelli, Olinto. "I limiti altimetrici in Comelico," in *Memorie Geografiche, supplemento alla Rivista Geografica Italiana*, i (1907), pp. 9–99.

Mayer, Robert. "Die Verbreitung der Kulturflächen in den Ost-Alpen und ihre obere Grenze, geomorphologisch betrachtet," in *Geographische Zeitschrift*, xxxii (1927), pp. 113–138. Excellent.

Moore, Barrington. "Physiological Requirements of Rocky Mountain Trees," in *Ecology*, v (1924), pp. 298–302. Example of tree requirements.

Peattie, Roderick. "The Conflent," in *Geographical Review*, xx (1930), pp. 245–257. Referred to in this chapter. See a critique by P. Arbos in *Revue Géographique des Pyrénées et du Sud-Ouest*, i (1930), pp. 505–508.

Peattie, Roderick. "Height Limits of Mountain Economies," in *Geographical Review*, xxi (1931), pp. 415–428.

Peyre, M. "La vigne en Suisse," in *Revue de géographie alpine*, x (1922), pp. 495–548.

Platt, R. S. "Six Farms in the Central Andes," in *Geographical Review*, xxii (1932), pp. 245–259.

Quervain, Alfred de. "Die Hebung der atmosphärischen Isothermen in den Schweizer Alpen und ihre Beziehung zu den Höhengrenzen," in *Beiträge zur Geophysik*, vi (1904), pp. 481–533.

Ratzel, Friedrich. "Höhengrenzen und Höhengürtel," in *Zeitschrift des Deutschen und Österreichischen Alpenvereins*, xx (1889), pp. 102–135. A classic and a review of previous work.

Reishauer, Hermann. "Höhengrenzen der Vegetation in den Stubaier Alpen und in der Adamello-Gruppe," in *Wissenschaftliche Veröffentlichungen des Vereins für Erdkunde zu Leipzig*, vi (1904), pp. 1–210.

Robbins, W. W. *Native Vegetation and Climate of Colorado in their Relation to Agriculture*, Fort Collins, Colorado, 1917. (Colorado Agricultural College, Experiment Station, Bulletin 224.)

Roletto, G. B. "Considerazioni Geografiche sulla Distribuzione del Castagno nelle Alpi occidentali," in *Bollettino della Reale Società Geografica Italiana*, serie vi, iii (1926), pp. 548–557. This makes an excellent trilogy with the articles on the vine by Peyre and the olive by Blanchard.

Roletto, G. B. "Les zones de végétation des Alpes Cottiennes dans leurs rapports avec l'économie pastorale," in *Revue de géographie alpine*, xii (1924), pp. 645–668.

Scharfetter, Rudolf. "Die Grenzen der Pflanzenvereine," in *Zur Geographie der deutschen Alpen Robert Sieger gewidmet* (Vienna, 1924), pp. 54–69.

Schimper, A. F. W. *Plant-Geography upon a Physiological Basis*, tr. by W. R. Fisher. Oxford, 1903. Chapter on Mountains.

Schindler, F. "Culturregionen und Ackerbau in den Höhen Tauern," in *Zeitschrift des Deutschen und Österreichischen Alpenvereins*, xix (1888), pp. 73–82. Historically a basic article.

Schindler, F. "Kulturregionen und Kulturgrenzen in den Oetzthaler Alpen," in *Zeitschrift des Deutschen und Österreichischen Alpenvereins*, xxi (1890), pp. 62–84.

Schindler, F. "Zur Kulturgeographie der Brennergegend," in *Zeitschrift des Deutschen und Österreichischen Alpenvereins*, xxiv (1893), pp. 1–20.

Schmoe, F. W. *Our Greatest Mountain: A Handbook for Mount Rainier National Park*. New York, 1925.

Schröter, Carl. *Das Pflanzenleben der Alpen*, 2. Aufl. Zurich, 1926.

Shaw, C. H. "Vegetation and Altitude," in *The Plant World*, xii (1909), pp. 63–65.

Shreve, Forrest. "Conditions indirectly Affecting Vertical Distribution on Desert Mountains," in *Ecology*, iii (1922), pp. 269–274.

Shreve, Forrest. "The Physical Conditions of a Coastal Mountain Range," in *Ecology*, viii (1927), pp. 398–414.

Shreve, Forrest. *The Vegetation of a Desert Mountain Range as Conditioned by Climatic Factors*. Washington, 1915. (Carnegie Institution of Washington, *Publications*, 217.) A most exact study.

Sieger, Robert. *Beiträge zur Geographie der Almen in Österreich*. Graz, 1925. One of the clearest of books on the Alps. Excellent.

Sorre, Maximilien. *Les Pyrénées méditerranéennes*. Paris, 1913.

Tate, G. H. H., and Hitchcock, C. B. "The Cerro Duida Region of Venezuela," in *Geographical Review*, xx (1930), pp. 31–52.

Taylor, W. P. "A Distributional and Ecological Study of Mount Rainier, Washington," in *Ecology*, iii (1922), pp. 214–236.

Tits, D. A. "Les zones altitudinales de végétation dans les Pyrénées orientales," in *Bulletin de la Société Royal de Botanique de Belgique*, lvii (1924), pp. 31–50.

Townsend, C. H. T. Vertical Life Zones of Northern Peru with Crop

Correlations," in *Ecology*, vii (1926), pp. 440–444. Zones up to 14,000 feet, or 4220 meters.

Warming, Eugenius. *Oecology of Plants*. Oxford, 1909. Chap. xxi.

Wettstein, R. "Die Pflanzenwelt der Alpen," in *Die Österreichischen Alpen*, ed. by Hans Leitmeier (Leipzig and Vienna, 1928), pp. 124–136.

Exposure to Sun

Almost every regional study takes up this important question. See also references on isolation at end of Chapter I.

Blanchard, Raoul. "L'habitation en Queyras," in *La géographie*, xix (1909), pp. 15–44, 97–110. Raoul Blanchard, the creator of the Institute of Alpine Geography at Grenoble, is one of the most prolific writers upon mountain geography.

Blumer, J. C. "A Comparison between Two Mountain Sides," in *The Plant World*, xiii (1910), pp. 134–140.

Bonaparte, Roland. "L'influence de l'exposition sur le site des villages dans le Valais," in *La géographie*, xi (1905), pp. 212–216. The importance of this article should not be measured by its length.

Huttenlocher, Friedrich. Sonnen- und Schattenlage. Oehringen, 1923. Of second importance for this discussion.

Levainville, J. "La vallée de Barcelonnette," in *Annales de géographie*, xvi (1907), pp. 223–244. Of first importance for its data and its point of view.

Peattie, Roderick. "La question de l'adret et de l'ubac," in *Revue de géographie alpine*, xviii (1930), pp. 175–187. A critique of European studies; incorporated in part in this volume.

Shreve, Forrest. "Soil Temperature as Influenced by Altitude and Slope Exposure," in *Ecology*, v (1924), pp. 128–136.

Vessereau, Marcelle. "L'adret et l'ubac dans les Alpes occidentales," in *Annales de géographie*, xxx (1921), pp. 321–333. The best article on the subject.

Andorra

Armet y Ricart, S. *Les Valls d'Andorra*. Barcelona, 1906.

Brutails, J. A. *La Coutume d'Andorre*. Paris, 1904. The great book on this little country.

Carrier, Elsé Haydon. *Water and Grass*. London, 1932. Chap. xix.

Chevalier, Marcel. *Andorra*. Chambéry, 1925. Has a topographic map.

Chevalier, Marcel. *El paisatge de Catalunya*. Barcelona, 1928.

Corey, Herbert. "A Unique Republic, where Smuggling is an Industry," in *National Geographic Magazine*, xxxiii (1918), pp. 279–299.

Dalmau de Baquer, Luis. *Historia de la República de Andorra*. Barcelona, 1849.

Newman, Bernard. *Round about Andorra.* London, 1928.

Peattie, Roderick. "Andorra; A Study in Mountain Geography," in *Geographical Review*, xix (1929), pp. 218–233.

Peattie, Roderick. "Wanderungen in Andorra," in *Der Erdball*, iv (1930), pp. 287–290.

Rios Urruti, Fernando de los. *Vida e Instituciones del Pueblo de Andorra: Una Supervivencia Señorial.* Madrid, 1920.

Whittlesey, Derwent. "Andorra's Autonomy," in *Journal of Modern History*, vi (1934), pp. 147–155.

The Tarentaise

Arbos, Philippe. *La vie pastorale dans les Alpes françaises.* Paris, 1922.

Arbos, Philippe. "La vie pastorale en Tarantaise," in *Annales de géographie*, xxi (1912), pp. 323–345.

Blanchard, Raoul. *Les Alpes françaises.* Paris, 1925.

Blanchard, Raoul. "Comparaison des profils en long des vallées de Tarentaise et Maurienne," in *Recueil des travaux de l'Institut de géographie alpine*, vi (1918), pp. 261–331.

Carrier, Elsé Haydon. *Water and Grass.* London, 1932.

Evrard, F., and Chermezon, Henri. "La végétation de la Haute-Tarentaise," in *Bulletin de la Société botanique de France*, lxv (1918), pp. 153–209.

Gex, François. *La plus haute commune de Savoie; Val d'Isère et la Haute-Tarentaise.* Chambéry, 1922.

Onde, H. "La transhumance en Maurienne et en Tarentaise," in *Revue de géographie alpine*, xx (1932), pp. 237–251.

Peattie, Roderick. "Height Limits of Mountain Economies," in *Geographical Review*, xxi (1931), pp. 415–428.

Peattie, Roderick. "La question de l'adret et de l'ubac," in *Revue de géographie alpine*, xviii (1930), pp. 175–187.

Rey, François. *L'exploitation pastorale dans le départment de la Savoie.* Chambéry, 1930.

CHAPTER V

FORESTS AND THEIR SIGNIFICANCE

TREE LINE AND FOREST LINE

THE *forest line* on mountains is the upper limit of the more or less continuous forest zone. The *tree line* marks the upper limit of scattered trees. The forest line approximates an average tree line. Where considerable clearing at the upper margin has taken place, tree line and forest line may coincide. Once a coincidence has been established there is little possibility of scattered trees encroaching upon the pastures, because of the destruction done to saplings by browsing and grazing. There is also to be considered the lower limit of forests. This is usually the upper limit of fields. This limit is an economic matter, which depends upon topography, soil, and ground water. On steep slopes the lower limits of the forest stand push downward. On gentle slopes field culture repels the lower limit of trees to a greater elevation. The extent to which lumbering operations are carried on determines in part the elevation of this lower limit. But lumbering to-day ordinarily consists in selecting suitable trees wherever found, and does not alter the total area of woods or cause the retreat of forest margins. In Southwestern America, where forests are primeval, there is a lower limit which is climatic. The basis of such a limit is, of course, a matter of rainfall, but in the more southern portions of the western American mountains there is also the determinant of soil temperatures. Bare soil there, unshaded by tree growth, prohibits the downward advance of trees, because the rock temperatures, well over 45 degrees C. in the sun, kill off the seedlings.

Is the upper limit of forests climatic? Imhof would define this margin as the result of the sum total of climatic factors. This is more true of the tree line than of the forest line. De Martonne has studied forest distribution in the Carpathians, where in the High Tatra there is little question of economic influences. There the limitation is more exactly climatic. There are always the factors of soil and topography present here, as in a consideration of any vegetation limits. Yet although, generally speaking, the limits of primeval forests in mountains are climatic, it is worth our attention to analyze the relative importance of the several factors.

There is no question in mountain geography concerning which writers more thoroughly disagree than the matter of forests. In France Mougin disputes the views of Lenoble. German and Austrian authorities are Fritsch, Reishauer, Imhof, and Marek. Topographic, climatic, and economic factors are, in fact, inter-related and seldom independent. Shreve, studying relatively simple conditions in our arid Southwest, sees moisture, tempera-ture, and light factors as all playing a part. In many studies temperature may well be more or less eliminated as a deter-minant in forest limitations, because the disheveled and crippled appearance of the trees definitely points to wind and evaporation as limiting factors. There is a coincidence between forest line and zone of maximum precipitation. The economic factor is illustrated where forests are found on the poorer ground or steeper slopes which cannot be pastured.

Forest limits at one place or another clearly show relationship to temperature decrease, amount of precipitation, duration of snow cover, exposure to wind, ground water, soil, and relief. Which of these factors does the following table show? Obviously the matter cannot be decided without detailed consideration of each exposure on which the observation was made. (Figure 30.)

FOREST LIMITS AND EXPOSURE

| Region | Exposure | | | |
	South	West	North	East
Lauterbrunnental (N. side of Alps)	1950 m.	1920 m.	1820 m.	1900 m.
Ortler Alps	2131	2154	2100	2120
Stubai Alps	1842	1974	1805	1815

The table on the opposite page is from Roletto, writing upon the Cottian Alps. The climate being Mediterranean, there is a lower limit of forest due to aridity. Exposure, precipitation, and soil, as well, perhaps, as economic factors, are here illustrated.

The figures for the Po valley are low because of the steep slopes found there. No figures are given for the nearby Plateau of Larches, because that territory is now exclusively reserved for pasturage. There is not even fuel enough for shepherds' use. The lack of evenness in the figures representing the difference between the heights on the two slopes shows that factors other

LIMITS OF CONIFERS IN THE COTTIAN ALPS

Valley	Upper limit	Lower limit	Exposure of upper limit	Side opposite to that of the upper limit	Difference	Predominant geological formation
Varaïta	2300 m.	1000 m.	NE	2000 m.	300 m.	Calcareous schist
Po	1840	1000	N	1550	290	Serpentine
Pellice	2300	1100	W	1550	750	Serpentine
Germanasca	2300	1000	W	1000	1300	Mica schist
Cluson	2450	1100	N	2200	250	Calcareous schist
Bardonnèche	2100	1100	NE	2100	0	Calcareous schist
Doire de Césanne	2350	1100	N	1900	450	Calcareous schist
Cenischia ..	2200	1100	NE	1800	400	Mica schist

than climatic control the elevation of the limits. The more general the figures, the more likely they are to show climatic influences. Clearing, avalanches, landslides, steep topography, and the like control the details of the forest limits rather than the average elevations. The physiographic influences in their effect on forest distribution are so patent that they do not require emphasis.

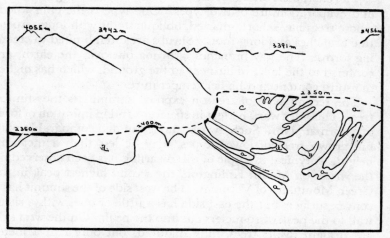

FIG. 30. FACTORS IN TREE LIMITS IN THE VAL ROSEG, SWITZERLAND

Solid line = Climatic tree line.
Broken line = Theoretical tree line.
Fine line = Actual tree line.

    a, lowered by avalanches; b, by talus and rock movement; c, by glaciers and moraines; d, by clearing for alp pastures. (*After Brockmann-Jerosch.*)

Physical Factors

The climatic factors, on the other hand, need elaboration. Wind is the most important factor in controlling tree lines. Nowhere in nature are the destructive environmental factors more effective against tree invasion than at the frontiers on mountain slopes. The last trees are gnarled and twisted, their branches growing on one side of the trunk and the trunks inclined. The uppermost trees are dwarfed. This is because the higher the location on a given exposure on a peak, the greater, in general, is the wind velocity. Isolated peaks have also greater wind velocity than protected slopes of the same elevation in the interior region of a massif. We have always to interpret the altitudinal importance of the wind in terms of relief and isolation of the station under consideration. Isolated peaks of moderate elevation are usually barren of trees, even though their altitudes are considerably below the level of critical temperature and precipitation. Evaporation thus accounts for the much-studied 'balds' of the Great Smokies of North Carolina.

The characters of the trees in the zone of struggle against wind and evaporation are of two types. One type is the elfin wood, whose trees have short, gnarled, oblique stems with long serpentine branches and long roots. Shrubs are often limited to creeping forms. The low branches, growing out over the earth, are confined to the layer of air near to the ground, which has higher moisture content and higher temperature.

The second type of tree on exposed summits is the stunted tree. This is a dwarf, perfect in structure and in imitation of form of a normal plant. Such dwarfs, though of age comparable with full grown trees of lower slopes, may be less than a meter in height. A typical example of this dwarfing has been observed by the writer on Mount Killington, the second highest peak in the Green Mountains of Vermont. The west side of the summit has a convex surface, but the east side has a little cirque, with a sheer wall to the peak of 10 meters cut into the peak. On the west side are straight dwarf trees, fully matured, but only half a meter high. In the shelter of the cirque trees stand 10 meters tall, their summits reaching only as high as the shelter of the rock cliff. Though temperature may play a part, the difference must be due largely to exposure and evaporation.

Since, regardless of altitude, the summits of peaks are fre-

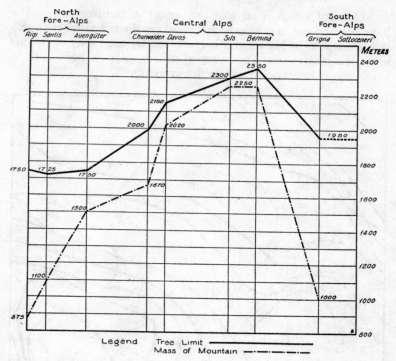

FIG. 31. TREE LIMIT AND MASS OF MOUNTAIN IN AUSTRIA
(*After Brockmann-Jerosch.*)

quently bare, the highest mountains, other things being equal, have the highest tree limits. The following table possibly illustrates the point, though mass of mountain must also be regarded as a factor.

THE HIGHEST MOUNTAINS HAVE THE HIGHEST FOREST LIMITS

	Mountain limit	Forest limit
Carpathians	2500 m.	2000–2100 m.
Massif Central (France)	1800	1400
Vosges	1300	1000

It must not be thought that only summits are affected adversely by evaporation. Winds are often factors in keeping alp lands free of trees and in determining the xerophytic nature of heath and grass cover. Moreover, evaporation without the assistance of winds is an effective agent in limiting trees. We have pointed out in previous chapters how the potential evaporation from soils at high levels is increased by the rarity of the air and high insolation. Exposure, of course, plays a part both in insolation values and in wind effectiveness.

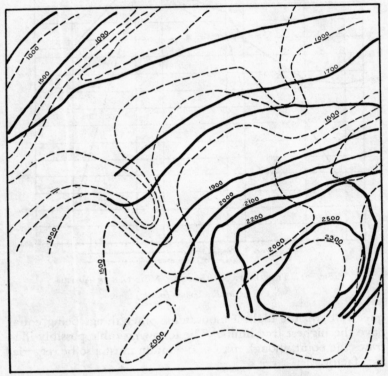

FIG. 32. FOREST LIMIT AND MOUNTAIN MASS IN SWITZERLAND

The solid line represents the forest limits and the broken lines the relative mass of mountain. (*After Brockmann-Jerosch.*)

It is said by some authorities that the main topographic and climatic factor in limiting tree and forest lines is the length of the growing season. Though most pines require three months free from frost, one type of pine is said to live where the frostless season is but 67 days. It has been suggested by others that the mountain forest limit is controlled by the same factors as the Arctic forest frontier, because each has an approximately equal July air temperature. The Arctic July average is about 10 degrees. The winter minima are probably of slight consequence to tree growth. Yet, conclusive as these data seem, we should be wrong in thinking that they offer a complete solution.

Mass of mountain, of course, affects temperature, but trees gain greater heights on massive mountains than the increased temperature would seem to imply. (Figures 31 and 32.) Thus an increased mass of mountain in inner Austria is said by Marek to have raised a forest line from 1511 to 2029 meters (518 meters difference), whereas the 8.26 degree mean annual isotherm was lifted from 1741 to 1890 meters (only 149 meters difference). Imhof says mass of mountain as a factor in forest limits outweighs exposure. His map of forest lines in Switzerland certainly shows high forest lines on the massive Monte Rosa and Weisshorn groups. It is true that in two groups whose peaks are of equal elevation the group with the lesser dissection has the higher forest lines. Considering a cross section of Austria on the 29th meridian east, one discovers a decrease of the mass and of forest line. The decreases are not, however, of the same rate. Whereas mass elevations lose 1222 meters, forest lines lose but 556 meters. A most common observation on forest lines is the excess of elevation in a central massif as compared with the lower and more dissected border ranges. Moreover, the greater the mass of mountain, the greater the difference between forest line and tree line. Reishauer gives the following table for six regions in the Stubaier Alps:

MASS OF MOUNTAIN, FOREST LINE, AND TREE LINE

Height of mass	Forest limit	Tree limit	Difference
2094	1812	1866	54
2358	1810	1894	84
2520	1850	1940	90
2746	1681	1875	194
2827	1930	2070	140
2863	2037	2199	162

Brockmann-Jerosch in his *Baumgrenze und Klimacharakter* offers perhaps the most searching and complete analysis of climate and tree limit. The following table is characteristic of the details he has collected. The stations are arranged so as to make a profile of the Alps, north to south.

CONDITIONS OF TREE LIMITS IN ALPINE STATIONS

	Altitude	Mean annual temperature range	Average tree limit	Mean mass
Rigi summit	1787 m.	39.3°	1750 m.	800 m.
Guttanen	1055	42.7	1880	1800
St. Gotthard	2096	41.1	1960	2150
Airolo	1141	40.5	2100	1900
Monte Generoso	1610	35.5	1950	800

It is probable that evaporation, soil, slope, ground water, precipitation, and duration of snow cover are more important here in limiting the upward advance of forests than temperature decrease. Both tables bring out the fact that though generalities may be constructed showing the temperature relations of forest lines, they are, in reality, of little value, for two reasons: (1) the details of control of temperature affect the details of forest elevations and (2) many other climatic factors play inseparable rôles.

De Martonne reports that the forest limit in the Carpathians is more or less coincident with the zone of maximum precipitation. Marek does not find this true for Austria. If there is a decrease of precipitation above a given zone, then, if the mountain range has sufficient altitude, there surely must be a limitation to tree growth. Undoubtedly this would be true for the Himalayas and Andes. One must remember also the additional factors active above the zone of maximum precipitation, such as greater evaporation due to increased insolation, lack of cloud, high winds, steep slopes, and deficient ground water. Generally the greater the precipitation the greater the percentage of area in forest, at least above the cultivated zone. This is partly true because the greater the precipitation the greater the degree of slope that will support trees. It is true again because precipitation means cloudiness and a consequent lessening of evaporation.

Ratzel in 1889 was one of the first to point out the relationship between forest line and snow line. The earlier conception was that the duration of snow cover restricted the growing season. Since it is soil temperature and plant temperature rather than air temperature which really determine the growing season in high altitudes, the relationship of snow cover to growing season is important. Marek, in Austria, judged the average length of snow duration at the forest line to be 221 days. Other things being equal, the forest line is about 800 meters below the climatic snow line.

Fig. 33. Avalanche Track in the Grisons, Switzerland

Fig. 34. Slope Farm in the Forest Zone, Stubaital, Austria
Note the hay barns on the valley floor and the post-glacial cutting of the stream.

Snow cover is important in other ways. It has been pointed out to the writer by Transeau, of Ohio State University, that trees in the High American Sierras are found on the ridges rather than in the ravines and valleys. The windswept exposures, having less depth of snow, are first bared by melting, and so permit seedlings to get an early start. A forest cannot be expected to reproduce itself over an area which has snow cover until late July or early August. Shaw shows conclusively still another effect of snow as a limitation on forests. By visiting the Selkirks in winter he proved his contention that the snow 'drowns' trees by preventing aeration and thus permitting fungous growth at the base of the trunk. This accounts for the dead branches of dwarf wood near the timber line. He states that alp pastures in the Selkirks are treeless because of the depth of snow cover.

PLANT FACTORS

The conception of plant zones is further challenged when one considers individual kinds of trees. In the Western Alps there are, to the casual observer, definite tree zones. Excluding the tree flora of the Mediterranean littoral, which extends only up to 300 meters, there are four tree zones. Many authorities assign altitudinal limits to these zones. The altitudes which they give may be true of the region for which they write, but the conditions are so variable in different regions, and on different sides of the same mountain, that it is better to leave precise altitudes out of consideration. It must not be supposed that these zones are everywhere developed with equal completeness. On the south slopes of the Maritime Alps they are crowded together, and only the first and third zones are well developed. Many trees shift through two zones. Thus, on the south slopes of the Maritime Alps, Pinus sylvestris occupies the north cold shaded slopes at low altitudes, but as high altitudes are reached, it switches around to the south or sunny slopes, leaving the north side to firs and larches.

The truth is that tree species and varieties have characteristic requirements as to

(1) Soil. This varies in physical and chemical nature with the geology, slope, and ground water.

(2) Length of growing season. A matter of great significance, which varies first with altitude and secondly with exposure.

(3) Soil temperature. This has been shown to have distinct relation to altitude.

(4) Moisture. A matter of precipitation totals, percentage in snow, seasonal distribution, character of storms, ground water, and evaporation.

The soil requirements of trees are many and various. The Aleppo pine, laurel, and holly are frequently found on lime soils. The Black Cluster pine and larch grow on more acid ground. Soil aeration, presence of available salts, particularly nitrates, phosphate, and potash, and the amount of ground water in greater or less degree control the prosperity of different types of trees. A needle-leaf tree and a broad-leaf tree certainly have different transpiration rates as well as different abilities to carry on photosynthesis. The abilities of the two types of trees in regard to these functions are for the moment in dispute. In the Maritime Alps, of which we are speaking, it is true that the needle-leaf trees predominate on exposed and steep slopes. The deciduous trees prevail in valleys and in hidden glens. There are, however, many other factors which control the distribution of these tree types.[1]

The moisture requirements of trees permit of no generalization. The pines, for example, differ greatly among themselves. A sharp contrast is also presented between the beech and the spruce. The beech avoids excessive ground water, but the beech leaf needs the atmospheric humidity of the *ubac*. The spruce requires a highly saturated soil, but will tolerate the very dry atmosphere of slopes exposed to wind and sun. Among the oaks also, great difference in requirements prevails. The common oak (Quercus robur) is a typical deciduous tree in its needs, but the holly oak will tolerate the arid and almost soilless precipices of the Fore-Alps of the Riviera.

The upward expansion of any species of tree is, then, the result of a complexity of factors, and it is impossible to ascribe definite altitudinal limitations. Altitudinal modifications of climate are, of course, factors in the height limit of any species. But even above that tree line, the same plant will appear as a bush to which the botanist assigns a variety name. Thus the Swiss Mountain Pine, whose limber branches, supporting great quantities of snow and ice without breaking, permit it to live at snowy alti-

[1] Data supplied by Donald C. Peattie.

tudes, will, because of the aridity of peak areas, appear at those levels as a bush, variety *pumilio*. Yet higher, it becomes a creeping shrub, variety *Mughus*.

This section is meant to show that in considering tree or forest zones one must study not merely the physical factors, but also the reactions of the tree-types to those conditions. The situation is analogous to the point of view of cultural geography, where one takes into account not only the influences of the earth on man but particularly man's adaptation of the earth to his purposes.

Economic Factors

The demands which increasing populations place upon forested areas for lumber and for fuel, the expansion of pasture and tilled land at the expense of the forest area, and the demand of certain industries, especially the manufacture of charcoal for forges, have forced back the margins of the forest in mountains as elsewhere. Mougin, judging that the word 'Savoie' once meant 'dark forest,' believes the rate of deforestation to be proportional to the increasing population. Encroachment of pasture area upon forest certainly has taken place. There has been definite clearing of forests to increase alp pasture. The fuel needed, especially on those alps where cheese is manufactured, and the bedding made by cutting young conifers, have lowered the upper limit of forests. The sudden ceasing of forest and the commencement of the grass lands without transition have been cited as evidence that forest lines have been forced back. Unfortunately for this argument, forest lines in the Western Cordillera of North America show this same lack of transition, and yet we know that there has been little artificial extension of the pastures there.

Not a little has been written, pro and con, as to the damage that cows, sheep, and goats do to forests. The goats certainly do the most injury, but in mountains where forests are worth considering the goat is not important. Sheep are alleged by some to do considerable damage and by others to do no damage. One's interest in sheep raising may well color the argument. There is the statement that the greater the size of the flocks of sheep, the lower the tree line. On the other hand, would it not be true that the lower the tree line, and so the greater the pasture area, the larger the flocks? It is the writer's observation, as well as that of others, that the elevation of forest lines as seen in the Alps and other European mountains is seldom the result of climatic factors alone. The demand for pasture or the demand for wood has altered the forest lines. It is only in countries with a shorter history of habitation that true climatic lines are found coinciding with actual forest limits.

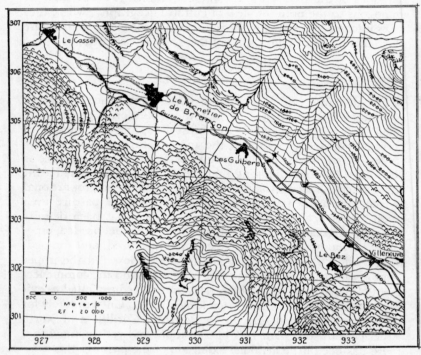

FIG. 35. EXAMPLE OF FOREST DISTRIBUTION IN THE FRENCH ALPS
The extent to which forests have been cleared from the *adret* is well shown.

The lower limit of the forest, where contact is made with agricultural lands, is almost always raised as increasing populations make demands for a larger tilled area. Koegel offers a detailed study of a local retreat of forest lines before the demands for farm lands.

The following table for the Sellraintal is given by Reishauer, and goes to show that the use of land for crops on the sunny side of the valley contracts the forest lines:

FOREST LIMITS IN THE VAL CAMONICA

	Average woods	Highest woods	Average tree	Highest tree
Sunny slope	1752 m.	1910	1822	2015
Shady slope with side valleys ...	1859	1950	1977	2140

It is interesting to note here that the differences between the highest woods is 40 meters, and between the highest trees, 125 meters, while the difference between the average woods is 107 meters, and between the average tree limits, 155 meters. Perhaps the maximum limit approximates the climatic limit.

The extent to which forest distribution is due to economic rather than climatic factors is shown by the fact that in low valleys, where evaporation is not a significant element, the shady or cool sides hold the forest. In the Vintschgau, 67 per cent of the forests are on the *ubac*, and in the Engadine, 60 per cent. In many valleys the percentage is even higher, as is illustrated by a valley in Queyras where the percentage is 93. This is not, however, the original distribution of forests in the valley. The sunny slope in the lower valleys is more favorable for trees, but has today been denuded of forests and given over to cultivated fields.

There is a debate among geographers, particularly in France, as to the extent to which mountains have been deforested. This debate is represented in part by the references given in the bibliography at the end of this chapter. The writings by Mougin and Lenoble cover the question. Certainly the Alps were no less forested in primeval times than today. Certainly there have always been topographic and climatic limitations of the tree lines. If one goes far enough back in history, larger ice and snow fields opposed the advance of trees. The Stone Age and Bronze Age were periods when the open spaces above the forest zone were occupied by men who preferred the high meadows to the terrifying and chilly shades of the forest. These upland clear spaces the German refers to as *Urweiden*. Deposits of stone tools have been found at 2700 meters in Valais.

But was there serious deforestation in, say, Roman times? There certainly was in the Apennines, and, even earlier, in the mountains of Greece. Though the Mediterranean buildings were largely of stone, the ships were of wood. The demands of Phoenician commerce aided in the denudation of the Greek mountains. The Etruscans made early demands upon the forests of the Apennines, and they were followed by the Romans. The climate of the deforested Mediterranean mountains was not suitable for natural reforestation. The Roman demands for timber then drove the woodcutter into the Alps. It is possible that logs were floated down the Rhone from as far north as Savoy. But it is in the later Middle Ages that deforestation of the Pyrenees and Alps is first evident. There appear in the archives of those periods numerous laws and regulations calculated to prevent undue spoliation of the forests. Examples are readily found in the local and regional studies, many of which have historical chapters (see end of Chapter VII).

Deforestation in the Alps and Pyrenees was less a result of commercial exploitation than of the overpopulation of the valleys. In the later Middle Ages, there was little movement of population, and isolated communities were compelled to provide for their own natural increase. Not only did the increased numbers require more cleared fields and pastures, they also needed a greater supply of fuel. The degree to which overpopulation caused excessive destruction of the forests is shown by the amount of destructive soil erosion which took place. Undoubtedly water resources were also lessened. Natural reforestation was hindered by the browsing of the herds and droves among the seedlings.

In the study of deforestation and the preservation of mountain forests, it is needful to appreciate the peculiar importance of forests in mountain regions. For two reasons there are extensive forest areas in mountains: much of the slope is too steep for any other use, and the zone of maximum rainfall gives the necessary water for tree growth. This is particularly important in arid regions. The dry states of Arizona and New Mexico, and dry countries like Spain, lean heavily upon their mountain forests. Mountains of the volcanic type are lacking in coal; the fuel, therefore, in such places, is wood. But forests in mountains have so many special local functions that they are guarded carefully against overcutting for fuel. The living tree is more important to the mountaineer than timber or fuel wood. The farmer will preserve trees on the borders of his fields and along irrigation ditches, which he will trim and so gather an annual crop of branches or twigs. These pollard trees, so familiar an aspect of European plains landscapes, are found also in mountain valleys, particularly in the Mediterranean mountains. The writer has

seen a chestnut stump twelve feet in height and seven feet in
diameter in the Mediterranean Pyrenees. Above the stump was a
bush of the last year's growth of shoots. Since this bush is cut
annually, the diameter of the stump testifies to the years in which
this cropping has been practised.

Erosion in mountains is severe. One of the best guards against
erosion is the maintenance of forest stands. Deforestation in the
French mountains, particularly in the Pyrenees, has caused such
almost catastrophic soil erosion as to excite national attention to
the reforestation of the denuded slopes. The same has been true,
though perhaps to a lesser extent, in every country sharing the
Alpine territory. Soil erosion in mountain valleys is a double
calamity. It not only destroys the slopes, but it also causes torrential fans of coarse detritus to spread over the valley fields and
clog the channels of the streams. A farm may be laid waste in a
single night by gravel washed down by the waters of a cloudburst.
Unfortunately, when once a gully or ravine is begun the erosion
is difficult to check. As a preventive, wicker or stone dams are
thrown up across the gully and then trees are planted there.
Forests maintain soil on steep slopes. Soil without proper covering of vegetation has an angle of rest which is much less steep.
The wide divergence of angle between these two slopes represents the possible amount of earth which may be eroded from the
slope and deposited over the valley fields.

It has been many times proved that forests and forest soils
largely prevent immediate run-off of storm waters and so preserve the ground water table and regulate the flow of streams.
The article by Toumey referred to in the bibliography sum-
marizes opinion upon this matter. Those who wish a quantitative study of the importance of forests to stream flow and flood
crests should turn to the article by Bates and Henry. These men,
both experienced in mountain climatology, determined conclusively that on a mountain in a semi-arid region deforested
land does not hold snow cover so long as forest, while flood
crests are earlier and more severe than in the forest area. Besides
the value of constant stream flow in providing an all year round
water supply for the mountain village or town, deep snow cover
means to mountain areas irrigation water, water for power, and
comparative freedom from floods. Mountains are important in
semi-arid regions because the heights provide water for irrigation of the valleys and piedmonts. The industrial future of most

mountain areas depends upon water power. One of the most active groups of agents in furthering reforestation has been the water power organizations. The danger of floods to inhabitants of the confined valleys hardly needs emphasis. There is yet another significance to mountain forests. The wood provides material for innumerable, often part-time, wood-working industries, and thus gives to the mountaineer a seasonal employment. A planning of the land utilization of mountains calls for an extensive area in tree growth.

BIBLIOGRAPHICAL NOTES

Forests

Bates, C. G. *Forest Types in the Central Rocky Mountains as Affected by Climate and Soil.* Washington, 1924. (United States Department of Agriculture, Bulletin no. 1233.) Tree requirements.

Bates, C. G., and Henry, A. J. "Forest and Stream-Flow Experiment at Wagon Wheel Gap, Colo.," in *Monthly Weather Review*, supplement no. 30 (1928). Difficulty of reforestation in a dry climate.

Brockmann-Jerosch, Heinrich. *Baumgrenze und Klimacharakter.* Zurich, 1919. Perhaps the most authoritative book on the question.

Buffault, Pierre. *Le Briançonnais forestier et pastoral.* Paris, 1913.

Chevalier, Auguste. "Le déboisement et la dégradation du manteau végétal dans les Alpes," in *Annales de géographie*, xxxii (1923), pp. 546–551.

Cowles, H. C. "The Relation of Snow and Ice to Mountain Timber Lines," in *Annals of the Association of American Geographers*, i (1911), p. 106.

Demontzey, Prosper. *Étude sur les travaux de reboisement et de gazonnement des montagnes.* Paris, 1878.

Flahault, Charles. "Les limites supérieures de la végétation forestière et les prairies pseudo-alpines en France," in *Annales forestières*, x (1901), pp. 385–401, 417–439.

Frödin, John. "La limite forestière alpine et la température de l'air," in *Botaniska Notiser*, 1920, pp. 167–176.

Gannett, Henry. "The Timber Line," in *Bulletin of the American Geographical Society*, xxxi (1899), pp. 118–122.

Gaussen, Henri. "Les forêts du pays d'Ossau," in *Revue géographique des Pyrénées et du Sud-Ouest*, ii (1931), pp. 431–447.

Gaussen, Henri. "Les forêts de la Vallée d'Aspe," in *Revue géographique des Pyrénées et du Sud-Ouest*, iii (1932), pp. 5–17.

Harvey, L. R. H. *A Study of the Physiographic Ecology of Mount Ktaadn, Maine.* Orono, 1903. (*University of Maine Studies*, no. 5.)

Heybrock, Werner. "The Interval between Tree and Pasture Lines and the Position of their Extremes," in *Geographical Review*, xxiv (1934), pp. 444–452.

Imhof, Eduard. "Die Waldgrenze in der Schweiz," in *Beiträge zur Geophysik*, iv (1900), pp. 241–330. A pioneer article and a classic.

Kerner, Anton von. *Der Wald und die Alpenwirtschaft in Österreich und Tirol.* Berlin, 1908.

Koegel, Ludwig. "Von der Alpinen Buchengrenze," in *Zeitschrift der Gesellschaft für Erdkunde zu Berlin*, 1929, Heft 1–2, pp. 33–35.

Künkele, Theodor. "Der Hochgebirgswald," in *Zeitschrift des Deutschen Öund sterreichischen Alpenvereins*, xli (1910), pp. 6–17. Excellent for details.

Lavauden, L. "Un example de dégradation végétale dans les Basses-Alpes," in *Revue des eaux et forêts*, lxxii (1934), pp. 33–36.

Lenoble, Félix. "La légende du déboisement des Alpes," in *Revue de géographie alpine*, xi (1923), pp. 5–116. One must be cautious in accepting his conclusions.

Lenoble, Félix. "Le valeur économique du reboisement des Alpes méridionales," in *Revue de géographie alpine*, xii (1924), pp. 5–29.

Marek, Richard. "Beiträge zur Klimatographie der oberen Waldgrenze in den Ostalpen," in *Petermanns Mitteilungen*, lvi, 1 (1910), pp. 63–69. Marek is an authority on forests in the Alps.

Marek, Richard. "Waldgrenzstudien in der österreichischen Alpen," in *Mitteilungen der geographischen Gesellschaft in Wien*, xlviii (1905), pp. 403–425.

Meylan, Réné. "La forêt du Risoud," in *Bulletin de la Société Neuchâteloise de géographie*, xxxiv (1925), pp. 5–15. A forest due to inversion of temperature.

Mougin, P. "Les forêts de protection en Savoie," in *Revue des eaux et forêts*, lii (1913), pp. 545–557.

Mougin, P. "La question du déboisement des Alpes," in *Revue de géographie alpine*, xii (1924), pp. 497–545. Disagrees with Lenoble.

Mougin, P. "Le déboisement des Alpes du Sud," in *Revue des eaux et forêts*, lxxii (1934), pp. 194–198.

Pearson, G. A. "A Meteorological Study of Parks and Timbered Areas in the Western Yellow-Pine Forests of Arizona and New Mexico," in *Monthly Weather Review*, xli (1913), pp. 1615–1629. The climate of open spaces versus forests.

Reishauer, Hermann. "Höhengrenzen der Vegetation in den Stubaier Alpen und in der Adamello-Gruppe," in *Wissenschaftliche Veröffentlichungen des Vereins für Erdkunde zu Leipzig*, vi (Leipzig, 1904), pp. 1–210. An instructive and valuable work.

Roman, Joseph. *Les causes du déboisement des montagnes d'après les documents historiques du XIIIᵉ au XVIIIᵉ siècle.* 1887.

Salvador, J. "Simples notes sur l'aménagement et l'exploitation des forêts pyrénéenes françaises," in *Revue géographique des Pyrénées et du Sud-Ouest*, i (1930), pp. 58–74.

Sclafert, Thérèse. "À propos du déboisement des Alpes du Sud," in *Annales de géographie*, xlii (1933), pp. 266–277, 350–360; xliii (1934), pp. 126–145.

Shaw, C. H. "The Causes of Timber Line on Mountains: The Rôle of Snow," in *The Plant World*, xii (1909), pp. 169–181.

Toumey, J. W. "The Relation of Forests to Stream Flow," in United States Department of Agriculture, *Yearbook*, 1903, pp. 279–288.

Zon, Raphael. *Forests and Water in the Light of Scientific Investigation.* Washington, 1927. Reprinted, with revised bibliography, from *Final Report* of the National Waterways Commission, 1912.

CHAPTER VI

ALP PASTURES AND ALP ECONOMY

What Is An Alp?

ALPS are, in the language of those who live amongst them, the grassy slopes above the tree line, the grassy areas in hanging valleys, the pastures on the mountain spurs, and the steppe vegetation of plateaus and about the peaks. The alp is, therefore, not a peak but a mountain pasture. The mountaineer has little interest in the peaks as compared with the utilitarian alp. He visits the barrens only to shoot game or to look for lost sheep. It is but in recent years that the mountaineer has learned alpinism from the tourist.

Sieger, quoting Spann, gives a topographic and economic definition. He writes of alps as those pastures in the mountains, at least 900 meters above the level of the sea, which offer during the favorable season grazing for cattle, and which, though managed separately from the valley farms, are an integral part of the farmer's economy. He then quotes with approval the definition of Wittschieben. Wittschieben speaks of alps as territorial establishments which carry cattle during the summer for a long and continuous period of grazing. Wittschieben excludes from his definition uplands where cattle go only for a short period or which are not pastured because of inaccessibility. No doubt such fine distinctions have a place in detailed economic studies of alps, but to us they are of little concern (Figure 36).

There is, in fact, no statement as to the elevation limits of alps which will hold universally. Alps are commonly above the tree line. In many places the alp zone is in contact with the agricultural zone. Such may be *petites montagnes*, and are relatively accessible. *Grandes montagnes* are the true alps and are distant from the agricultural village. Spann would refer to the *petite montagne* as an elevated farm pasture in distinction to an alp. The difference lies in that the one is managed from the base farm, while the alp has a separate administration. A true alp should have seasonally inhabited shelters, if not villages.

The alp is treeless. Botanically it is grass land which grades from steppe to tundra. Not only may the plants have xerophytic characteristics, but they are adapted to a short growing season. The plants are in many cases light-loving. In the upper reaches

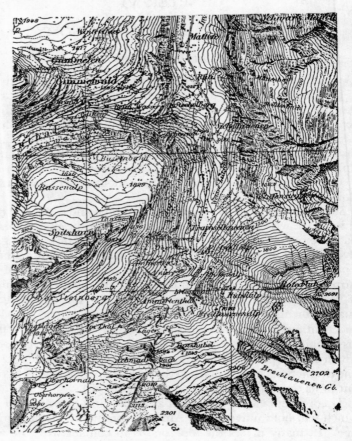

FIG. 36. TOPOGRAPHIC RELATIONS OF ALP PASTURES

Note Bussenalp, Ober Steinberg and Hubelalp. These are summer pastures above the level of the inhabited zone. Scale 1/50,000. Contour interval 30 meters.

the subsoil may be frozen and tundra aridity is a dominant control. Even though day temperatures, especially soil temperatures, are high, it must be remembered that the minima are most significant. As one ascends, the plant associations less and less resemble those of the valley. The grass becomes thinly scattered as in deserts. The pioneer lawn plants give way to plant bunches or plant cushions. Above, on the almost barren peaks, are rock plant associations. One essential difference between the alpine climate and an arctic climate of equivalent mean annual temperature is the great noon insolation of the alp land as compared with that of the true tundra. A difference in the plant life results. Alpine peaks have many more varieties of plants than arctic fields.

One of the most common of limiting factors in the upward expansion of alp pastures is topography. A steep cliff frequently marks the approach to a peak. Literally the alp grows upon a cone surface of mantle rock which does not extend completely to the peak. Because of the structure of the bed rock, the cone when found on sedimentary masses has a declivity whose slope is interrupted by cliffs or steep areas. These steepened portions may be barren, in forest, or in grass. Each step of the pastoral ladder which the herds mount is known to the Germans as a *Staffel*, i. e., ladder round.

If the alp is, in a way, an alluvial cone clinging about the peak, the height of the peak is of prime importance. One must remember, however, that the height of the peak is only a partial measure of the mass of mountain. The greater the mass of mountain the higher the summit, and, therefore, ordinarily the higher the limit of the alp. Also, if the mass is great, the area of the alp is correspondingly extensive. This is true because massive mountains in most cases have convex rather than concave slopes. Massive mountains may have an extent of alp land quite out of proportion to the area of the valley hay lands. Such is true of the schist uplands of the Tarentaise. Therefore, in order to utilize fully their alp pastures, the peasants must import beasts each summer (*transhumants*) in addition to the animals they are able to winter on the valley hay. In contrast there are the limestone border Alps, such as the Chartreuse, where mass is less than in the Tarentaise and slopes are more concave. Alp pastures there are deficient. In the Tarentaise alp pastures make up three-fifths of the area. In the Chartreuse such lands are but one-fifth of the area. The Stubaier Alps, a part of the core range of Austria, have considerable mass. Alp pasture limits there mount to the great height of 3000 to 3100 meters, whereas in the adjacent limestone border ranges the limit of pastures is 2400 meters.

Though mass of mountains is an important factor in the height limit and area of high pastures, yet topography can counterbalance mass as a factor. There are areas of alp which have peaks higher than 3000 meters yet alp limits of only 1600 to 2500 meters. The Italian Dolomites are an example in point, with their steep cliffs in the upper reaches of the peaks.

However, air temperatures are not so significant in limiting alp pastures as they are in limiting cultivated fields. In high altitudes, it must be remembered, low air temperatures are counteracted in part by high soil and plant temperatures. This is well illustrated by fine pastures on sunny slopes under the same air temperatures as permanent snow fields lying on the shady side.

Snow cover will, of course, control the length of the growing season. Snow cover, it will be remembered, is the result of the amount of snowfall, exposure to wind, exposure to sun, and position in regard to drifting snow or avalanche, as well as other factors. An area which is free from snow but a month a year cannot be expected to maintain grass cover.

The matter of soil temperatures deserves further remark. Soil temperature depends upon the physical character of the soil, the direction of exposure, the duration of sunlight on a given exposure, the angle of slope, and the vegetal covering. Shady slopes may have soil temperatures lower than the already low air temperatures. Soil temperatures on sunny slopes, especially where there is protection from wind, may be surprisingly high.

By way of résumé, the following are the more important factors in limiting the elevation of alp pastures:

1. Mass of mountain.
2. Topography.
3. Soil.
4. Exposure.
5. Precipitation.
6. Evaporation.

There are a number of terms connected with alps and alp exploitation with which the student searching through European literature should be familiar. As with any specialized industry, there has arisen a set of terms characteristic of mountain pastoral life. Moreover, the multiplicity of mountain dialects has given a variety of forms based often on the same root. A few of the more common are here reproduced.

The alp is, of course, the upland pasture. Such has been the use of the word throughout this book. The term alp is perhaps the most universally used. Some American physiographers have selected the term *alb* for use. The writer sees little reason to use other than the widely accepted *alm* or *alp*. There are the following equivalents, or partial equivalents:

alpe	*berg*	*galen*
alpo	*berge*	*pla*
arpe	*olbe*	*planina*
alpage	*monti*	*plaroure*
albe	*montagne*	*jasse*
alm	*montagna*	

In the maps one frequently see descriptive combinations, as Sennberg, Kuhberg, or Viehberg. Arbos indicates a few of the numerous place names which involve alpine pursuits. They are such as Alpettaz, Arpette, Aups. *Calmis,* an ancient term for pasture, has given Lachat, Bellachat, la Chalmette, les Chalps, and many other words. Another ancient term for pasture is *Laie, Lée,* or *Lex.* We have then L'Allée Blanche, L'Aile-Froide, and Vers l'Allée. From *la Montagne* we have le Mont Bas, le Mont Froid, etc., etc. There are also La Vacherie, le Col des Génisses, le Jas des Agneaux, la Cabane des Mulets. The other languages may be expected to have an equal number of variations. The first *Staffel* or more nearly level area of the alp holds a temporary dwelling. Here hay is cut, in some cases land is tilled for field crops. This is known as the *montagnette, Voralp, mayen, Vorsass,* or *Mainensass.* Following are a series of French terms demonstrating the character of alp exploitation: le Col du Fruit (cheese), le Fruit Commun, la Vacherie, la Vélière, le Col des Génisses, le Roc des Boeufs, la Cabane des Mulets. The following terms describe in a collective word portions of alps. L'Aoup grand is a large alp and l'Arpilhoun a small alp. The side of a little alp is Couesta de l'Aoupet. A poor alp is l'Aoupenas. A short grass pasture, as for sheep, is Pelouniera. One special term is worth note: a *Kuhstoss* is a cow's portion of grass. A *Kuhstoss* is thought of as supporting two heifers, three sheep, four pigs, or eight goats.

The enumeration of terms is partly to give an idea of the multiplicity of provincial dialects, and the reader must remember that the lists are not complete, but rather indicative of the variety.

Within a single dialect there are numerous terms for the shades of distinction. This is characteristic of primitive peoples who are highly specialized in their economic pursuits. The nomad of the steppes has an interminable vocabulary for the shades of horses. The French Canadian has a large specialized vocabulary for the kinds of ice that clog the mill races in winter.

Alp Economy

Certain economic aspects are peculiar to mountain pastoral life in distinction to pastoral life on plains. Some of these have to do with the relative isolation or difficulty of access of the alp pasture. Others have to do with qualities inherent in the pastures themselves.

Most alp pastures are more or less within sight of the valley settlements in whose economy they are involved. Yet, especially in a valley with a decided glacial U-shape, there may be difficulty of access which isolates the alp in terms of effort and hours of climbing so as to affect its economy.[1] Indeed the alp which is easily attainable from the valley settlement is thought of in special terms and hardly considered a true alp. These alp lands which are at no great distance from the winter settlement or even adjacent to it are often owned in separate parcels and are treated like so much pasture land on a plain. In any case they do not have the economic organization of the true alp, located high on some mountain shoulder or hanging valley. The isolation of these true alps is not so much an isolation of distance as difficulty of access. This difficulty is not only in the labor of climbing but in the problem of road building and maintenance. That the arduous and expensive maintenance of a road is demanded, calls ordinarily for corporate efforts. Alps are for this reason, as well as others, owned ordinarily by communes, corporations, or syndicates.

More important than the difficulty of access are certain qualities inherent in the alps themselves. Because the cattle enter upon the lowest rung or *Staffel* of the alps while the upper reaches still lie under snow it is impossible to grant small areas to private ownership. The alp is a land which because of topographic

---

[1] The accessibility of an alp must be thought of partly in terms of cow travel. Even alps near to the permanent village hold the cattle from nightly return to the stables because travel impairs the health of the cow and the milk yield.

climate must be a range land. Also, if any portion of the alp
suffers erosion because of misuse, areas below may suffer torrential deposition, and areas above may experience gullying
from headward erosion. Alp use implies access to water supply

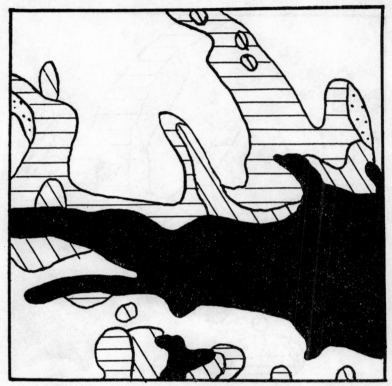

Fig. 37. Ground Plan of Up-Mountain Movements, Murau Region of
Austria

Black = permanently inhabited. Diagonal lines = occupied May 15.
Horizontal lines = occupied June 15. Dots = occupied August 1.
Blank = unoccupied. (*After Spreitzer.*)

and, if cheese is made, to fuel. In short, alps because of their nature should ordinarily be operated as a unit. Alps may, in fact,
be owned privately, by corporations, or by the commune. The
private ownership is not always the most fortunate. The private
owner may not have money to preserve and care properly for the

alp. Moreover, he is less subject to public opinion and may permit erosion or other deterioration of the alp. The communal ownership is by far the best. The economy of the valley village is not complete without utilization of the alp pastures. When a

Fig. 38. Ground Plan of Down-Mountain Movements, Murau Region of Austria

Blank = uninhabited. Fine dots = occupied until September 15. Coarse dots, until October 1. Horizontal lines, until October 15. Diagonal lines, until December 27. Black = permanently inhabited. (*After Spreitzer.*)

commune owns the alp a committee decides the dates of pasturing, the number of cows permitted on the alp, the amount of manuring, and improvement of the grass.

The right to pasture a cow upon an alp is characteristic of this system. Such rights are sold or inherited. The right properly should, and usually does, go with a piece of valley land. That land should be at least of a size and soil that will provide winter hay for the beast. But less overgrazing and the attendant destructive soil erosion come about if the number of cows on an alp is strictly limited. An example of pasture regulation is shown in the case of the Beaufort alp in Savoy. Here on an alp of 150 hectares, half of which is barren, there are 150 cattle for 82 days. The alp lies between 1500 and 2000 meters. Had the pasture zone been higher, the number of beasts might have been decreased.

There are in most mountain areas, but particularly in the drier mountains, two types of mountain pastures. One has more ground moisture and lusher grass. This is pasture for cattle. Such lands are found on gentle slopes, in valley bottoms, and in cirques and other hollows. The second type of pasture has less ground water, less succulent grass, and is reserved for sheep. It is found on steep slopes, at great altitudes, or on summits exposed to considerable evaporation.

If there is an excess of summer cattle pasture, cows are either underfed in the winter, or, what is more likely, are sold in the autumn. This occasions the autumnal cattle fairs in so many of the commercial valleys. Such a fair is that of Chur in Eastern Switzerland or of Moûtiers in the French Alps. Andorra, with an excess of summer pastures, has a series of fairs to sell the stock that cannot be wintered there. So important are these fairs that great seasonal discrepancies appear in the statistics of animal populations. The summer figures are in excess of those of winter.

This lack of balance between hay supply for winter and summer pasture is compensated for in a number of ways other than the selling of cattle in the autumn. Pasturage is rented to owners of stock that live on the plains, a subject that is discussed later in this chapter.

Again, the *Voralp* or *mayen* may be used partly for hay production. Also portions of the alps not easily accessible for beasts, or dangerous for them, are devoted to hay. These wild meadows may even be so dangerous for men as to call for public restrictions as to their use. Often a deficiency of alp land is made up at the expense of the forest area.

Where, on the other hand, a deficiency of pasture exists, and there is excess of hay land, cows may be pastured in the valley about the permanent settlement, or a commune or corporation may lease or own lands outside its watershed. Indeed, the water divide in the pass head or on the mountain crest will often be such as not to hinder the wandering of cattle outside the valley proper. In places the cattle are driven over snow, and even glaciers, to gain remote grazing grounds.

The character of ownership of the alp pastures is sometimes of geographic consequence. A *petite montagne* is ordinarily divided into plots privately owned. The accessibility, the usually gentle slope, and the contiguity or nearness to the fields of the valley bottom, impose none of the conditions which cause the *grande montagne* to be owned by common interests. This private ownership of pieces of alp pasture is characteristic of the Fore-Alps of Savoy and of the Inntal of Austria. The ownership is sometimes a communal affair, or it may pertain to a syndicate or corporation. There are, of course, alp lands held by a single individual who rents cow rights to others. So important is the summering to each pastoral-agriculturist of the valley, so complementary are the summer pastures to the valley hay fields, that individual ownership of alps runs counter to the geographic set-up of the valley economy. The common ownership seems to have been decreed by nature.

MOUNTAIN NOMADISM

The alps set the scene for a seasonal movement of the cattle and the herders. It would not be far amiss, philosophically, to say that the alps impose this nomadism upon mountain regions. This mountain pastoral nomadism is the periodic seeking of the grass of the upland pastures. The valley land furnishes hay for the winter stabling and perhaps the field crops for food for the village. But the valley is really subsidiary to the upland pastures. Another characteristic of mountain nomadism is that it is ordinarily within a single region. If the vertical distance of the wandering of mountain nomadism is not greater than the horizontal, it is at least more significant. There are cases not a few where stock is taken beyond the limits of the basin into neighboring regions. In one Swiss example, the cattle actually migrate 70 kilometers and mount 1000 meters, climbing over a glacier. Ordinarily, however, the distant pastures are continuous with the home pastures, and the generalization holds that mountain nomadism is a wandering within a region.

Both the nomadism of the plains and that of the mountains

FIG. 39. THE DAY OF THE CATTLE DOWN-DRIVE IN ANDORRA

Cattle descending to winter stables in late October. (Courtesy of the *Geographical Review*, published by the American Geographical Society of New York.)

FIG. 40. TRANSHUMANCE IN ANDORRA

Part of the 30,000 sheep that leave Andorra in autumn for the Spanish plains.

have a rhythm, and imply a return to the starting point. Plains nomadism ordinarily has an extent of movement much greater than that of the mountains. In each case the termini of the annual wandering are complements. The plains nomad carries a tent or collapsible hut. The mountain nomad has stone huts at intervals along the short course of his summer migrations. There is one group in the high French Alps that has a separate set of huts for almost every week of the summer.

The degree to which people migrate from their so-called permanent or winter villages depends largely upon the topographic set-up of the valley. Generally, severely glaciated regions have considerable altitudinal differentiation between the valley bottom and the alp pastures. The simplest form of seasonal rhythm developed through mountain nomadism is that of the Chartreuse. This massif is a steep-sided portion of the Savoian Fore-Alps. Its valleys are considerably higher than the main valley of the Isère. The villages and hamlets of the interior of the massif are near to, or at, the lower limit of the alp pastures. The summer alp area and the hay and stable area of winter support are adjacent. Near the Chartreuse is the area of the Belledonne range. Here the winter granges and stables are isolated from the villages. The granges are at the lower edge of the summer pastures, where, on the first *Staffel*, hay is made. The villages are much lower. The cattle then winter above the villages. In the Central Pyrenees the same type of seasonal movement is observed. The difference between the Chartreuse and Belledonne system is largely topographic. There is a forest zone on the Belledonne between the 1000- and 1800-meter contours. Practically the entire population lives below 1000 meters and most of it below 800 meters. In the winter the granges are visited daily by a caretaker.

Another type of nomadism is discoverable in the Conflent in the French Pyrenees. Here there are no high-level summer villages. Living in a Mediterranean climate, the cattle in winter not only eat hay in the stable, but graze in the fields. In summer, accompanied by a herder or several herders, the droves and flocks ascend the mountains. The cattle go to the moist pastures of the *jasse* areas in the forest or cirques, and the sheep still higher to the *pla* pastures.

A complex nomadism is characteristic of the *mayen, Voralp,* or *montagnette*. As defined before, these three analogous terms mean

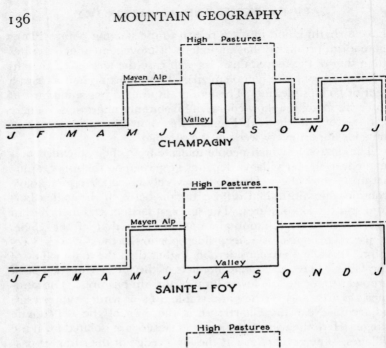

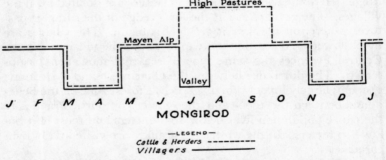

FIG. 41. MOUNTAIN NOMADISM IN THREE REGIONS OF THE FRENCH ALPS
Top to bottom: Champagny; Sainte-Foy; Mongirod. (*After Arbos.*)

the lowest alp, used for grazing in combination with haying and perhaps agriculture. This alp is ordinarily occupied by man and beast for a period in spring and autumn. It is usually above or near the upper forest limit, or, at least, is allied with the true alp, the *grande montagne*, by a topographic separation from the valley floor.

The Tarentaise offers the simplest form of the more compli-

cated migration. Let us consider two types of Tarentaise nomadism. The Val de Tignes is a portion of the uppermost valley
of the Isère. The town of the same name is 1849 meters above
sea level. Its highest satellite village is at 1936 meters. The surrounding peaks are from 1900 to 2272 meters. The town of
Tignes is practically at the lower limit of alps and is so high as
to have a critically short snow-free period. Here the beasts leave
the permanent village for shelters on the *montagnette*. The family
abides with them for a period in the spring. Hay is gathered.
Then the cattle, herders, and cheese-makers go up the mountain, while the remainder of the population descend to the valley to make hay. The cattle coming down from the true alp
in autumn are met again by the population at the *montagnette*,
where hay is cut once again. People and cattle then remain at
the *montagnette* until the hay in the grange is exhausted. This is
perhaps until Christmas. All then come down to the valley
village.

The Bourg-Saint-Maurice type is more characteristic of other
regions, and perhaps comes close to an average. Bourg-Saint-
Maurice is a town of the lower valley. Between May 15th and
June 1st each family sends its beasts to the *montagnette*. The household — even the children — accompany the beasts. Within a
month the animals with the herdsmen and shepherds go up to the
true alps, while the family descends to the valley. During the
spring and autumnal sojourns hay is cut on the *montagnette*. For
a time in autumn the stock eat in the little pastures neighboring
the *montagnette* village. Later they eat the hay of the grange.
People and animals then make their way to the lowland village,
where during the summer hay and vegetables have been harvested. In all, the beasts are on the lower level some seven
months. The people, aside from the herdsmen, are absent from
the permanent village but two one-month periods.

The Champagny type of nomadism is illustrated by Figure 50.
From January to early May, people and cattle are in the permanent village. There is an early summer sojourn of some six
weeks in the *montagnette* village. During the summer, when the
cattle are on the true alp, the people are alternately in the valley
and on the *montagnette*, taking in harvests, principally hay. Because of the several summer visits to the *montagnette* the autumnal
visit is barely a fortnight. There is a return to the *montagnette*
village for more than a month in midwinter to consume the

very considerable store of hay and such vegetables as are left there.[1]

There are further aspects of alp land and valley that affect nomadic movements. Latitude, altitude, steepness of slope, continuity of slope, exposure, and percentage of local alp land all enter into the question. In some cases, physical conditions are such as to require as long a residence on the mountain as in the lowland, indeed, perhaps longer, though of broken continuity. Arbos recounts two such instances, both in the French Alps. At Mont-Aimont from January to late May, and from September to November, people and cattle are in the valley village. A few workers, and perhaps the very old and very young, remain in these villages all summer. Even these are in the *mayen* village for the early winter period. The summer period sees the cattle and a part of the population on an alp. Between seasons the cattle remain pastured in the vicinity of the *mayen* village.[2]

A second type is that of Ceillac. During the winter season men and beasts stay in the valley village. Spring, summer, and autumn, men and beasts are above. Part of the population settles in the *mayen* village for the summer, while another part of the group goes higher up the mountain with the cattle. Here the occupation of the so-called 'permanent' village is of shorter duration than that of the 'temporary' habitation.

Even though there has been in recent years a trend from general farming to pastoral pursuits, there is, nevertheless, a decay of pastoral life in the European mountain valleys. This is due in part to the decrease in the number of available workers, but is more largely the result of hydro-electric developments. The royalties received for water rights free numbers of the people from the necessity of pastoral labors.

In the French Alps many of the highest granges are today in ruins. Thus in the commune of Saint-Christophe, mentioned earlier in this book as having a winter duration of snow that is Siberian, thirteen out of the twenty-one summer chalets have been abandoned. Today but half the folk of the Briançonnais ascend the mountains in summer. Elsewhere the proportion is even less. Where, as in L'Argentière, factories exist because of the

---

[1] Jules Blache has simplified the classification of mountain nomadic movements. See *Revue de géographie alpine*, xxii (1934), pp. 525-531.

[2] *Montagnette* and *mayen* are here used interchangeably. The first is more characteristic of the French Alps and the second of the Swiss. *Mayen* seems the preferable term.

electrical power, the decay of migration is most significant. Valloire, which since the beginning of the nineteenth century has lost one-half its population, has abandoned five-sixths of its alp pastures.

In the Val d'Anniviers

The most extraordinary example of nomadism is found in the Val d'Anniviers. The writer, unfortunately, has not had the advantage of visiting this valley, but its pastoral industry has been often studied. The Val d'Anniviers is pendant above the south slope of the Upper Rhone. The valley is drained by the Navigenze which rises in the massif of Mont Collon and the Dent Blanche. It flows into the Rhone at Sierre. The valley has a north-south trend. It is 20 kilometers in length. The valley is abruptly set in the massif and yet 'hangs' at a considerable elevation above the gorge of the Rhone.

The chief village is Zinal. The journey from Sierre, in the deep gorge of the Rhone river, to Zinal in the hanging valley requires six to seven hours on foot. After an hour and a half of travel from Sierre one has mounted a thousand feet along a roadway built with great difficulty upon the precipitous side of the Rhone valley. Beyond Zinal are yet higher villages — indeed, some of the highest in Europe.

The visitor to the valley is surprised to find that always a part of the population is on the move. Month by month the people move up and down the mountain slope. Because of the rigors of the climate, each halting place requires substantial protection. There must be shelter for the family, stable, granary, and cellar. A plentiful wood supply makes the multiplication of barns and outhouses easy, and leads to an exaggerated estimate of the population.

This valley, of all valleys of the Alps, is noteworthy for its seasonal migrations. With the change of the seasons there is to be seen the movement of the people impelled by the climate. Up and down the mountain go processions, moving from the *mayen* village to the valley village, and from the valley village to the village among the vineyards far below in the bottom of the Rhone valley. In addition to this migration, there is the movement of cattle and herdsmen to the high alp pastures. The procession is a picturesque sight. The migration from the five villages of the Rhone valley to the high Val d'Anniviers is taken together. The priest and mayor of each village lead the companies. The women and children follow on foot. Behind come the crowding cattle, goats, and sheep, driven by an ancient shepherd. With the family are carried the household utensils and impedimenta.

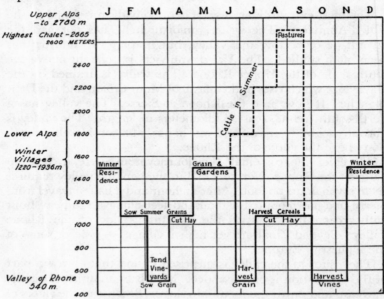

FIG. 42. SEASONAL MOVEMENTS IN THE VAL D'ANNIVIERS, SWITZERLAND

Let us recount month by month the typical movements of a village (Figure 42). February finds the inhabitants at the principal village. It would be wrong to call this the winter village, for they are not here most of the winter. Nor is it the permanent village when it is occupied but little more than four months of the year. These villages are elevated 1220 to 1936 meters above sea level. At the end of February the vineyards of the Rhone valley are free from snow. The people of the high valley own lands in the main valley. The villagers then descend a thousand meters to tend the grapes and to sow some crops. The end of March sees the groups mounting again to the chief villages — shall we call them datum villages? The end of April means an ascent to the *mayen* villages, where hay is gathered and cattle are pastured near by. Nightly the cattle are collected so that manure may be accumulated. Here people and cattle rest for perhaps seven weeks. In late June the herders and cattle, as well as the cheese makers, mount to the true alp. The villagers descend. We must follow their separate fortunes.

The cattle and their attendants mount by stages (1800 meters and 2780 meters) to the final and highest alp at 2800 meters. The most elevated *cabane* of the herders is at 2665 meters. The mountain pasturage begins earlier and ends later than in most Swiss valleys. It may last, indeed, for 100 days. Towards the end of September the cattle descend, not to the *mayen*, but to the datum village. What has been happening to the villagers during the summer? When they parted from the cattle on the *mayen* in late June, they descended past the datum village to the Rhone village. Here for a month they were busy with the harvest of grains and vegetables. By late July they mounted to the datum village in the side valley, where they gathered the hay harvest. October and part of November find the villagers again by the Rhone working among the grapes. Late in November, villagers and cattle are again found in the *mayen* villages, where the cattle are consuming the *mayen* hay crop.

This is one of the most complicated of nomadisms.[1] The full horizontal range of movement may amount to 20 kilometers. The altitudinal range amounts to almost 2300 meters. There are three villages for each group. The villagers have fewer resting periods than the herders, yet the villagers make eight separate moves annually.

So completely are the special resources used that there is a high density of population. In 1900 the valley held 2238 people. And it must be remembered that many of these people had three or four houses. Generally speaking, in the valley itself there are not definite towns, but groupings of houses. The people migrate to such an extent that the commune has not the complete functioning of a plains commune. The commune is merely a political unit. Though the curé is a functionary of the political unit, the schoolmaster is of the settlement or village. The distinction dates back to feudal days and the division between temporal and spiritual power, but its preservation is due to the unimportance of place in a nomadic régime.

---

[1] The movements of the people of Chandolin of the same valley are so complicated as to be quite confusing in description or diagram.

Pastoral Buildings of the Central Pyrenees

A type of study which is frequently made is of the variety of form and purpose of the dwellings involved in nomadic life. A number of these are to be found in the bibliographies. The writer offers some notes upon a partial investigation in the French Pyrenees.

The number and distribution of buildings of the *gaves* of the Central Pyrenees of France is misleading unless interpreted in the light of the seasonal movements of the people. The problem of the houses of these *gaves* is increased because of the difficulty of classifying their uses. There are 'permanent' and 'temporary' dwellings, villages, stables, isolated stables, and various types of hay barns (*fenils*). Their uses are many, in that they fit into the seasonal rhythm of labor required of the people by the topography of the countryside. In these valleys, generally speaking, there is little or no separation between the hay meadows of the valley and the pastures of the high slopes. What, under natural conditions, would have been the forest zone is now woodlots and little meadows, each with its hay barn. The summer hamlets are within an hour's, or even half hour's, walk, of the winter villages. Winter stables for beasts are in many cases in the meadows or at the edge of the alp pastures. Some are within ten minutes of the village. They are *near the hay field*. This is to save the hauling of the hay — in some cases down steep slopes. Their absence from the village means better sanitation there.

In the Conflent the cattle are pastured on the alp or *jasse* in the summer time and are quite separated from the permanent village. In the winter the beasts are stabled in the valley or allowed to feed in the meadows. In the Central Pyrenees a different system prevails. The alp pastures are nearly continuous with the valley lands. Moreover, heavy snows in the valleys prevent any winter pasturage on the hay meadows. Cold weather, snows out of season, or overgrazing frequently force the herds from the upper pastures to the lower limit of the alp pastures. Hence there are settlements or isolated hay barns and stables near the lower limit of the alp pastures or among the meadows of what was once the forest zone. Even in summer the cattle may be driven nightly to a rude settlement at the lower limit of the alps. These groups of huts are known variously as *cortals*, *bordes*, or *pardinas*. They are ordinarily merely herders' refuges, but some patches of land are

Fig. 43. Pastoral Establishments near Pralognon, French Alps
Looking down from the heights of the Vanois upon cheese huts and stables.

Fig. 44. Cheese Huts of the Marjelen Alp, Bernese Oberland, Switzerland

on occasion devoted to vegetables. The writer has visited one, far above the tree line and in a region lacking fissile stone, which was shingled with squared cow-dung. There is frequently a stone corral, into which the cattle are herded so that their droppings of the night may be collected. This manure is then accumulated and carried in season to the valley fields by cart. This means fertilizing of the fields at the expense of the pastures. Were the beasts stabled in the villages in the winter these manure depots would probably not exist. Such a depot exists in the Vallée de Griff where one turns to the trail for the Pic du Midi.

To illustrate more clearly the seasonal movements of the region, let us consider the Barèges valley. It is by this valley that one mounts from Luz to the Col de Tourmelet. Along the valley lie the villages of Esterre, Viella, Betpouey-Barèges, and Barèges. The altitude of Luz is 660 meters and of Barèges 1232 meters. One slope town, Sers, lies at 1340 meters. Barèges is a large town for its altitude, but few of its people live from agriculture or herding. The town is a tourist center, has mineral springs, and boasts a military hospital. Above Barèges are some chalets and barns and stables occupied in the winter. In summer the stables are deserted. The cattle are high on the mountain pastures under the care of a community *vacher*, while the sheep and their *bergères* wander among the yet higher and more remote pastures.

The summer villages at the edge of the alp are the equivalent of the *mayen* villages of the Swiss, but they are less well organized and of a less concentrated form. The family comes to them in May before the cattle have left. Commencing in June, four crops of grass are harvested. By September 15th, snow has fallen on the higher alps and the cattle descend to their winter barns. The families and the ever-present pig descend to the valley villages. Milch cows are taken to the valleys. The Pyrenees are more noted for beef production than cheese. The comparative absence of the cheese industry explains the primitive form of the *bordes* as compared with the *fruitières* or *Sennhütten* of the Alps.

In winter the cattle and sheep are stabled, ordinarily, above the winter village level. These stables are the hay barns in the forest zone or in the summer village zone. The stable is a dark, almost hermetically sealed building situated at a spring or over a stream. The beasts are allowed the freedom of the building. They seek their water at the trough or the hay at the feeding rack. The nearer barns are visited at intervals to renew the hay.

In some, the more isolated stables, high on the mountain, and actually buried in snow, there lives a miserable guardian of the beasts. He sleeps on straw, as do the animals. Amid the darkness and stench of the stable he spends his winter in silence except for the occasional lowings of the kine.

TRANSHUMANCE: THE FRENCH ALPS

Though the term *transhumance* is variously defined, there is ordinarily a distinction made between it and nomadism. Transhumance strictly is merely nomadism. When applied to mountains, the term implies an exchange between the pastures of plains and the high pastures of mountains. The beasts find winter forage on the plains and summer on the alp lands. Frequently the animals are sheep with a sprinkling of goats. In transhumance, as distinct from nomadism, the pastures of the two seasons are remote from each other. Ordinarily in European mountain transhumance today the families do not take part in the movement, but only the sheep and the herders.[1] This driving of beasts from plain to distant alp is best developed in Mediterranean lands. Where winter rains provide pasturage in that season in the Mediterranean area, in summer the pastures are burnt and dusty, the supply of drinking water is scarce, and the heat too intense for the well-being of the animals. Mountain pastures are looked upon as a necessary complement to winter forage.

Therefore Spain, Southern France, Italy, the Balkans, and the Southern Carpathians are all lands where transhumance has a long history and a modern phase. The sheep from Southern France move seasonally by the thousands to the Massif Central and to the Alps of Haute-Savoie and Dauphiné. The movement of animals from the delta of the Rhone and the Provençal lowlands into Tarentaise and Maurienne is especially important.

The monotonously flat lands of the Rhone delta and the stony plain of Crau near by are ill fitted for sheep in summer. They are dry, the forage is poor, and the heat is bad for the animals. It is from these regions that vast numbers of sheep repair annually to the alp pastures of Tarentaise and Maurienne. In terms of the pastoral industry, the two regions are complementary. There is also what has been called an inverse transhumance. Sheep

[1] The Balkans form a notable example.

owners living in the mountains send sheep to winter on the plains about the mouths of the Rhone. This is of secondary importance as compared with the normal transhumance.

The means and ways of travel of sheep, herdsmen, and impedimenta between the two areas of forage were a matter of much concern in the Middle Ages and early modern periods. The narrow roadways, the lack of provision for rest areas for the weary sheep, the tolls at bridges and in towns, the expense of feeding and watering led to special sheep-ways being constructed. These *carraïres* were rights of way, three to seven meters wide, which avoided towns and farms. Areas were assigned for rest places (*relargs*) and for the night (*pousadous*). Narrow routes (*drayes*) led to the high pastures. The organization of a migration of so many sheep, together with the materials of living loaded upon donkeys, was not unlike the organization of an army. As many as 40,000 head of sheep would make up a single movement.

Even today large droves of sheep move from Provence and Gard towards the highest and least accessible alpages of the French Alps. The interesting scene is enacted every year. As summer approaches, the advance guard of donkeys burdened with the shepherds' impedimenta puts in its appearance. The sheep and the goats follow, some of them bearing huge booming bells. They literally cover the road. Hundreds succeed hundreds. Forty thousand are pastured each season in the remote Alps of Maurienne and Tarentaise. But the long journey on foot is largely a thing of the past. The sheep and goats are driven from the Crau and the mouths of the Rhone and the plain of the Midi to Arles, Pont d'Avignon, and Nîmes, where they are taken by rail to the very valleys above which lie the summer pastures at such centers as Bourg-Saint-Maurice and Mondane. Modern transportation has made the *carraïres* superfluous.

There has been an interesting change in the totals of transhumance since 1913 in Tarentaise and Maurienne:

24,000 beasts in 1913
41,000 " " 1926
44,000 " " 1928
41,000 " " 1930

This is contrary to the usual course of transhumance today. In most regions the practice is decreased as compared to the time before the war. Here the figure for 1930 exceeds that of 1913.

In Provence, wool and especially meat have increased in price. The alps of the high communes of Val d'Isère, Saint-Martin-de-Belcher, and Tignes have raised their rentals and receive 40 times the amount which was paid for pasturage in 1913.

Generally speaking, transhumance in Europe is on the decline. The large-scale importation of wool from the Americas, Australia, and Asia has offered severe competition. Substitutes for wool have lessened the market. In Provence there is now a considerable trade in fattening African sheep for the market. Because less land in Alpine valleys is being used for grain crops, more forage is raised for winter feed. Hence the mountaineers make greater use of the pastures for their own flocks. Moreover, the overgrazing which was a phase of unrestricted transhumance created a reaction against the system. Briot, a vigorous critic of transhumance, was the chief enemy of this annual visitation of hungry animals. Ten years after Briot's attacks, the number of beasts visiting alp pastures had been greatly reduced.

For further details of these movements one should see especially Arbos's great work, the article by Onde, the readable book by Miss Carrier, and the excellent treatise by Blache. Arbos has excellent details on the French Alps, while the survey of Blache covers many lands and types.

In the Balkans

Nowhere is transhumance of more local importance than in the Balkans. The following material is largely condensed from Miss Carrier's study on nomadism. The writer has visited Dalmatia and Albania casually.

In Balkan territories the Vlachs are, as a race, nomadic. They have clung with remarkable tenacity to their time-honored ways of life. From their flocks they derive milk, cheese, and meat for food, and skins, wool, and leather for clothing. They practice transhumance, except where modern conditions are too restrictive. In a region where the plains in the summer are burnt brown, the green pastures of the mountains at that season are irresistibly tempting. The seasonal rhythm of movement is from steppe to mountain upland. A distinction between Balkan transhumance and that of the Alps lies in the fact that in the former type the whole family moves. This, however, is in gradual process of change.

Wallachia is the Rumanian portion of the Danube plain. Between this semi-steppe and the flat-topped Transylvanian Alps is the chief Balkan transhumance. The Vlachs dwell in piedmont villages where life is partly agricultural. In winter the pastures of the plain support the sheep. In summer the sheep are pastured on the mountains in areas known as *plaiouri*. Formerly there were special ways for passage between these seasonal grazing grounds. These sheep roads were called *drumul oilor*, the equivalent of the *carraïre* of Provence.

The movement involves the entire village. On the mountain the summer home is a *stina*. The way of living in the summer is primitive, to say the least, and it is said that a *stina* can be smelled before it is seen. Much of the summer season is taken up with the making of sheep's cheese. Swine are raised on whey. Early in September the entire group, people, sheep, swine, beasts of burden, with the children and impedimenta, begin the trek to the valley. The flocks have by their milk and cheese supported the family during the summer except for such grain as was brought for bread. The profit comes from selling the surplus cheese, the natural increase of sheep, and the by-product of swine. There is also the crop of wool.

There is a people of Vlach origin who live in the Pindus range in Northern Greece. They maintain their proper villages in the mountain grazing zone. Since the immediate piedmont of the range is settled and not open to them, they travel considerable distances to Thessaly, Macedonia, and the lowlands of Albania. This is an example of an inverse transhumance, for the true culture of these Pindus Vlachs is derived from the upland environment. The movement from the plain to the mountain upland is begun by the sheep and their herders. The animals clog the roads. A traveler may see 60,000 migrant sheep in a day. The entire movement from Albania to Greece may involve 3,000,000 goats and 5,000,000 ewes. Here again transhumance has declined in the last few decades. Italian interests in Albania are creating a market for corn, olive, wine, and citrus fruits. The one-time Turkish rule permitted free passage of the flocks. To-day custom duties are being charged at the national borders.

Yugoslavia has several phases of transhumance. A normal movement is from valleys of the Adriatic littoral to mountain pastures in Bosnia, Herzegovina, and Montenegro, some three to six days distant. As part of the littoral is on the islands, the writer has seen the last part of the autumnal down drive accomplished in boats, the cattle with their heads over the rail of the little sail boat, the sheep crowded beneath, and the goats standing adventurously on the fore-deck. Except for Northern Dalmatia, this migration does not involve families.

Winter on the east side of the Dalmatian range is more severe. The permanent villages found on the upper levels of this gentle Pannonian slope exile their flocks in winter time to the valley of the Save in the care of shepherds. At one time there was a swine transhumance in Bosnia to let the swine feed in autumn upon the acorns of the mountain oak forests.

There are many other types of Balkan transhumance. Enough has been said to show the complexity of types as depending upon geographic variations.

BIBLIOGRAPHICAL NOTES

Alp Pastures and Alp Economy

The Bibliographical Notes at the end of Chapter VII will also include much material on alp pastures.

Arbos, Philippe. "L'économie pastorale dans quelques vallées savoyardes," in *Recueil des travaux de l'Institut de géographie alpine*, i (1913), pp. 45–71.

Arbos, Philippe. "L'économie pastorale en Suisse," in *Recueil des travaux de l'Institut de géographie alpine*, iv (1916), pp. 355–363.

Arbos, Philippe. *La vie pastorale dans les Alpes françaises.* Paris, 1922. Published also as *Bulletin de la Société scientifique de l'Isère*, xliii (1922), 716 pp. This is the great book on mountain pastoral life. Bibliography of 400 titles.

Briot, Félix. *Les Alpes françaises: Études sur l'économie alpestre.* Paris, 1896. A book which greatly influenced alp management.

Briot, Félix. *Les Alpes françaises: Nouvelles études sur l'économie alpestre.* Paris, 1907. Factual.

Briot, Félix. "Économie pastorale de la vallée de l'Ubaye," in *Annales de la science agronomique française et étrangère*, 3e sér., iv (1909), pp. 218–227.

Cardot, Émile. *L'économie alpestre et la genèse du régime pastoral.* Besançon, 1897.

Cavaillès, Henri. "L'économie pastorale dans les Pyrénées," in *Revue générale des sciences*, xvi (1905), pp. 777–783.

Cavaillès, Henri. *La vie pastorale et agricole dans les Pyrénées des Gaves de l'Adour et des Nestes.* Paris, 1931.

Décombaz, Édouard. *L'économie alpestre dans le Canton de Vaud.* Lausanne, 1908. (*Statistique des alpages de la Suisse*, 7.)

Flahault, Charles. "Les hauts sommets et la vie végétale," in *La montagne*, i (1905), pp. 165–184.

Lefebvre, Theodore. *Les modes de vie dans les Pyrénées atlantiques orientales.* Paris, 1933.

Maas, Walther. "Die Almwirtschaft in der Ostkarpathen," in *Zeitschrift der Gesellschaft für Erdkunde zu Berlin*, 1930, Heft 5–6, pp. 185–199.

Martonne, Emmanuel de. "La vie pastorale et la transhumance dans les Karpates méridionales," in *Zu Friedrich Ratzels Gedächtnis* (Leipzig, 1904), pp. 225–245. Excellent.

Peintinger, Alfred. "Zur Geographie und Statistik der Almen im Hochschwabgebiete," in *Mitteilungen der Geographischen Gesellschaft in Wien*, liv (1911), pp. 324–335. Great detail.

Pittioni, Richard. "Urzeitliche 'Almwirtschaft,'" in *Mitteilungen der Geographischen Gesellschaft in Wien*, lxxiv (1931), pp. 108–113.

Rabot, Charles. "La vie pastorale dans la Savoie septentrionale," in *La géographie*, xxvii (1913), pp. 348–357.

Rebsamen, Henri. *Zur Anthropogeographie der Urner Alpen.* Zurich, 1919.

Roletto, G. B. "L'économie pastorale d'une commune du haut Val Trompia," in *Revue de géographie alpine*, viii (1930), pp. 163–174.

Roletto, G. B. "La zona pastorale delle Valli di Lanzo," in *La Geografia*, ix (1921), pp. 3–25.

Sieger, Robert. "Almstatistik und Almgeographie," in *Mitteilungen des Deutschen und Österreichischen Alpenvereins*, xxxiii (1907), pp. 225–226.

Sieger, Robert. *Beiträge zur Geographie der Almen in Österreich.* Graz, 1925. Defines *Alm* at length.

Spann, Joseph. *Alpwirtschaft.* Freising, 1923. A much quoted work. The economics of alp economy in much detail.

Strüby, A. *Die Alp- und Weidewirtschaft in der Schweiz.* Solothurn, 1914. Very important.

Strüby, A. *Die Alpwirtschaft im Kanton Graubünden.* Solothurn, 1909.

Thallmayer, R. A. *Österreichs Alpwirtschaft.* Vienna, 1907.

The Val D'Anniviers and Valais

Berndt, G. *Das Val d'Anniviers und das Bassin de Sierre.* Gotha, 1882. (*Petermanns Mitteilungen*, Ergänzungsheft Nr. 68.)

Biermann, Charles. "La vallée de Conches en Valais," in *Bulletin de la Société Vaudoise des sciences naturelles*, xliii (1907), pp. 39–175.

Brunhes, Jean. *La géographie humaine*, 4ᵉ éd. Paris, 1934. 3 vols. Chap. viii.

Brunhes, Jean, and Girardin, Paul. "Les groupes d'habitations du Val d'Anniviers comme types d'établissements humains," in *Annales de géographie*, xv (1906), pp. 329–352.

Carrier, Elsé Haydon. *Water and Grass*. London, 1932. Chap. xxxiv.

Courthion, Louis. *Le peuple du Valais*. Geneva, 1903.

Desbuissons, Léon. "La vallée de Binn," in *La montagne*, iv (1908), pp. 221–230.

Desbuissons, Léon. *La vallée de Binn (Valais)*. Lausanne, 1909.

Jegerlehner, Johannes. *Das Val d'Anniviers*. Bern, 1904.

Schröter, Carl. *Das Pflanzenleben der Alpen*, 2. Aufl. Zurich, 1926. Special attention to the Val d'Anniviers.

Wolf, F. O. "Les vallées de Tourtemagne et d'Anniviers," in *L'Europe illustrée*, nos. 106, 107, 108.

Movements of Mountain Peoples

Arbos, Philippe. "Le nomadisme dans les hautes vallées savoyardes," in *La montagne*, ix (1913), pp. 324–340.

Arbos, Philippe. "La transhumance savoyarde en Provence," in *Revue de géographie alpine*, viii (1920), pp. 665–666.

Arbos, Philippe. *La vie pastorale dans les Alpes françaises*. Paris, 1922. A classic on nomadism and transhumance; exhaustive for the region.

Blache, Jules. *L'homme et la montagne*. Paris, 1933. An excellent resumé, beautifully illustrated, written authoritatively for the general public.

Blache, Jules. "Le types de migrations pastorales montagnardes," in *Revue de géographie alpine*, xxii (1934), pp. 525–531.

Bladé, J. F. "Essai sur l'histoire de la transhumance dans les Pyrénées françaises," in *Bulletin de géographie historique et descriptive*, 1892, pp. 301–315.

Blanchard, Raoul. "Migrations alpines," in *Annales de géographie*, xxxi (1922), pp. 308–312.

Brunhes, Jean. *La géographie humaine*, 4ᵉ éd. Paris, 1934. 3 vols. Chap. vii.

Carrier, Elsé Haydon. *Water and Grass: A Study in the Pastoral Economy of Southern Europe*. London, 1932. One of the most informative books on the subject in English.

Cavaillès, Henri. *La transhumance Pyrénéenne et la circulation des troupeaux dans les plaines de Gascogne*. Paris, 1931.

Chevalier, Marcel. "La transhumance et la vie pastorale dans les vallées d'Andorre," in *Revue des Pyrénées*, xviii (1906), pp. 604–618.

Dedijer, Jevto. "La transhumance dans les pays dinariques," in *Annales de géographie*, xxv (1916), pp. 347–365.

Fabre, L. A. "L'exode du montagnard et la transhumance du mouton en France," in *Revue d'économie politique*, xxiii (1909), pp. 161–200.

Flückiger, Otto. "Die Wanderungen der Berner Bauern," in *Mit-*

teilungen der geographisch-ethnographischen Gesellschaft in Zürich, xxi (1920), pp. 65–74.

Fournier, Joseph. "Les chemins de transhumance en Provence et en Dauphiné," in *Bulletin de géographie historique et descriptive*, 1900, pp. 237–262.

Fribourg, André. "La transhumance en Espagne," in *Annales de géographie*, xix (1910), pp. 231–244. A famous article.

Gasperi, G. B. de. "Le casère del Friuli," in *Memorie Geografiche, supplemento alla Rivista Geografica Italiana*, viii (1914), pp. 295–461.

Khristianovich, V. P. *Mountainous Ingushiya (Gornaya Ingushiya)*. Rostov, 1928. Reviewed by J. V. Fuller in the *Geographical Review*, xxi (1931), pp. 154–155. Included as a study of transhumance in the Caucasus.

Lefebvre, T. "La transhumance dans les Basses-Pyrénées," in *Annales de géographie*, xxxvii (1928), pp. 35–60.

Lencewicz, Stanislas. "La transhumance dans le val de Réchy," in *Bulletin de la Société Neuchâteloise de géographie*, xxv (1916), pp. 106–121.

Mouralis, D. "L'émigration alpine en France," in *Revue de géographie alpine*, xi (1923), pp. 223–240.

Onde, H. "La transhumance en Maurienne et en Tarentaise," in *Revue de géographie alpine*, xx (1932), pp. 237–251.

Robert-Muller, C., and Allix, André. "Un type d'émigration alpine: Les colporteurs de l'Oisans," in *Revue de géographie alpine*, xi (1923), pp. 585–634.

Roletto, G. B. "La transumanza in Piemonte," in *Rivista Geografica Italiana*, xxvii (1920), pp. 114–120.

Sayce, R. U. "An Ethno-Geographical Essay on Basutoland," in *Geographical Teacher*, xii (1924), pp. 266–288.

Sieger, Robert. "Zur Geographie der zeitweise bewohnten Siedlungen in den Alpen," in *Geographische Zeitschrift*, xiii (1907), pp. 361–369.

Spreitzer, H. "Der Almnomadismus des Klagenfurter Beckens," in *Zur Geographie der deutschen Alpen Robert Sieger gewidnet* (Vienna, 1924), pp. 70–86. Excellent details.

Wallner, Hans. "Die jährliche Verschiebung der Bevölkerung und der Siedlungsgrenze durch die Almwirtschaft im Lungau," in *Mitteilungen der Geographischen Gesellschaft in Wien*, liv (1911), pp. 358–403.

Wopfner, Hermann. "Eine siedlungs- und volkskundliche Wanderung durch Villgraten," in *Zeitschrift des Deutschen und Österreichischen Alpenvereins*, lxii (1931), pp. 246–276.

CHAPTER VII

LAND UTILIZATION AND ECONOMICS

THE ECONOMIC BALANCE IN LAND UTILIZATION

MOUNTAIN lands should be studied in three dimensions. Previously we have been studying the use of land in the dimension of height or depth. Now we shall do well to consider those two dimensions which make for horizontal area. This study resembles an areal study of a plain countryside, but even here there are certain elements which are peculiar to mountains. This will be seen when one realizes that the amount of land used and the character of the use depends upon morphological and climatological conditions arising out of the orography. Moreover, there is a struggle maintained in mountains to balance the areal distribution of alpland, forest, and field because, since one cultural zone lies above the other, erosive agencies, water supply, landslide, and avalanche in one zone may affect the prosperity of the zone lower down.

Rude climate, barren peaks, and the comparative inaccessibility of large areas may reduce the inhabited territory. In Austria, uninhabited areas amount to 54 per cent in the Fore-Alps of Salzburg and 36 per cent in the Julian Fore-Alps. The difference is largely due to relief. Escarpments in portions of the Dolomites cause 85 per cent of the area to be uninhabited. The uninhabited zone, the *anoekoumene*, in the Adamello Group, is 87 per cent of the total, and in the severely glaciated Silvretta Massif it is 94 per cent.

The density of mountain population then should be considered as the number of persons divided not by the total area of the mountain zone but by the area of the inhabited portion. The density of population in mountains considered in this manner proves to be very high. This is shown without the need of statistics by the rapid succession along the valley of agricultural, commercial, and industrial centers. Generally, in the Alps the inhabited land lies between 700 to 2000 meters and the uninhabited area is from 30 to 90 per cent. The inhabited and productive area maintains a population of 15 to 150 persons to the square kilometer. Mountains, if considered in terms of total area, are not economically important. On the other hand, there are many prosperous and populous towns in mountain districts. Such towns lie in the productive area.

Früh gives the following figures on unproductive areas: Upper Rhine area, 36 per cent; Upper Engadine, 51 per cent; Tirol, 25 per cent. Arbos gives details of land utilization for the entire

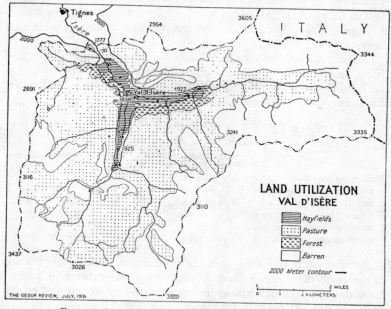

FIG. 45. LAND USE IN THE VAL D'ISÈRE, FRENCH ALPS

This is a high valley above the true agricultural zone. Figure 37 pictures some of the existing fields. (Courtesy of the *Geographical Review*, published by the American Geographical Society of New York.)

French Alps. Norbert Krebs has a discussion and a map of land utilization in his great work on Austria. His article on populated and unpopulated areas of the Eastern Alps shows a geologic influence upon percentage of unproductive lands in the following table:

GEOLOGIC FACTORS IN THE AREA OF UNOCCUPIED LAND IN THE EASTERN ALPS

	Percentage of unoccupied lands
Gneiss Alps	68 per cent
Schist Alps	66 "
North Limestone Alps	64 "
South Limestone Alps	47 "

Generally speaking, the percentage of waste land increases as one penetrates the mountain chain. Much of the waste land of the Bernese Oberland or the Mont Blanc massif is actually under snow and ice. The valley of Ubaye has not only the usual subtractions from total area because of height, slope, and relief, but much of the land that might otherwise be productive for field, forest, or pasture has infertile soil. About one-half of the valley is unproductive because of barrens, scrub lands, and torrential areas.

A large part of the area of mountain valleys is in pasturage and hay. Incidentally this percentage devoted to hay, as compared with other crops, increases with altitude. André Gibert offers the following table:

HAY AND ALTITUDE IN THE VALGAUDEMAR (FRENCH ALPS)

(Communes increase in altitude, left to right)

	Saint-Firmin	Saint-Jacques	Saint-Maurice	Villard-Loubière	Clémence-d'Ambel	Guillaume-Peyrouze
Per cent of hay, pasture, and common land to total surface	39.6	40.4	63.2	81.6	67.1	34.5
Per cent of hay, pasture, and common land to cultivated surface	122	265	1270	1758	3331	2211

A chief element in the value of productive land in mountains is the ratio of cropped land to pastures. Farm land in Alpine mountains has slight value unless adequately accompanied by summer pasture area.

Because of the interplay of economic conditions and the topographic and climatic peculiarities of each region, there is at any particular time a proper norm for the use of land. How much land is best left in field, in forest, and in pasture depends on the physical and on the economic factors. There are a great many relationships between topography and the use of land which will readily suggest themselves. The high communes, for example, have often an excess of high sheep pastures, which, in spite of the perhaps difficult economy of sheep raising during the winter period, can be devoted to nothing else. Field culture on the alp pastures may be restricted by the need for pasture. Mountaineers have become more and more conscious of the fact that the economy of a valley is best served by the preservation of a considerable extent of forests.

To understand the causes controlling height limits of forests in any particular region, one should study the amount of upland pastures, the amount of land devoted to crops, and the amount devoted to hay. On a farm on a plain, outside the mountains, the amount of land left in woodlot is an economic, not a climatic, affair. Though the case is not so simple in a mountain valley, economic factors nevertheless must here also be taken into consideration. Because of the commonly prevailing partial communal ownership in valleys an entire basin may be thought of as an economic unit, and adjustments of land use made in the light of that consideration.

How land utilization, altitude, and economy are interrelated is best shown by regional descriptions. The writer made a brief investigation of the economy of the commune of Naves. This commune comprised a hanging valley tributary to the Upper Isère in the Tarentaise. The valley has a north-south trend and an elevation of 900 to 2413 meters. The difference in elevation between the valley of Naves and the main stream is covered by a cascade. The commune has four villages and a number of summer hamlets. The population in 1928 was 487 people. In 1911 there had been 550 persons, and in 1860 there were 673 persons. Even down to 1900 the commune had had almost complete economic independence. The railroad in the valley of the Isère did not make its appearance until after 1880, and a good paved and well planned road did not greatly precede 1900.

Since the improvements in transportation, grain culture has been on the decrease. The failure of a community to raise its own breadstuffs is a measure of the decline of economic independence. In 1925–26, only 22 hectares were devoted to the raising of bread grains. This would not suffice for half the flour consumed. The wheat ordinarily does not grow above 1200 meters. Barley and oats are here forage crops. Vegetables are not too common and fruits are neglected. Half of the commune is in pasture. Of the pasture, at least one-half is high altitude pasture of such inferior quality as to serve only for small beasts, that is, chiefly sheep. Some hay is cut on fields so isolated as to call for six hay cables to transport the hay down steep cliffs to the level of the barns. Four of these cables center on the hamlet of Grand-Naves. The longest runs two kilometers with a drop of 150 meters.

Cows are the important beasts. The milk which is the by-product of the cheese industry makes swine second in importance.

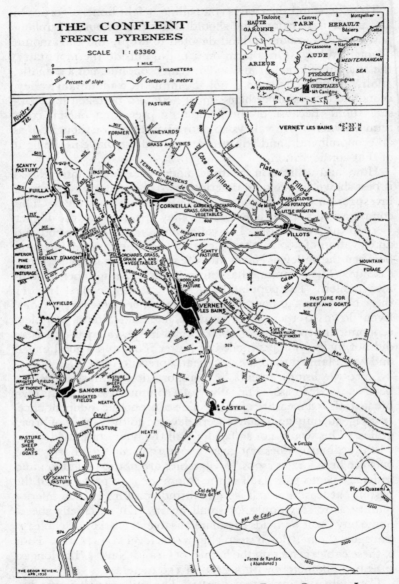

THE GEOGR. REVIEW.
APR., 1930

FIG. 46. CHOROGRAPHY OF THE CONFLENT, FRENCH PYRENEES, I

The map is significant only when used in conjunction with Figure 47. One hundred per cent slope equals 45 degrees. (Courtesy of the *Geographical Review*, published by the American Geographical Society of New York.)

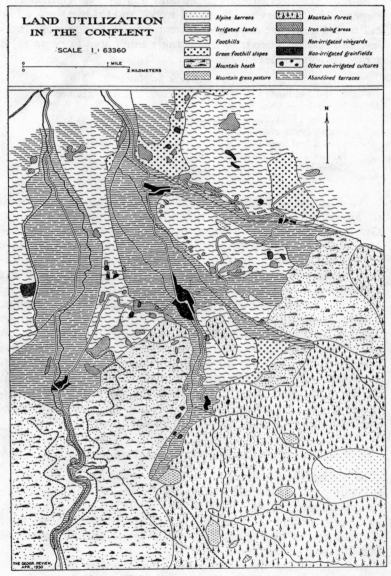

LAND UTILIZATION
IN THE CONFLENT

SCALE 1 : 63360

Alpine barrens
Irrigated lands
Foothills
Green foothill slopes
Mountain heath
Mountain grass pasture

Mountain forest
Iron mining areas
Non-irrigated vineyards
Non-irrigated grainfields
Other non-irrigated cultures
Abandoned terraces

THE GEOGR. REVIEW,
APR., 1930

FIG. 47. CHOROGRAPHY OF THE CONFLENT, FRENCH PYRENEES, II
Should be read in conjunction with Figure 46. (Courtesy of the *Geographical
Review*, published by the American Geographical Society of New York.)

The high pastures support sheep and goats. The cash income depends on (1) dairy products, (2) wood, and (3) live stock. The cultivated lands are devoted to wheat, barley, forage crops (barley, oats, clover, beets). A surprisingly small area (4 hectares) is set out in vegetables for the table.

LAND UTILIZATION IN NAVES

Cultivated lands	222	hectares
Natural meadows	356	"
Pastures	1554	"
Marsh lands	3	"
Woods and forests	764	"
Fallow	308	"
Other lands	31	"
	3238	

An example of economy in a remote and elevated area is found in Tavetsch. This area lies at the headwaters of the Rhine in Graubünden. It has a topography which has resulted from violent forces. Glaciers, torrents, avalanches, and landslides have played their parts in making the land forbidding. A high altitude is accompanied by a rude climate. The high valley provides 45 hectares of arable land. Most of this is devoted to hay to feed the stock, which in summer roams the extensive alpine pastures. The highest village is at 1650 meters. Agriculture is precarious and grain does not always ripen. Today the growing of grain has lost its importance, because transportation by road and rail has broken down what was an extreme instance of economic independence. The region continues to have, however, a certain degree of isolation. This may explain the fact that, though possessed of but meager resources, the region has not suffered depopulation, but continues to maintain 800 to 900 inhabitants.

MODERN CHANGES IN LAND UTILIZATION

More instructive than these fragmentary examples in the utilization of land are the changes in the use of land which have occurred largely in the last half century. It is difficult, however, to discuss modern changes in the utilization of mountain land without first discussing changes of population and the increased facilities of transportation.

Mountain areas in Europe have suffered severe depopulation in the twentieth century. The causes of depopulation, so far as they lie in the mountains themselves, are the impoverishment of agriculture and the decline of pastoral pursuits. Impoverishment of the soil, soil erosion, and deforestation have been some of the causes of decay. An example of impoverishment is found in the Val d'Egesse (Conches), which supported 500 cattle in the beginning of the fifteenth century. Now but 220 cattle pasture there. Many an alp is today barren because of soil erosion or of avalanches, landslides, and torrents. Generally speaking, the causes of change have been:

> Depopulation.
> Increase of facilities of transportation.
> Increase of agricultural knowledge.
> The development of forage crops.
> Better animal husbandry.

Mountain regions are difficult to farm. Economically they are the last places which are chosen. They are overflow areas of the plains, and the number of people that they are compelled to maintain depends upon the economic condition and pressure of population of the adjacent plain. The height limits of culture in mountains in any one century, and almost, one may say, in any one decade, is a function of this pressure and of such economic matters as price fluctuations. The depopulation of mountain areas has increased pastoral pursuits as against agricultural pursuits. When few workers are available, a unit area of land, a holding, is operated better as a hay and herding organization than as a farm for field crops. The following table is from Arbos:

VARIATION OF AREA IN CEREALS AND ITS RELATION TO POPULATION

Natural regions	Cantons	Dates	Pop.	Grain in hectares	Hectares per 100 pop.
Bauges	Le Châtelard	1874	10429	2221	21
		1913	8029	1364	16.9
Vercors	Villard-de-Lans	1857	5888	2254	43.3
		1913	4490	2048	46
Baronnies	Rosans	1857	3448	2094	60
		1914	2381	1159	48.6
Haut-Verdon	Castellane	1857	5617	2693	47.7
		1913	3132	1663	53
Beaumont	Corps	1857	5593	1454	26
		1914	3673	1157	31.2
Tarentaise	Bourg Saint-Maurice ...	1874	8771	809	9.2
		1913	8079	643	8
Maurienne	Lanslebourg	1874	5314	608	11
		1913	4352	474	10.4
Briançonnais	Le Monêtier	1836	5482	899	16.1
		1914	3734	545	14.6

The increased facilities of transportation had many far-reaching results. They brought to the isolated village contacts with the easier life of the plains which drew away many of the young people. They also brought in the knowledge of better farm methods, of which we shall speak. But, most important, they made cattle and cheese a better cash crop. The farm had been an economic unit where considerable area and labor was devoted to breadstuffs. In the twentieth century the farmer sells the 'crop' for which his land is most adapted, that is, dairy products and beef. The author, visiting a public house in a summer village high in the valley of the Schandigg, Grisons, was served with bread and cheese. Inquiring about the cheese, he found that it was sent in from the Swiss plain, and that the cattle of this summer alp were sold as far as Basel for beef. The grain field has disappeared. Its area is today devoted to hay meadows. The grist mill may still grind cattle feed, or it may stand a picturesque ruin beside a broken dam. In the Pays d'Allevard, in the French Alps, the cereal area has decreased since 1801 from 528 hectares to 81 hectares. Barley and millet, common in the medieval mountain agriculture, are disappearing. The periodic fluctuation of height limits of cereals is economic rather than climatic. Flax, a crop of the days of more independence, has disappeared. Rapeseed for oil for lighting has been replaced by the introduction of electricity. It is significant that the field area in the Tirol decreased in some cases 12 per cent in the period from 1875 to 1922. In Vorarlberg the decrease was 30 per cent.

The following table from Arbos shows a decided decrease in pastoral activities in the last forty years or so for stations in the French Alps. It is interesting to note, however, that in several cases, as in Bauges, though there is a decrease of cattle, there is an increase of the ratio of cattle to population. In other words, the population has decreased at a greater rate than the cattle.

It is clear that the decrease of the fields is not due to an increase in the pastures. Pasturage area was decreasing in the same period, though to a much smaller extent. The numbers of beasts in many mountain regions have declined. Plant rotation, chemical fertilizers, and plant selection have increased the crop yield per hectare. As cereals on mountain fields were entirely for home consumption, fewer hectares were necessary to feed the people even had the population remained constant.

The Lower Tarentaise, French Alps, is an east-west valley

FIG. 48. CULTIVATION OF A FORTY-FIVE DEGREE SLOPE, FRENCH PYRENEES

Summer rains in the Central Pyrenees support a heavy grass cover. The grass is cut four to six times a season, developing a lawn-like cover which maintains soil even on so steep a slope.

FIG. 49. TERRACED FARM IN PROVENCE, FRANCE

In this unglaciated valley there is no original level land. Farming is possible only after terracing.

occupied by the river Isère, between the towns of Moûtiers and Bourg-Saint-Maurice.[1] The High Tarentaise is the Val de Tignes. Down to the end of the nineteenth century Tignes was isolated from the rest of the world. The descent in winter was dangerous because of avalanches. The climate rendered harvest precarious. Snow lay upon the fields in places until June. Even in July there were sometimes frosts.

RELATION OF THE NUMBER OF CATTLE AND SHEEP TO THE NUMBER OF PEOPLE IN THE FRENCH ALPS

Natural regions	Canton	Dates	Total Number Cattle	Sheep	Cattle to 100 people	Sheep to 100 people
Bauges	Le Châtelard	1873	7930	1400	75	13
		1913	7398	595	92	7
Vercors	Villard-de-Lans ...	1857	6054	3439	103	58
		1913	4899	731	87	16
Diois	Châtillon	1852	428	29075	6.5	440
		1913	246	21666	5.5	500
Baronnies	La Motte-Chalançon	1852	486	18549	7	265
		1913	85	17575	2.5	500
Beaumont	Corps	1857	3084	10020	55	179
		1913	2485	4912	64	127
Champsaur	Saint-Bonnet	1857	6580	25372	56	215
		1913	3850	13062	43	147

The Lower Tarentaise was more favored for tillage and harvest. It was economically independent. A variety of conditions of soil and the comparative isolation made the district a little world in itself. Wine, bread, meat, cloth stuffs, and building materials all came from the valley. The peasant had all demands satisfied. But the essential economy of the valley was determined by the need of utilizing the vast upland pastures. Their extent was unusually great in comparison to the valley lands. They were the real basis of the life of the communes.

Increased transportation greatly increased the emphasis upon pastoral pursuits. Any harvest, as the grain harvest, giving mediocre returns, was abandoned. The area devoted to wheat, rye, barley, and oats was greatly diminished. After the ravages of the phylloxera the vine never regained its importance. A considerable emigration followed improved transportation.

So much of the valley land had been devoted to field crops

[1] The following paragraphs are largely based upon a classical article by Philippe Arbos, "La vie pastorale en Tarantaise," in *Annales de géographie*, xxi (1912), pp. 323–345.

that there was not enough hay for the beasts in winter. With the change in economy, the bringing in of food stuffs and the decrease of population, more hay land was available. Cattle raising became so considerable and so characteristic of the Tarentaise that a special breed of cattle, the *race tarine*, was evolved there.

The products of the Tarentaise are today almost purely pastoral. Generally speaking, there is an excess of summer pasture over hay lands. Many of the beasts cannot be stabled through the winter. Therefore in a series of fairs many cattle are sold, largely for beef direct to consuming centers. The lambs born in September are strong enough to climb to the alps in spring. Not so with those born in January. In the spring these are sold for butchering. There is accordingly a secondary fair in springtime.

The summer is a period of considerable cheese production. Again during the winter more cheese is manufactured. Butter is made also during this period. The necessity of raising young cattle to take the place of those sold in the autumn means that much milk must be kept for the calves. Thus the economy of the region is almost exclusively pastoral. The importance of dairying is indicated by the following figures for 1903:

The Dairy Industry in Tarentaise

Canton	Number of cows	Cheese	Butter
Aime	3200	66,000 Kgr.	3580 Kgr.
Bourg-Saint-Maurice	3700	147,700	8950
Moûtiers	4900	201,000	45200

Level Land and Terraces

An obvious limit to the amount of productive land in mountains is the degree of slope (Figure 50). Nothing is more valued in mountains than level land. In a rough way, level land is a measure of the population, other things being equal. If level land is subject to floods or covered with torrential deposits it may be useless. If high in elevation or too isolated it has less value than if at a lower level. But one is impressed in the Western American mountains with the fact that every considerable piece of level land is or has been the site of a farm. Mountaineers prize level land as a dweller in an oasis prizes land with water rights. Houses are built on slopes to preserve level land for the plow. The piled villages of Tibet are an extreme case of houses built on steep slopes to save the gentler slopes for tillage. So little level land is found in some valleys and ravines that in Hochgallmig in the Tirol there is a saying that "Here the hens have to walk on crampons and the cocks use Alpine poles." In Oberinnthal they say, "If the swallows can't find any walls of suitable height in the rest of Tirol, they come to Taufers to build their nests on the slopes of the valley." In this valley crampons (spikes fastened to the sole of the shoe, especially useful in snow) have been worn by people going to church. In the Wild-Schonau, also in Tirol, it is reported that houses are built on such steep slopes that they are moored with chains. In Moos, a village not very far from the Brenner, having a population of 800 inhabitants, it is reported that more than 300 men and women have been killed, since 1758, by falls from the incredibly steep slopes upon which the pasturages of this village are situated. So steep are they, in fact, that only goats, and even they not everywhere, can be trusted to graze on them, and the hay for the larger cattle has to be cut and gathered by the hand of man. These almost unbelievable circumstances are, of course, not normal. Nevertheless, that level land is at a premium is attested to by the extent to which terracing is resorted to to accommodate the expanding populations of the valley bottom.

Mountains may or may not have level valley land. The young valley of a mature mountain group has steep sides and little that represents a valley bottom. The mature valley has a floor width proportional to the stage of maturity. The glaciated valley of the classical U-shape has, of course, level valley land. In this section we use the term level for anything approximating a level and not classified under distinct slope. The glaciated valley frequently has a step profile, so that the level land consists of more or less isolated stages, one above the other, along the valley. Moreover, unequal deposition in glaciated valleys, definite moraines, and the presence of *verrous* [1] will form basins which are either lakes, swamps, or fill plains. Both unglaciated and glaciated valleys have open places where two streams or two glaciers have joined. Such a basin area may be seen in process of formation at the broad Concordia Platz of the Aletsch glacier in the Bernese Oberland.

Mountain valleys in maturity normally have natural terraces.

[1] A *verrou* is a bed rock barrier in a glaciated valley. The writer knows no American examples. The origin is not satisfactorily explained.

Without diastrophism or interruption of the cycle of erosion, a stream in the processes of meandering and lateral leveling leaves terraces. The significance of geologic structure in the formation of terraces is an elementary and oft-told tale.

Valleys have level land and area for farms, for road building, and for sites for towns. But there are few cases where level land is sufficient to permit even a moderate expansion of the population. In lieu of level land of natural origin, men build terraces. The fields above the retaining walls may be large or the size of a table. They are hand-made fields. The dirt behind the walls washes down to lower levels and must be carried up again. The fields are ordinarily too small for pasturage and so manure must be carried up to them, usually on men's backs. Miss Semple has called this 'desperate agriculture.'

The labor connected with terraces is not slight. Not only are walls built with stones brought together with great effort, but soil must be level where irrigation is practised. Irrigation is often necessary on terraces to maintain a reasonable water table. The soil, perhaps dug from below the surface zone, lacks humus and requires heavy manuring. Ordinarily the manure is brought up from the valley. Manure is heavy.

The remarkable thing is the degree of perfection attained by primitive people as terrace engineers. Primitive negroes on the steep western face of the rift valley near Lake Tanganyika farm upon terraces. A savage negro tribe in the Murchison Range of Northern Nigeria have mapped their land in an elaborate terrace system. Some of the remarkable terraces of the world are in the mountains of Szechuen. Here in remote Western China whole mountain sides are devoted to terraces. In Western Tibet each lamasery has its terrace culture developed to high degree. The primitive peoples of Central Luzon are accomplished terrace engineers. No more surprising terraces are known than those of the Incas. At Salamanca in Peru the terraces extend up the mountains to the frost line. It has been estimated that in certain valleys the Incas had turned every possible usable slope into terraces and that no room was left for an increase of cultivation or support of population.

Terrace culture is not confined to primitive peoples. It is found generally in the mountains of Europe (Figure 49). The valley of the Rhone about Sierre, on the route of the Simplon Express, is carefully terraced. This section is mentioned because it has been observed by so many travelers. Generally speaking, the drier the mountain slope the more important the terracing. The Eastern or Mediterranean Pyrenees have more terraces than the moister central portion. The Italian slope of the Alps has more terraces than the northern slope. Two reasons stand back of this. Agriculture on the drier slopes depends upon irrigation to a greater extent. Dry slopes have poor grass cover and are thus more subject to erosion. Grass is harvested in the *gaves* of the Central Pyrenees on slopes of 50 degrees without destructive soil erosion. (Figure 48.)

The social implications of terrace culture and of irrigation are much the same as those arising from the communal ownership of pastures. There is, of necessity, a series of communal regulations controlling terrace building, replacing of soil, access to terraces, building of trunk canals, and regulation and distribution of water, and these force upon the people a group organization which tends towards the formation of syndicates and a socialistic attitude.

THE FACTOR OF RELIEF: ANDORRA

The writer has prepared a map of Andorra which illustrates strikingly the amount of territory which must be subtracted from the whole because of relief. The map shows areas which are so steep as to be barrens. Even the high peaks of this region are used as pasture where the slope angle is not prohibitive. Most of the steep areas are in a middle zone rather than the highest zone. (Figure 52.) There were no areal statistics in Andorra at the time (1928) this investigation was made. The map offered is the result of personal observation and of the study of the single topographic map existing. This is on the scale of 1:50,000 with a 25-meter contour interval.

Four symbols are used on the map prepared by the writer. (1) The horizontal lines represent the area of continuous cultivated fields on the valley bottoms or alluvial slopes, whether they are irrigated or farmed normally. Isolated fields, as fields upon the shoulders of the canyons, are not included. (2) The pointed symbol or inverted V indicates areas of accessible timber of commercial value. Over this area the stand varies greatly and for most sections the measure in board feet is not great. The tree which predominates and is of prime value is the mountain pine. The finer trees which once stood on the better watered areas in the high mountains have been cut and the land given over to pasturage. (3) The vertical lines indicate cliff or land of over 100 per cent (45 degree) slope. Much of this area has slight timber value; most of it is barren of even sheep forage, and some of it has talus which is a menace to the tilled lands below. (4) The dotted area is of upland pastures. The *plas* are grassy plateaus, of value chiefly for sheep. The *comas* are green parks devoted to cattle and horses. Many of the high points to the north are knobs rather than peaks, and here pasture — not of the best quality, it is true — covers the heights. Elsewhere it is topography, rather than climate, which limits the altitude of the grass. Land which is park land, that is, alternate forest and open area, has been mapped here as forest or pasture according as one or the other economy represents the predominant industry.

A striking feature of the map is the amount of territory which must be considered barren because of too great declivity. This is a feature of land utilization which is commonly slighted in mountain mapping. A second noteworthy element of the map is that there are huge areas devoted to pasture. It is well that this should be emphasized, for certainly it stands first in the elements of the country's economy. The largest pasture area is to the north. This area is the little dissected portion of the summit plateau of the Pyrenees. Much of this area, though of high level, is flattish. Still a further factor in the large amount of pasture to the north is the altitude. The tree line is somewhere between 2000 and 2400 meters. This latter contour encloses considerable areas of the north.

The unequal distribution of the farmed area is a geological and topographical matter. Between the wider basins, the farmed land may narrow down to a mere strip of grass land lying in the deep shadowed gorge and chilled by the stream. Here precipitous walls prevent the farms from creeping up the valley sides. Where the valley is wider, the slopes are more gentle and the height limits of the fields are generally greater.

The map may well stimulate interest in a more detailed description of the landscape. The 495 square kilometers of the country are largely in one drainage basin; but the main stream, the Riu Valira, has two distinct branches and, in all, six open basins. These basins are caused by the unequal resistance of metamorphic rocks found in the southern part of the country. The northern portion, referred to previously as the *pla* country,

Fig. 50. Relation Between Slope and Culture, Central French Pyrenes

Fields creep up the gentler slopes of the alluvial cones but shun the steeper mountain sides. Here there is an interlocking of tilled areas and forest rather than a continuous zone of tillage.

Fig. 51. Land Use in a Canyon, Andorra

There is no level land in this picture taken from the brink of the canyon. Terraces in the lower left-hand corner. Grass lands beside the stream have 30 degree slope and are irrigated and devoted to grass because the sunlight is not sufficient for grains. Poplars represent source of fuel. Path up slope leads to goat pastures.

(Courtesy of the *Geographical Review*, published by the American Geographical Society of New York.)

represents the granitic core of the range. As the valleys are gorges with slight bottom area, there is a great deal of the high level land represented in the southern portion. (Figure 51.) Here the uplands are of a different character, for glaciation has been much more severe in the more easily eroded rocks. Cirques, compound cirques, glacial lakes, and hanging valleys are common. Both the northern and southern portions of the upland represent summer pastures, but the organization of the industry is different in the two cases. On the *plas* large droves of sheep and goats, largely transhumants from France and Spain, feed in the summer time. The increased precipitation due to the altitude joins with the level surface and the impermeability of the granite rocks to provide excellent pasture for small stock. The highlands of the dissected southern portion consist of peaks and serrated ridges with steep cirque walls which separate cirque bottoms and high level valleys. Here the steep slopes have only enough soil and ground water for the mountain pine. The small areas of valley bottom soil offer excellent pasturage. On these *comas* the Andorran pastures his own beasts, largely cattle, mares, and young mules. These *comas* are not leased but are used by the communes. There are, then, two topographic levels of life in the country, the pastoral and the agricultural. The difference in relief between these two levels is 1000 to 1500 meters. In contrast to the mountain nomadism represented in many higher groups of mountains, as the Alps, ordinarily only a few shepherds take part in the seasonal movement.

The valleys are distinctly glaciated. The forms of erosion are much more severe than in most parts of the Pyrenees, and the general aspect of the landscape is savage. The basin of Andorra la Vieja is a little Yosemite. Since glacial times there have been canyons cut which are still so youthful as to offer serious barriers to communication between the basins. Thus the gorge of Sant Antoine between the basin of Andorra and La Massana has today but a mule path hewn from the rocks. The gorge from Andorra to Encamp has a road along its wall considerably above the stream (Figure 51), but from Encamp to Conillo the trail is forced up 320 meters over the shoulder of the mountain to pass the gorge of Meritxell. The climb is an arduous one for man or mule. The villages are on terraces which are lateral moraines. Whereas the glacial terraces in places offer high level agricultural land, elsewhere the morainic deposits are so rough and

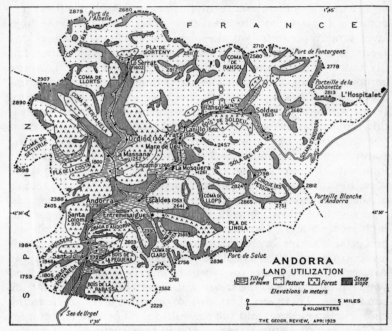

FIG. 52. LAND UTILIZATION MAP OF ANDORRA

   The area of continuous cultivated fields on the valley bottoms or alluvial slopes is shown, whether irrigated or farmed normally. Isolated fields upon the shoulders of the canyons are not included. Under forest are shown areas of accessible timber of commercial value, chiefly the mountain pine; but the stand varies greatly and generally the board-foot measure is not high.

   Land of over 45° slope is distinguished: much of it has slight timber value; most is barren even of sheep forage; some of it has talus which menaces the tilled lands below. The upland pastures include the *plas*, grassy plateaus used largely for sheep, and the *comas*, green parks devoted to cattle and horses. Many of the high knobs of the north are covered with pasture of sorts to the summits; elsewhere it is topography rather than climate that limits the altitude of grass. Mixed forest and grassland has been mapped according to predominant use. The scale is approximately 1: 290,000. (Courtesy of the *Geographical Review*, published by the American Geographical Society of New York.)

strewn with huge boulders as to be unfit for use except for pasturage between the rocks. On the whole, glaciation has improved the Andorran valleys as a place of habitation. The greatest contribution the ice made was in creating a terminal moraine on which Santa Coloma stands. A lake of short duration existed in the valley upstream. Alluvial deposits from the side walls have encroached upon the lacustrine soils.

The region is to be classed as of a moist Mediterranean climate in distinction to the dry Mediterranean climate to be found in Spain just without the borders of the country. Farming is both of the irrigated and the normal type. The mown grass, tobacco, and vegetables are grown by irrigation; the cereals are a dry land crop. All level land or slopes that lie adjacent to and below canals on the valley walls are irrigated. These slopes are usually terraced and then are devoted to grass. As in all regions where beasts are pastured in the high mountains in summer, the greatest part of the cropped land is devoted to hay production for feed for the animals during the winter. Andorra has an excess of high pasture. Therefore the economic pressure for the hay land as against field crops is great. The more hay, the more beasts of Andorran ownership on the uplands. The number of cuttings of grass varies from one on the natural meadows at the edge of the *plas* to four on the irrigated fields. There is in Andorra, considering the Mediterranean type of climate, a remarkable flow in the streams. That the uplands have a considerable duration of snow cover is an element in this condition, but the relative levelness of the uplands as well as the number of lakes plays a part. There is always an excess of water for the amount of land to which it can be easily conveyed.

BIBLIOGRAPHICAL NOTES

Regional Works on Mountain Geography

Allen, W. E. D. "The March-Lands of Georgia," in *Geographical Journal*, lxxiv (1929), pp. 135–156.

Allix, André. "L'économie rurale en Oisans," in *Revue de géographie alpine*, xvii (1929), pp. 469–610. Stubborn agriculture.

Allix, André. *L'Oisans*. Paris, 1929. The thoroughness of the work is indicated by the fact that 800 pages are devoted to one small area of the French Alps.

Atwood, W. W. "Utilization of the Rugged San Juans" (Colorado), in *Economic Geography*, iii (1927), pp. 193–209.

Bernhard, Hans. *Die Wirtschaftsprobleme des Vallemaggia (Tessin) als typischen Gebirgsentvölkerungsgebiet*. Zurich, 1928. An excellent local study.

Biermann, Charles. "La vallée de Conches en Valais," in *Bulletin de la Société Vaudoise des sciences naturelles*, xliii (1907), pp. 39–175. Excellent.

Blache, Jules. *Les massifs de la Grande-Chartreuse et du Vercors.* Grenoble, 1931. 2 vols. Blache is one of the promoters of the Grenoble school of Alpine geography, which, under the leadership of Blanchard, has caused the French Alps to be one of the best studied territories in the world. This work is a model for a regional study.

Blanchard, Raoul. "Aiguilles," in *Revue de géographie alpine*, x (1922), pp. 127–165.

Blanchard, Raoul. *Les Alpes française.* Paris, 1925. Preliminary to the volumes upon the French Alps which are now being written by this master of mountain geography.

Blanchard, Raoul, and Seive, F. *Les Alpes françaises à vol d'oiseau.* Grenoble, 1928. (*Les beaux pays.*) Illustrated by 137 heliogravures of mountain scenery.

Bleicher, Gustave. *Les Vosges, le sol et les habitants.* Paris, 1890.

Bouchet, Jeanne. "La vallée de la Roizonne en Taillefer: Enquête économique," in *Revue de géographie alpine*, xvi (1928), pp. 179–192.

Bowman, Isaiah. *The Andes of Southern Peru.* New York, 1916. A study in which carefulness of detail is combined with breadth of view.

Brunies, Stephan. *Der schweizerische Nationalpark*, 3. Aufl. Basel, 1920. In the nature of a guide book. There is a French translation.

Cavaillès, Henri. *La vie pastorale et agricole dans les Pyrénées.* Paris, 1931.

Cholley, André. *Les Préalpes de Savoie et leur avant-pays.* Paris, 1925.

Dainelli, Giotto. *Le Condizione delle Genti.* Bologna, 1924. (Spedizione Italiana de Filippi nell' Himàlaia, Caracorùm, e Turchestàn Cinese, 1913–14, Relazioni Scientifiche, serie ii, 8.) Anthropogeographic material on Himalaya of a most scientific nature.

Dainelli, Giotto. *Il Monte Bianco.* Turin, 1926. Though it is not Dainelli's most serious work, nevertheless this is an informative book upon the Italian side of Mont Blanc.

Desbuissons, Léon. *La vallée de Binn (Valais).* Lausanne, 1909.

Flahault, Charles. *La mise en valeur des terres pauvres par le boisement.* Montpellier, 1920.

Forrer, Niklaus. *Zur Anthropogeographie des Alpinen Thurtales.* Bülach, 1925.

Früh, Jacob. *Geographie der Schweiz.* St. Gallen, 1929–33. 2 vols. The great book on the geography of Switzerland.

Gex, François. *Dans les Alpes françaises.* Paris, 1929.

Gibert, André. "Le Valgaudemar," in *Revue de géographie alpine*, xi (1923), pp. 663–782.

Gos, François. *Zermatt and its Valley*, tr. by F. F. Roget. London, 1927.

Gradmann, Robert. *Süddeutschland.* Stuttgart, 1931. Chapter on the Bavarian Alps.

Gsteu, Hermann. *Beiträge zur Anthropogeographie von Vorarlberg.* Stuttgart, 1932.

Hedin, Sven. *Southern Tibet.* Stockholm, 1916–22. 9 vols. Many other books of exploration could be mentioned. This is included as a splendid example.

Hettner, Alfred. *Die Kordillere von Bogotá.* Gotha, 1892. (*Petermanns Mitteilungen,* Ergänzungsheft Nr. 104.)

Krebs, Norbert. "Die bewohnten und unbewohnten Areale der Ost-Alpen," in *Geographische Zeitschrift,* xviii (1912), pp. 443–454.

Krebs, Norbert. "Die Dachsteingruppe," in *Zeitschrift des Deutschen und Österreichischen Alpenvereins,* xlvi (1915), pp. 1–42.

Krebs, Norbert. *Die Ostalpen und das heutige Österreich.* Stuttgart, 1928. 2 vols. The great book on the regional economy of a mountain area. Instructive and philosophic.

Krebs, Norbert. "Die Verteilung der Kulturen und die Volksdichte in den österreichischen Alpen," in *Mitteilungen der Geographischen Gesellschaft in Wien,* lv (1912), pp. 243–303.

Leemann, Walter. "Zur Landwirtschaftskunde des Tavetsch," in *Mitteilungen der Geographisch-Ethnographischen Gesellschaft in Zürich,* xxix (1928–29), pp. 13–122.

Levainville, J. "La vallée de Barcelonnette," in *Annales de géographie,* xvi (1907), pp. 223–244.

Machatschek, Fritz. *Die Alpen,* 3. Aufl. Leipzig, 1929. A primer.

Machatschek, Fritz. *Landeskunde der Sudeten- und Westkarpathenländer.* Stuttgart, 1927.

Martonne, Emmanuel de. *Les Alpes.* Paris, 1926. A review.

Martonne, Emmanuel de. "The Carpathians: Physiographic Features Controlling Human Geography," in *Geographical Review,* iii (1917), pp. 417–437.

Martonne, Emmanuel de. *La Valachie.* Paris, 1902. Deals with the Carpathians.

Newbigin, Marion Isabel. *Southern Europe.* London, 1932.

Ogilvie, A. G. *Geography of the Central Andes.* New York, 1922. (American Geographical Society, *Map of Hispanic America,* Publication no. 1.)

Reynier, Élie. "La région Privadoise," in *Recueil des travaux de l'Institut de géographie alpine,* iii (1915), pp. 1–56.

Robequain, Charles. "Le Trièves," in *Revue de géographie alpine,* x (1922), pp. 5–126.

Roletto, G. B. "La Valle dell' Orsigna," in *Rivista Geografica Italiana,* xxiii (1916), pp. 432–440; xxiv (1917), pp. 24–38.

Sieger, Robert. *Die Alpen.* Leipzig, 1900.

Zur Geographie der deutschen Alpen Prof. Dr. Robert Sieger zur 60. Geburtstage gewidmet. Vienna, 1924. Some of the essays in this *Festband* are noted elsewhere.

Sorre, Maximilien. *Les Pyrénées,* Paris, 1922.

Sorre, Maximilien. *Les Pyrénées méditerranéennes.* Paris, 1913. The more elaborate work.

Telker, Minnie J. "The Cascade Mountains," in *Journal of Geography*, xiii (1914–15), pp. 242–250.

Ténot, Suzanne. "Le massif de Belledonne," in *Recueil des travaux de l'Institut de géographie alpine*, vii (1919), pp. 601–689.

Tivollier, Jean. "Monographie de Ceillac (Hautes Alpes)," in *Bulletin de la Société d'études des Hautes-Alpes*, xlv (1926), pp. 71–140.

Vallot, Charles; Vallot, Joseph. *Le massif du Mont-Blanc*. Versailles, etc., 1921–23. 2 vols. An example of a scientific guidebook.

Vila, Pau, and Chevalier, Marcel. *La Cerdanya*. Barcelona, 1926. See also the review by Philippe Arbos in *Revue de géographie alpine*, xv (1927), pp. 363–367.

Wissman, Hermann von. "Das Mitter Ennstal," in *Forschungen zur deutschen Landes- und Volkskunde*, xxv (1927), pp. 1–144.

Economic and Industrial Changes in Mountain Economy

See also the works named in the preceding note. The French have a special fondness for historical studies of this sort.

Allix, André. *L'Oisans au Moyen-Âge*. Paris, 1929.

Blache, Jules. "L'essartage, ancienne pratique culturale dans les Alpes dauphinoises," in *Revue de géographie alpine*, xi (1923), pp. 553–575.

Blache, Jules. *L'homme et la montagne*. Paris, 1933.

Blanchard, Raoul. *Grenoble: Étude de géographie urbaine*. Paris, 1911. The story of urban development in mountains.

Blanchard, Raoul. "L'industrie de la houille blanche dans les Alpes françaises," in *Annales de géographie*, xxvi (1917), pp. 15–41.

Blanchard, Raoul. "The Utilization of Water Power in France," in *Harvard Business Review*, VI (1927–28), pp. 176–187.

Brutails, J. A. *Étude sur la condition des populations rurales du Roussillon au Moyen-Âge*. Paris, 1891.

Brutails, J. A. *Notes sur l'économie rurale du Roussillon à la fin de l'ancien régime*. Perpignan, 1889.

Clouzot, E. "À propos de la haute vallée du Vénéon à la fin du XVᵉ siècle," in *Recueil des travaux de l'Institut de géographie alpine*, vi (1918), pp. 333–340.

Coulter, J. W. "Land Utilization in the Santa Lucia Region," in *Geographical Review*, xx (1930), pp. 469–479.

Jorrè, Georges. "L'aménagement hydroélectrique de la vallée d'Ossau," in *Revue géographique des Pyrénées et du Sud-Ouest*, ii (1931), pp. 317–336.

Lorin, Henri. "L'industrie rurale en pays basque," in *Le musée social*, 1906, Mémoires et documents, pp. 349–375. The part of little industries.

Mathieu, André. "Les petites industries de la montagne dans le Jura français," in *Annales de géographie*, xxxviii (1929), pp. 439–459. More of little industries.

Méjean, Paul. "Le bassin de Bonneville, Haute-Savoie," in *Revue de géographie alpine*, xvi (1928), pp. 5–168. A valley given over to workshops.

Plandé, R. "L'utilisation industrielle de la vallée d'Aspe (Pyrénées Occidentales)," in *Revue de géographie alpine*, xvii (1929), pp. 41–54. A development due to water power.

Sclafert, Thérèse. *Le Haut-Dauphiné au Moyen Âge*. Paris, 1926.

CHAPTER VIII

MOUNTAIN POPULATIONS AND THEIR DISTRIBUTION

GENERAL ASPECTS

RELATIVELY speaking, mountains are agriculturally unproductive. Miss Semple has it that man, as a part of the mobile envelope of the world, like air and water, always feels the pull of gravity. Mountains, like the sterile portions of plains, have, for the most part, been occupied only after the more favored lands. Some peoples, indeed, entered mountain regions at an early date, usually remnants of defeated folk who could not successfully resist their enemies in the lowlands. The Caucasus Mountains have so many such relics as to be called the graveyard of nations. Except for a tendency of the impoverished inhabitants to raid the richer lowlands, mountains have played a passive rôle in history. Once a race is established in a mountain fastness, isolation and defensibility of position have tended to preserve ethnic and cultural characteristics. Vidal de la Blache has said that mountains not only bring populations into being, but preserve them. The first part of the statement would seem hardly true, for mountains are, in fact, populated by the overflow of plains. The latter part of the statement is not true since 1850. Before that date the mountaineer was held to his home by the difficulty of transportation. The mountain spurs confined him to his valley settlement. But since 1850 the reverse has been the fact.

Until 1850 mountain populations grew by natural increase. Population had become so dense that an economic crisis existed. One may read of economic conditions in a high isolated valley in the nineteenth century in the historical study by Allix of the Oisans, in the French Alps. Always in mountains tillable land is scarce and labor arduous. Crop returns are commonly pitiful. With populations increasing in certain valleys as greatly as 34 per cent between 1800 and 1850, man power, to use an old phrase, was sorely exceeding bread power. This increase of population continued until the middle of the century, when a great flow of emigration commenced. The figures for Savoy are instructive.

POPULATIONS AND DISTRIBUTION

POPULATION OF SAVOY

Year	Population	Year	Population
1723	337,184	1838	564,137
1783	423,166	1901	518,514
1828	538,567	1906	513,914
		1911	503,027

The figures in the above table representing the present century do not fully reveal the great decrease in rural population. Savoy includes some growing industrial centers. Gex calls attention to their growth. A purely rural region in Savoy is the valley of the Ubaye. Between 1851 and 1901 the population of this valley fell from 17,585 to 12,538 souls. Whole hamlets were abandoned. The same rural exodus is found in the Pyrenees. A few of the easily accessible valleys have increased in population during the last thirty years, because of the growth of industrial, commercial, or religious centers. But the higher and more remote valleys have decreased in population until some villages are only one-fourth their former size. Of the thirty-one mountainous departments of France, several increased between 1800 and 1850 at the rate of 10 to 50 per cent. Between 1850 and 1911 great losses were sustained. The Basses-Alpes lost 31 per cent, and Ariège, 26 per cent. In the 31 mountainous departments, 26, between 1901 and 1906, lost 107,000 persons "because of soil erosion." Certainly soil erosion was a factor. But in this period the peripheral centers of Nice, Marseilles, Perpignan, Toulouse, Bordeaux, and Lyons all increased in size, no doubt at the expense of the adjacent mountain regions. Almost always a decrease of population in a mountain region denotes an increase of an urban center. This is usually a valley town. In the Val Pellice of the Italian Alps a population of 6000 in 1805 had increased to 9000 by 1911. In this valley is the town of Torre. The growth of the population of that center from 2000 in 1805 to 5500 in 1911 not only accounts for the increase, but indicates a slight decrease in the rural population.

Improved facilities of transportation permitted and encouraged the flight. Many authors concur in this opinion. This was the period of road-building and rail-laying. One is surprised at the number of communities at the beginning of this period without roads to the outside world. It has been estimated that Spain had 2000 such communities, largely in the mountains. Arbos gives a fragmentary table indicating the meager communication of certain regions of the French Alps and showing the progress of road building.

PROGRESS IN ROAD BUILDING

Region	Total number of communes	Number of communes without roads in			
		1860	1880	1900	1914
Canton of Châtelard (Bauges)	14	10	2	0	
Arrondissement of Albertville (Tarentaise, Beaufortin, Combe d'Arly)	42	25	20		1
Arrondissement of Moûtiers (Tarentaise) .	56	42	36	4	2
Arrondissement of St.-Jean-de-Maurienne	68	45	33	18	11
Arrondissement of Castellane	48		18	8	4
Canton of La Javie (Préalpes de Digne) ..	10		6	3	3

It needed but a few roads to engender more. Road-building went forwards by leaps and bounds in the whole of the Alps. After the advantages of better communication had been demonstrated, the passive mental attitude of the mountaineer quickly changed. Ease of communication in mountain regions is not merely a function of topography and relief, it is an expression of the economical and mental needs of the mountaineer.

It is possible that the nomadic life of mountaineers, especially of the Swiss, prepared them psychologically for the emigration. In addition certain valleys, because of meager economy, had long practised the custom of sending forth mercenary soldiers, peddlers, itinerant merchants, and theatrical troupes. One writer, Miss Semple, in referring to these migratory habits, rather overstates the matter in saying that mountains, like the sea, breed travelers. These annual migrants were the exception rather than the rule. With the coming of the modern period and better transportation, there was indeed a factor which tended to keep people at home. This was the increasing importance of the cottage industries. An element outside of the mountains directly responsible for a large part of the emigration was the attraction of new lands in the Americas. Mountain people, living under as great economic pressure as any in Europe, logically took part in the American settlement. Sections of the Haut-Diois in the French Alps, which lost in two decades as much as 30, 40, and 44 per cent of their populations, sent great numbers to Mexico and the United States. Latin America took its quota of mountaineers. Another factor in the emigration was the general flight from the land towards the cities, a migration common to all European rural districts at this time. This, we have pointed out, did not greatly decrease the populations of districts where cities existed on valley plains within their limits.

Maull has said, "The upper limit of population distribution is the battle ground of the denser centers of population."

POPULATION AND ALTITUDE

If an average were taken for all European mountains, it would be fair to presume that increasing altitude would show decreasing population. Five per cent of the population of Switzerland is found above 1000 meters, and yet the area lying above that elevation is a considerably larger proportion of the total area of the country. Within limits, certainly below the climatic snow line or zones of long snow duration, the scant population of the upper levels is a result of the meager resources. The relation between meager resources and paucity of population is even more direct than that between percentage of level land and density of population. The severity of the decrease with ascent is well illustrated by the canton of Grisons, which has a density of population only a thirty-fifth that of the canton of Zurich. Most of Zurich is on the Swiss plain, while Grisons is mountainous upland. The upland is incapable of supporting large numbers of people. The climate is rude; harvests are limited in quantity and character; much of the area is actually barren. In the high cantons of Uri and Valais, Switzerland, more than half of the area is barren, and this is true of the Austrian provinces of Tirol and Carinthia.

The decrease of population with altitude is not, however, a regular matter (Figure 61). A reason for this is that zones of increasing altitude do not always show a decreasing acreage available for habitation. Forest zones and steep zones are more thinly populated than open lands and gentler slopes at higher altitudes. There are exceptions. Most zonings of population are taken in a valley cross section. If one took the density of population of valley floors alone, and arranged the densities according to increasing altitudes along the valley, a much greater regularity of decrease would appear.

Blanchard has one of the more exact studies of altitude and population. He has figured the mean altitudes of certain zones in the French Alps and the percentage of those zones which are inhabited. There is an approximate regularity of decrease only up

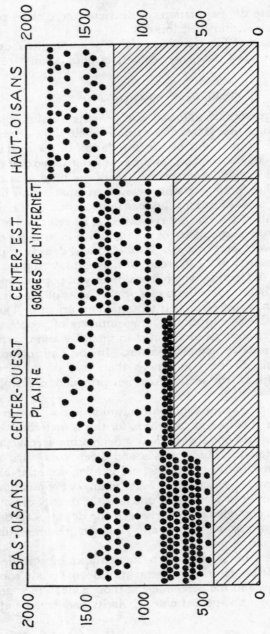

FIG. 53. POPULATION BY ALTITUDE IN THE OISANS, FRENCH ALPS

Hatched area shows height of valley bottom. Each point represents 25 inhabitants. (*After Allix.*)

to 1900 meters, and even that must be looked upon as a chance occurrence.

INHABITATION BY ALTITUDE AND MASS

Mean altitude	Percentage of inhabitation
1408	58
1419	56
1433	58
1650	40
1660	35
1712	40
1722	40
1834	23
1911	56
1954	50
1980	27
2105	42
2160	37
2203	34
2429	26
2556	12
2396	15
2279	31

Populations in tropical mountains are again another matter. Lowlands there have exhausting and debilitating climates because of heat and excessive humidity. Elevations of 1000 meters and above are more favorable. India is said to be ruled from over 2100 meters. The majority of the people of Ecuador and Bolivia live above the contour line of 2000 meters. In Peru there is permanent habitation between 3200 and 4500 meters. One shepherd's home is reported by Bowman at 5215 meters. Whereas not one-fifth of the population of Grisons live above 1500 meters, the mountain mass of Ethiopia, in equatorial Africa, recently supported five chief cities between the elevations of 1857 and 2500 meters.

South America illustrates the fact that in inter-tropical regions elevation makes for health and greater human activity.

HEIGHTS OF SETTLEMENT IN PERU

Cuzco (15,000 inhabitants) .... 3200 meters
Sicuani ('the Paradise of Peru') 3534   "
Cruciro 3953   "

Indeed, in Peru the most densely inhabited zone is between 1500 and 3500 meters. There is Cerro de Pasco, a min-

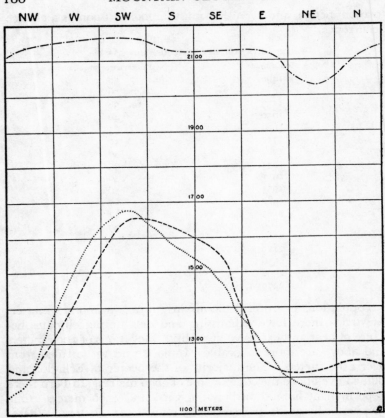

Houses: ·······························
Grain: – – – – – – – – – – – –
Forests: –·–·–·–·–·–·–·–·–

FIG. 54. PERMANENT HOUSE LIMITS AND GRAIN AND FOREST LIMITS IN THE ORTLER ALPS, AUSTRIA. (*After Fritsch.*)

ing camp, which has 13,000 souls living at 4350 meters, far beyond the timber line. Bolivia is largely a land of a high plateau. The climate is far more healthful than that of the Amazonian lowlands. The following cities have surprising size for their elevation:

HEIGHTS OF SETTLEMENT IN BOLIVIA

City	Population	Altitude
La Paz	100,000	3600 meters
Oruro	22,000	3617 "
Potosí	29,000	4000 "

The altitude of human occupation in Tibet is, in view of the principle of economic returns diminishing with elevation, almost a paradox. Villages dependent upon tillage are common at a height of 4000 meters. One finds clusters of permanent dwellings up to 4880 meters, where not only herdsmen but agriculturists are found. Barley is grown at 4400 meters, vegetables at 3600 meters. Crops at these extreme elevations are in response to low latitude, the dryness of the air, high insolation, and irrigation.

Some high settlements in the Alps are worth note:

St. Moritz	1856	meters
Arosa	1892	"
Chanolin	1936	"
Cresta	1956	"
Findelen	2075	"
Juf	2133	"

St. Moritz and Arosa, both in Grisons, originally villages depending on the land, are now great health resorts. Chandolin in the Val d'Anniviers is, curiously enough, above many of the pastures, so that the cattle in spring begin their migrations by descending. Findelen, in the same valley, has an anomalous agriculture. There, on steep slopes facing the sun, rye and barley ripen. Immediately opposite, on a shady slope, is a belt of Arctic-Alpine plants, and near by are two glaciers. Cresta has but five houses, while, at the end of the century, neighboring Juf, holding the Swiss record for altitude, had but 24 inhabitants. One summer village within the Val d'Anniviers, Alp de Lona, lies at the height of 2665 meters.

DETAILS OF POPULATION

Among the factors which control the details of distribution of population in mountains are altitude, relief, mass of mountain, distribution of critical temperatures, distribution of rain, duration of snow cover, winds, nature of bed rock, thickness and character of the soil, character of the vegetation, danger of floods, degree of accessibility, height of mountain passes, economic conditions, and the social character of the people. The question comes early to mind as to how high man may go in mountains before he meets physiological difficulties. In Bolivia there is a colony of miners living at 5000 meters. Here the barometric pressure approximates half of that at sea level. In Tibet there are permanent hamlets and agriculture of a sort at 4400 meters. Matters such as heart palpitation and mountain sickness seem of minor importance if men mount slowly, by generations as it were. Adjustment to very high altitudes, certainly of selected persons, seems quite possible. In European mountains, however, the mountain top or the permanent snow line is reached before physiological limitations are met. We shall discuss health and altitude in a later portion of the chapter.

In Alpine Europe, groups living at high altitudes are agricultural or pastoral. The so-called permanent or agricultural dwellings of these people are not often at great heights. The traveler may easily obtain false impressions as to the altitudinal distribution of the people and the density of population if the temporary or pastoral shelters are not eliminated from consideration. The number of buildings is not evidence of the distribution or numbers of inhabitants. Many peoples have a complete permanent village on the valley floor and another at the lower edge of the pastures. One Swiss group actually has four villages. At Courmayer, on the Italian side of Mont Blanc, each family has a dwelling and a barn in the valley village, a summer chalet higher up the valley, and on the high alp a herdsman's hut. We cannot, therefore, take the number of houses as indicative of the size of population, nor can we take the highest houses as indicative of the economic limits of 'permanent' habitation. Though numbers of people go to the higher villages for short periods some two or three times a year, we must regard the permanent residence as that in the lower valley. Also the number of people who follow the herds to the higher pastures is small. One of the few noteworthy exceptions is in portions of the Carpathians, where the summer population is sixteen to the square kilometer. The houses at the lower levels are the primary homes, but their inhabitants have an extensive zone of activity. This is a broad zone on the mountain flanks, most of which is above the dwelling. The high-level temporary villages are auxiliary homes. In Switzerland the permanent house limit is perhaps 100 meters below the forest line, and 800–900 meters below the permanent snow line.

In the Alps the details of distribution of population are so many and so interwoven that it is difficult to state the situation in a paragraph. The complexity is suggested by a French study of the Italian Val d'Aoste. This valley, with an east-west trend, has a sunny and a shady slope, and great geologic and topographic variety. Here are ancient crystallines, glacial deposits, terraces, and alluvial cones. The valley floor has the greatest amount of level land and the greatest number of inhabitants. On 7 per cent of the land one finds 18 per cent of the people. The second zone of concentration is one common to many Alpine valleys. This is the zone of the slope villages. Here on 3 per cent of the area live 9.5 per cent of the people. The third zone is the region of a commercial town, for the valley is on a route into France. This distribution is typical for east-west valleys; a dense concentration in the valley bottom, and a secondary concentration midway on the sunny slope. The shady slope is ordinarily little inhabited. Topographic and geologic conditions complicate matters, as do a number of climatic factors. There cannot be a simple statement of details of distribution of population in Alpine mountains.

A definite limitation to the density of rural population in mountains and a factor in the distribution is the restriction of productive land. Sixty-six per cent only of Alpine Europe is productive. In the Grisons, Switzerland, but 40.6 per cent is productive. Much of this productive area is, in the nature of things, pastoral land and supports relatively few people. The Alps as a whole support some twenty-five persons to the square kilometer, but if we consider only the productive areas, the population is forty to fifty persons to the square kilometer. The density of population on the valley bottoms is high as compared even with agricultural regions of the plains. But relief and barren ground separate these settlements. Mountain populations are generally in isolated chambers or corridors.

A study has been given us by Tonilio of the upper Valcamonica, which, because of its detail and because of the exceptions noted, is especially worth our attention. The valley is an east-west valley and is, a most important fact, a route to the Passo del Tonale. Within the fifteen kilometers which comprise the study, the elevation of the valley floor mounts from 850 meters to 1883 meters. The summits of the flanking walls mount to 3554 and 3278 meters. Geologically, the region is in the schist which flanks the crystalline massif. The valley walls show evidence of three terraces, the highest of which is pre-glacial. The elevations of the terraces are 1150–1376 meters, 1450–1800 meters, and 1600–2000 meters. The valley floor is divided into three basins.

The valley is overpopulated. Considering the total area of the drainage basin, the population is but 29 persons to the square kilometer. But in terms of the land cultivated the density is of 394 to the square kilometer. In spite of this large population there was a twenty-five per cent increase in the valley from 1861 to 1911. This period was one generally of depopulation in French Alpine valleys. Previous to the commencement of the World War in 1914, the surplus population was supported by seasonal migrations to Germany and Austria in search of work. For this purpose each summer a third of the men left the valley.

Practically all of the people live on land of little slope. Thirty-nine per cent of the people live on alluvial fans, 38 per cent on fluvial glacial terraces, 16 on orographic terraces, and but 7 per cent on mountain slopes.

As we have said elsewhere, most people in high valleys 'live in the sun,' that is, on the *adret* exposure. The table on page 185 is from Mademoiselle Vessereau, and needs no discussion.

ECONOMIC FACTORS

It might be supposed that the building of roads and the laying of rails into mountain regions after 1850 would improve the economic conditions there and so encourage the people to remain. The outward flood was not, however, to be easily stopped. An economic revolution within the mountains did take place, but it was the direct result of decreased population rather than of improved communications. Hitherto agriculture had been a mixed farming of the subsistence type. With the decrease in farm hands it necessarily changed to a pastoral and dairying economy. Grain areas decreased. The high fields, laborious to till, were abandoned first. In the Metnitztal, Austria, the highest grain field fifty years ago was above 1400 meters. Today there is none in the valley above 1150 meters. True, railways in mountains have made possible the use of chemical fertilizers and so doubled the production per hectare, but the decline of population is still evident. Generally the more precarious the regional economy, the greater the recent decrease in population. This is well illustrated by Tenot in a study of the Belledonne Massif. Another statement of rather general application is that the more remote the commune, the greater its decrease of population. By the same token, satellite communities suffer depopulation more severely than the commercial centers.

The economic crisis due to overpopulation had literally left

Proportion of Population Living on the *Adret* and on the *Ubac* in Certain Valleys

(Names of north-south valleys are underlined. In these cases the western exposure is reckoned the *adret*.)

Valleys studied	Pop. on *adret*	Pop. on *ubac*	Total population	Proportion of the pop. on the *adret*	
Aigue Blanche (Queyras)	536	0	536	100	per cent
Aigue Agnelle "	272	0	272	100	"
Cristillan "	344	0	344	100	"
Tarentaise, from Tours to l'Arly ...	513	0	513	100	"
Tarentaise, from Bourg-St. Maurice to Ste.-Foy	1919	63	1982	96.8	"
Torrent d'Arvieux in Queyras	495	40	535	92.5	"
Oetztal	?	?	?	91	"
Torrent de Landry in Tarentaise...	950	110	1060	89.6	"
Pongau.......................	8431	1504	9935	84.8	"
Pinzgau	9645	2036	11681	82.7	"
Doron de Beaufort	2942	642	3584	82	"
Val de Conches	3124	868	3992	78.2	"
Guil	1966	585	2551	77	"
Pellice	7405	2360	9765	75.8	"
Cluson	11744	4355	16099	72.9	"
Tarentaise, from Bourg-St.-Maurice to Moûtiers.................	6570	3074	9644	68.1	"
Vintschgau	11272	5317	16589	67.9	"
Doire Ripaire	61582	27084	88666	69.4	"
Val d'Anniviers	1498	755	2253	66.4	"
Valais (according to Lugeon)	26000	14000	40000	65	"
Tarentaise, from Moûtiers to Tours	4672	2791	7463	62.6	"
Maurienne, from Montsapey to the confluence	2436	1472	3908	62.3	"
Maurienne, from the source to St.-Jean	11729	7741	19470	60.2	"
Maurienne, from St. Jean to Montsapey	7886	5843	13729	57.4	"
Val d'Hérens	3141	2671	5812	54	"
Tarentaise, from Val de Tignes to Ste.-Foy	920	832	1752	52.5	"
Inntal	33763	33517	67280	50.1	"
Vallouise	1148	1157	2305	49.8	"
Val de Suse	26072	39264	65336	39.9	"
Val d'Ossola	5618	13810	19428	28.9	"
Val Chiese	3020	11272	14292	21.1	"
Tarentaise, from the source to the Val de Tignes	0	271	271	0	"

scars on the mountain sides which were difficult to heal. One of the most serious of things that may happen to a mountain region is excessive deforestation. Trees had been ruthlessly cut for lumber, fuel, and for clearings for fields and pastures. Deforestation means excessive soil erosion of the slopes, torrential deposits on

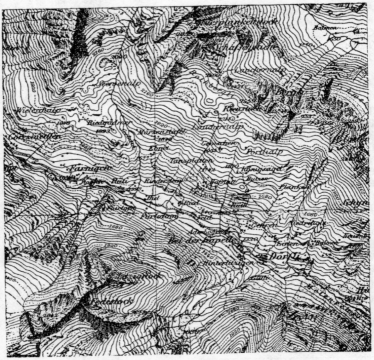

Fig. 55. Population about Dörfli, Switzerland

Note how many houses lie on the *adret*. Scale 1/50,000. Contour interval 30 meters.

valley fields, and loss of ground water. Danger of landslide and avalanche is increased. Moreover, the tilled fields had been over-cropped and impoverished. The pastures had lost area to make way for crops. The cattle, confined to smaller areas, were underweight. Manure for the fields was lacking because of the decrease in livestock. Let me give an extreme example of decay. On October 28, 1888, the inhabitants of Chaudun, in the French

Alps, petitioned that the state acquire 2027 hectares of the mountainous portion of the commune, which was so sterile that the inhabitants were starving. The commune was purchased and politically abolished in 1895.

The increased prosperity expected from the betterment of transportation did come, if tardily. Since 1900 conditions in even the remote valleys are decidedly improved, in spite of the flight from the land characteristic of the post-war period. The Haut-Diois, previously referred to, is an example in case. Railways have made markets accessible and have brought in chemical fertilizers. Sown meadows are now increasing in area. The yield of cereals per hectare has increased. Animals are now raised for shipment and there is a local slaughter-house. Previous to 1900, the region was poverty-stricken. Now there is an increasing prosperity and we may expect increasing population.

The valley of Roizonne, in the French Alps, illustrates the economic struggle of high and isolated valleys. This valley is oriented north-south and so has no true *adret*. The soil is poor. The climate is rude. Snow lies on the ground from the end of November to the last of March. Bouchet tells us how the ignorance bred of isolation has delayed until recently the use of artificial fertilizers. Agriculture suffers from depopulation. The young people making trips in the winter to the factory towns beyond the mountains have been unable to return. Valnoire (a sinister name) sixty years ago had 30 people. Today it is abandoned. La Morte (also sinister), though the highest commune in the valley and surrounded by desolation, is the best preserved because it has the best economy. Agriculture has decreased in importance, while pastoral pursuits have gained. In the last decade, however, the use of chemical fertilizers has been leading to a revival of cultivation. There is hope for the future.

LOCATION OF DWELLINGS

The location of dwellings is, of course, decisive in the distribution of population. An excellent study on this question is that of Flückiger. Valley by valley, rather than by massifs, he takes up the Swiss mountain areas and analyzes in a masterly fashion the factors in the distribution of population. With the Siegfried Topographical Atlas of Switzerland as a basis and with the aid of Imhof's study on forest line and Jegerlehner's study on snow line, he brings out the climatic, orographic, and economic factors. He sees two zones of population: one the zone of permanent houses, and the other the zone of temporary houses. It is the permanent house upon which the census is based, and in this portion of the chapter we shall not concern ourselves with the houses of the upper zone.

The factors influencing forest line and snow line likewise play a part in fixing the upper limit of elevation of isolated permanent houses, but, because in the limit of houses there is the element of human choice, the parallelism of the several lines is not exact. Just as with the snow line and forest line, the greater the mass the higher the dwelling line. Generally house lines are 100 meters below the forest line and 800 meters below the orographic snow line. But man often makes a poor adjustment of house location to climatic conditions because of economic or social factors. He may, as sometimes along pass routes, locate his house in defiance of climatic conditions. On the other hand, the Italian dislikes isolation, and so, living in villages, fails to elevate his house site to the climatic-economic limits.

Exposure is of utmost importance in the location of houses which stand apart. In mountains of middle or high latitudes, people having the choice always live in the sunlight. Many an Alpine valley has no settlement and few houses on the shady side. Even those villages that are on the valley floor have a smaller and less valuable portion of their land area on the *ubac* side of the valley stream. Houses of elevation on the *ubac* slope are ordinarily upon secondary *adrets*. This is true, for example, of the two slopes of the Brenner. Houses of surprising elevation are to be found in high valleys favorably situated for insolation.

In the French Pyrenees of Ariège in two valleys there is the following distribution of dwellings:

PER CENT OF DWELLINGS IN TWO VALLEYS ACCORDING TO EXPOSURE

Region	Adret	Valley floor	Ubac
Sillon Ariégeois ...	42	46	12
Vic de Sos	27	37	36

Of the first situation, all of the dwellings on the *ubac* were on secondary *adrets*. In the second situation, the 36 per cent on the *ubac* included 26 per cent on secondary *adrets*. The secondary *adret* is used as the site for isolated houses much more frequently than for villages.

Houses are located with due appreciation of inversion of temperature and the consequent thermal belts. The depth of snow in the valley bottom has some influence on locations. Cold winds from glaciers have caused to be left uninhabited upper portions of valleys which might otherwise hold a house site. In the Pinzgau, 24 of the settlements are on fans, 9 in basin and valley bottoms, and 7 on terraces.

The topographic factors are many. A glaciated valley may have all houses confined to the exact valley bottom, because the slope of the valley wall is everywhere too steep for houses. Where slopes are gentle, houses may mount to a considerable elevation above the valley floor. If there is little level land in a valley, the houses will be on slopes in order to leave all level land for fields. Extreme cases of this are the 'piled' houses or Ladakh, which literally cling to cliffs rather than encroach upon tillable land.

Not a little of what is said here is of necessity repeated later in this chapter. There are social factors which enter into the question of the isolated dwelling as over against the hamlet or village. It is well known that in uninterrupted plains there are regions of villages and regions of isolated farmsteads. Historical conditions and habits of gregariousness affect racial choice. Generally the Italians avoid the isolated dwelling to a greater extent than do the German mountaineers. The man who depends to an extent upon wood-cutting for a living will live apart. The scarcity of springs or water supply on certain slopes will force people to live in villages where water is accessible. These conditioning factors apply particularly to the permanent habitations. Yet another set of conditions control the location of the alp homes and shelters. It is hoped that Chapter VII deals sufficiently with these.

TOWNS AND VILLAGES

The height limit of towns and villages is affected by some of the same conditioning factors as limits of dwelling sites or of culture and vegetation. Particularly do these limits have climatic factors in common. There are some topographic factors which are peculiar to towns as distinct from hamlets or isolated dwellings.

To recount completely the climatic factors in the location of towns would be to repeat much that has been said in previous sections. But once again the two elements of exposure to sun and mass of mountain should be noted for their almost disproportionate importance. The greater the elevation the more important the matter of exposure. The high valleys of the Hohen

Tauren have 90 per cent of their village population living on the *adret*. Frequently the percentage of population living on an *adret* of a valley is not one hundred simply because the villages are on the valley bottom and some people live immediately across the stream. The settlement across the stream is technically on the *ubac* and may have a separate name. People living in the shade are frequently socially looked down upon. Mass of mountain has the same climatic significance and topographic implications in the location villages and towns as in limits of culture. There are, of course, exceptions. Méolans in the French Alps lies on a steep *ubac*. On the day of the winter solstice this town experiences but one hour of direct sunlight. Rochebrune, another *ubac* town, has but four and one-half hours of sunlight on the day of the winter solstice.

Sieger gives the following table showing factors of exposure in the height limits of permanent settlements:

HEIGHT LIMITS OF SETTLEMENT AND EXPOSURE

	Adret	*Ubac*
Runtental	1244 m.	1233 m.
Echödergraben	1236	1172
Ratchtal	1140	1080

Flückiger says that on the average in all of Switzerland the *adret* settlements are 75 meters higher than the *ubac*. Lugeon offers figures to show that the greater number of settlements are in the sun. In the upper valley of the Rhone 34,000 people live in the sun and 20,000 are on the shady side of the river. The valley of Conches, a high valley in Valais, having an east-west axis, has flanks of almost equal inclination. Three thousand of the mountaineers of this valley reside on the *adret*, whereas but 700 to 800 persons live on the *ubac*.

The topographic factors deserve rather special attention. Villages may not always require level land, but towns ordinarily do. Moreover, towns require considerable area as garden space. Hence towns are ordinarily situated in open basins. Innerkirchen, in the Bernese Oberland, is located where a basin has been formed by two tributary streams joining a main stream. There is a *verrou*, or barrier of bed rock across the valley, immediately below the town. Luz in the French Pyrenees is in a basin which is typical of the valleys of that range. Arosa lies in an open basin at the head of a main valley and so has the advantage of long hours of sunlight.

A most common location for towns lies on contact zones between regions of contrasted culture. In the Sierra Nevada of Spain, practically all the towns lie along a geological contact, because here is the juxtaposition of two cultures founded upon the geological contrasts. Towns in mountains frequently lie along the zone between vine and chestnut culture, woods and pasture culture, vine and wheat culture, valley and slope culture.

Several zones of town and village settlement within a single valley are not uncommon. The valley floor is likely to be the chief zone, though where there is a post-glacial gorge the concentration there may be lacking. Above the valley bottom there may be terraces, structural or superficial in origin, which hold lines of settlement. Such terraces may be found on both sides of the valley or upon only one. A terrace may afford communication along its course, and so bind those villages together as a series of communes. Yet communication with the valley floor may be of such difficulty as to develop separate cultures for the terrace village and the valley village lying plainly in view.

The menace of catastrophes in mountains limits village sites. Areas of frequent avalanches are out of the question. Occasional avalanches are guarded against at no small cost to certain communes. Floods keep many villages to the cones and fans, and so above the flood mark. Thus Chur, Trimmis, and lesser towns lie upon a single cone of dejection which has been washed down upon the plain of the upper Rhine valley. The towns are well above danger of flood. Towns have been known to be undermined by soil creep or land slide. Advancing talus on cones restricts the location of settlements at the foot of steep cliffs. Lastly, winds influence town location. Cold mountain winds that occur with the setting of the sun may make location near the stream unsuitable. Indeed the stream itself can be a refrigerating influence. Elsewhere winds in gorges or in line with a pass may be too violent for comfort. Hamlets have had to be abandoned because of strength of winds.

ALTITUDE AND HEALTH

There is a physiological limitation to the altitude at which man may live with comfort. Potosí, in the Andes, situated at 4000 meters, once had a population of 150,000 inhabitants. Cerro de Pasco in the same mountains, with 13,000 persons, lies at 4350 meters. This is higher than the peaks of most European mountains. But were these people healthy? Could they work efficiently? Could children be born in safety? Was permanent group acclimatization possible? The answer is that those who came to the high elevations without gradual adjustment were unable to work at full capacity without strain on heart and lungs. Those with weak hearts died. Pneumonia or lung troubles were likely to be fatal. At these high stations childbearing for women of the valleys was dangerous for the mother and usually fatal for the child. There is, on the other hand, no reason why any race may not live at high altitudes if it becomes acclimated gradually through the course of generations. Adjustments of the body will come about, and there will be a racial adjustment to the altitude by the processes of selection.

Rapid ascent of mountains results in an illness similar to that experienced by aviators and men subjected to artificial reduction of pressure. The fact of mountain sickness (altitude illness, *puna*, *soroche*, *chuno*, *mal de montagne*, and *Bergkrankheit*) has been long known, but the scientific study of its various aspects is rather recent. Medical authorities, mountaineers, and others still differ greatly concerning the causes and effects of mountain sickness, the usual height at which illness first appears, the height at which it is most prevalent, and the possibility of man's acclimatization to high altitudes. The symptoms of mountain sickness are dizziness, nausea, accelerated respiration and heart action, dimness of vision, and inability to move. Mountain sickness presents a field of study as complicated as those of mountain climates, life, and vegetation. Conditions vary so greatly, and the factors involved are so closely interwoven, that it is very difficult to isolate the causes of symptoms in any particular case. Symptoms vary greatly in different persons and under different conditions.

Some assert that the deficiency of oxygen at great heights is the explanation of all symptoms. The result is an anaemic condition in the blood. A high haemoglobin content, and thus an increased capacity to absorb oxygen, is characteristic of both animals and humans living at high altitudes. Visitors, as they become acclimated, may have an increase of red blood corpuscles of more than 50 per cent.

That persons arriving at altitudes without exertion, as by train, are often affected with illness, somewhat contradicts the theory that mountain illness is the result of fatigue. Nevertheless there is support for those who believe that fatigue is a factor in mountain sickness. Severe exertion does aggravate such illness, particularly in the matter of heart action. The writer has often worked without illness at elevations considerably over 3350 meters, and yet at that elevation he once suffered acute nausea. This was on an ascent of Mount Etna. The climb had been largely in sliding volcanic ash. The fatigue of the writer and another man had been unusually great in the climb on foot from a station at 600 meters. A woman companion had ridden the worst of the climb on muleback. She was unaffected, whereas the men were seriously affected by nausea and palpitation of the heart. A third theory looks to diminished pressure as the main cause of the illness. From these several viewpoints a great variety of explanations have been evolved. Each theory seems to account for some of the symptoms but not for all. The statement that reduction both of oxygen and of pressure plays an important part in causing mountain sickness is probably nearest the truth.

A phase of the theory of pressure is that the sickness is caused by the effect on the organs of the body of the loss of equilibrium between the pressure of the external air and the gas of the interior of the body. Among other things, it is thought that diminished pressure disturbs the circulation in that portion of the spinal cord immediately concerned with the nutrition and muscular control of the legs. The partial loss of power of the limbs is due to the collection and stagnation of blood in these portions. Perhaps the change of pressure produces a more contracted state of the lungs, causing a stagnation of the venous circulation, the resulting shortage of oxygen in the body being the cause of the symptoms. The extreme of pressure in its relation to man is found at San Vincente in Bolivia at 4575 meters, where the pressure is less than 18 inches. At the convent of Hanle in Tibet at the same elevation the pressure is 17 inches.

Analogies are made with the experiences of men working under high pressure in caissons. The use of a lockout chamber or room, in which a man is allowed to become accustomed to increasing pressure, suggests that mountain climbers should become gradually acclimated to greater altitudes. This was done in the case of the climbers who attacked Mount Everest.

Balloonists have complained of symptoms the same as those experienced in mountain sickness. Since the preponderance of oxygen is in the lower atmosphere, this might indicate that supply of oxygen is the most important factor to be considered.

However, in 1875, two French balloonists who reached 6939 meters died with oxygen still in reserve, so that death could not have been due to lack of oxygen. The fact that the mouths of both men were clogged with blood caused many to believe that death was due to the effects of the sudden change in pressure. Others believe their deaths to have been due to suffocation by gas released in the rapid rise of the balloon. More recently German balloonists in an open basket have survived 10,980 meters.

The difference in pressure, or the lack of oxygen, no doubt accounts for many of the symptoms of mountain sickness, but once again stress may also be laid on the similarity existing between the symptoms of mountain sickness and those of ordinary fatigue. It is known that excessive fatigue produces a tired feeling in the limbs, rapid, feeble, and irregular pulse, rise of temperature, and vomiting. These are all symptoms common to mountain sickness. Mountain ascents entail an amount of work the extent of which is not always recognized. Exertion is inseparably bound up with consumption of oxygen, and since there is less oxygen at the high levels fatigue will declare itself sooner there. However, early beliefs of mountaineers that bodily weakness increases more or less regularly with increasing altitude have been somewhat modified. All other things being equal, the higher one goes, the less should be the effect of any given rise, since atmospheric pressure diminishes less rapidly as one ascends. Consequently the difference in effort required between one stage and another should be less with each succeeding stage of altitude. Mountain climbing exhausts not only through physical effort but also through the mental anxiety due to the dangers of the ascent. The inability to carry any but concentrated foods, and the fact that cooking by boiling becomes increasingly difficult with altitude, result in an inadequate diet. A disordered stomach enormously decreases one's power of resistance. Hill men of Asia chew clove and ginger while crossing high elevations in order to avoid the danger of indigestion.

Hepburn goes so far as to reach a conclusion that mountain sickness experienced below a certain height (probably 5000 meters) is due largely to fatigue alone. The fact that practised climbers do not complain so much about mountain sickness as the casual visitor is due, he believes, to their better preparation for the ascent. On Aconcagua in Chile (7010 meters) an alpinist reports that his party suffered much at various times at altitudes

FIG. 56. WINTER VILLAGE IN THE VALLEY OF THE PLESSUR, GRISONS

FIG. 57. SUMMER VILLAGE IN THE VALLEY OF THE SAPÜNERBACH, GRISONS
This valley is a tributary of the valley of the Plessur pictured in Figure 56.

over 4900 meters. In Kashmir the people who live at an elevation of 1800 meters often suffer from mountain sickness after passing 3000 meters. Whymper and his companions on the slopes of Chimborazo were affected at 5100 meters, but Wolf and Whymper did not suffer at all on the summit of Cotopaxi at 5960 meters, although they spent a night at this altitude.

There is much disagreement as to the degree to which man can acclimatize himself to the higher altitudes. The conclusion that after a period of acclimatization man can live at the higher altitudes without a great deal of discomfort is no doubt true. Experience tends to show that with a sufficiently slow change of altitude, allowing time for the body to adjust itself to changes of oxygen and pressure, mountain sickness can be escaped.

Indians bringing sulphur from the summit of Popocatepetl, living at an altitude of 4000 to 5000 meters, seem strong and healthy after being engaged at the occupation for from twenty to thirty years. The experience of workmen engaged in the construction of a railroad tunnel in Peru at the height of 15,645 feet was that after several weeks, in extraordinary cases after several months, acclimatization was so complete that the men were capable of doing full work. Many people, mostly railway men, living and working at altitudes of fourteen or fifteen thousand feet along the Railway of Southern Peru have never experienced mountain sickness. On the other hand, acclimatization to high altitudes over a period of generations no doubt takes the form of natural selection of the most fit. The Bolivian Indian with his deep chest and great endurance, living at altitudes of 8000 to 14,000 feet, is a good example.

Since mountain sickness is influenced by a variety of things, such as the human constitution, habits, exertion, and the attendant natural circumstances of relief, pressure, wind, weather, and so forth, it is not surprising that the altitude at which the sickness appears varies greatly.

Among the subjects which involve the relation of altitude and man is the therapeutic influence of insolation at high altitudes. So great is its importance that sanitariums, solariums, and hotels concentrated at favorable positions have created towns at high altitudes. There is, indeed, a considerable population above the winter haze.

This haze over valleys is a feature worth mentioning. Peaks and the flanking alps have greater cloudiness in summer than do valleys. But the moisture of valleys in winter rises only a short distance before it is condensed. Ordinarily by the time the alps are reached the haze has been passed. The writer recalls starting from Montreux on a December day. The air was cold but the skies were 'clear.' Upon arriving by funicular at the Chesières Alp the light was dazzling, and the valley below was seen through a heavy haze. The 'clear' sky as seen from below was in reality a haze. Air temperatures on the alp were so high that a topcoat was a discomfort. Children from the solariums and health schools were skating or skiing with shoes, stockings, and abbreviated trunks as their only clothing.

The intensity of insolation has been treated in the foregoing pages. All that need be said of the intensity here is the contrast between winter intensities in valley and on alp.

The significant aspect of the therapy of sunshine at high levels is the degree to which the short wave length ultra-violet rays come through unabsorbed. The importance of rays from the 'finer' end of the spectrum is a matter for the medical dermatologist rather than the geographer. The curative values are attested by the number of famous sanitariums and institutes for medical research at high altitudes. Davos, Aroso, Leysier, Montana, and Andermatt are famous the world over as health resorts. There seems to be under the stimulating sunshine an increase of red-blood corpuscles, healing of respiratory organs, reduction of tumors, building up of nerves, invigoration of the heart, cure of rickets, and particularly the cure of tuberculosis.

The health resorts are ordinarily situated in high valleys which are not too enclosed. As many hours of sunlight as possible is the desired thing. A notable character of the sun in these high altitudes is its intensity from the moment of sunrise. Here, amid dramatic splendor, the sick recover in the rays of a beneficent sunshine at an elevation greater than Snowdon, the highest peak of South Britain. This is at a time when invalids in London and Berlin lie in rooms darkened by fog.

Not only the sick, but thousands of healthy people, seek the higher resorts in winter for sport and sunshine. The electric funiculars bear thousands each week-end to high resorts, the most famous of which is St. Moritz in the Engadine. The beauty of the Alpine scene is no less important than the sunshine. The spiritual values are not less than the physical renewal.

For sick or for well, there is a large group of permanent inhabitants who minister to their wants. Cities exist above the winter clouds. Sunshine, particularly ultra-violet sunshine, is responsible for the greatest anomaly in the altitudinal distribution of man.

Some of the curative properties of insolation at high altitudes are:

It adds vitamin A to certain foods.

It increases the calcium and phosphorus content in the milk of alp pasture cows as against the high citric acid content of milk from cows of the lowlands or fed on dry fodder.

It increases phosphorus in human blood. A few minutes of body exposure each day is said to double the phosphorus content in a baby's blood.

The thyroid gland is richer in the secretion of iodine.

Human mechanical energy is increased.

It cures rickets and lung diseases.

It is generally detrimental to germ life.

BIBLIOGRAPHICAL NOTES

Mountain Population

All regional, economic, and historical references on mountains are likely to contain information on population.

Allix, André. *L'Oisans au Moyen-Âge*. Paris, 1929. An example of the many studies in historical regional economy which treat of population.

Arbos, Philippe. "Évolution économique et démographique des Alpes françaises du Sud," in Comité des travaux historiques et scientifiques, *Bulletin de la section de géographie*, xxviii (1913), pp. 296–306. Another typical historical-economic study.

Bauer, Andrä. *Entvölkerung und Existenzverhältnisse in Vorarlberger Berglagen*. Bregenz, 1930.

Bernhard, Hans, Koller, Albert, and Caflisch, C. *Studien zur Gebirgsentvölkerung*. Bern, 1928. (*Beiträge zur Agrargeographie*, 4.) Excellent.

Bowman, Isaiah. "The Distribution of Population in Bolivia," in *Bulletin of the Geographical Society of Philadelphia*, vii (1909), pp. 28–47.

Clerget, Pierre. "Le peuplement de la Suisse," in *Bulletin de la Société royale belge de géographie*, xxx (1906), pp. 73–97.

Corcelle, J. "La dépopulation des Alpes," in *La nature*, xxxi, 1 (1903), pp. 188–190.

Dainelli, Giotto. "La Distribuzione della Popolazione in Toscana," in

Memorie Geografiche, supplemento alla Rivista Geografica Italiana, xi (1917), pp. 3–260.

Edwards, K. C. "Valley Settlement in North Tirol," in *Geography,* xvi (1931), pp. 197–206.

Fabre, L. A. *L'évasion contemporaine des montagnards français.* Nancy, 1911.

Flückiger, Otto. "Die obere Grenze der menschlichen Siedelungen in der Schweiz," in *Zeitschrift für schweizerische Statistik,* 1906, i. Band, pp. 145–162.

Folliasson, Mme. J. "Mouvement de la population en Maurienne au XIXe siècle," in *Recueil des travaux de l'Institut de géographie alpine,* iv (1916), pp. 1–187.

Gex, François. "La population de la Savoie de 1921 à 1926," in *Revue de géographie alpine,* xvi (1928), pp. 221–250.

Krebs, Norbert. "Die Verteilung der Kulturen und die Volksdichte in den österreichischen Alpen," in *Mitteilungen der Geographischen Gesellschaft in Wien,* lv (1912), pp. 243–303.

Letonnelier, G. "L'émigration des Savoyards," in *Revue de géographie alpine,* viii (1920), pp. 541–584.

Lugeon, Maurice. "Quelque mots sur le groupement de la population dans le Valais," *Étrennes helvétiques,* 1909.

Meuriot, Paul. *La population de la Savoie par altitude.* Paris, 1907.

Montbas, Hugues. "Le peuplement des Alpes suisses: Sa répartition et ses limites d'altitude," in *Mémoires de la Société fribourgeoise des sciences naturelles,* série géologie et géographie, viii (1919), pp. 155–240. Also printed separately, Fribourg, 1919.

Peattie, Roderick. "Notes sur les populations des montagnes européennes," in *Annales de géographie,* xl (1931), pp. 386–395.

Perriaux, L. "L'agonie et la mort des villages des Alpes niçoises: Différents processus dans le passé et dans le présent," in *Bulletin de l'Association de Géographes français,* no. 75 (1934), pp. 6–7.

Privat-Deschanel, Paul. "The Influence of Geography on the Distribution of the Population of Scotland," in *Scottish Geographical Magazine,* xviii (1902), pp. 577–587.

Reynier, E. "La région Privadoise," in *Recueil des travaux de l'Institut de géographie alpine,* iii (1915), pp. 1–56. An example of a region with so meager an economy as to have a slight population.

Robert, Jean. "La densité de population des Alpes françaises d'après la dénombrement de 1911," in *Revue de géographie alpine,* viii (1920), pp. 5–124.

Sauvan, E. "L'évolution économique du Haut-Diois," in *Revue de géographie alpine,* ix (1921), pp. 521–624. A changing economy.

Sion, Jules. "Le Tibet méridional et l'expédition anglaise à Lhassa," in *Annales de géographie,* xvi (1907), pp. 31–45.

Toniolo, A. R. "Per uno Studio sistematico sullo spopolamento della

Vallate Alpine," in *Atti dell' XI Congresso Geografico Italiano*, ii (Naples, 1930). Statistical.

Toniolo, A. R. "Ricerche di Antropogeografia nell'alta Valcamonica," in *Memorie Geografiche, supplemento alla Rivista Geografica Italiana*, vii (1913), pp. 245–363. Reviewed at length by Philippe Arbos in *Recueil des travaux de l'Institut de géographie alpine*, iv (1916), pp. 259–267. A complete study.

Toniolo, A. R. "Lo spopolamento montano nella Venezia Tridentina," in *Bollettino della Reale Società Geografica Italiana*, serie vi, viii (1931), pp. 99–111.

Wopfner, Hermann. "Eine siedlungs- und volkskundliche Wanderung durch Villgraten," in *Zeitschrift des Deutschen und Österreichischen Alpenvereins*, lxii (1931), pp. 246–276.

Locations of Dwellings and Settlements

Allix, André. "La limite supérieure de l'habitat permanent dans les Alpes," in *Revue de géographie alpine*, xi (1923), pp. 293–297.

Allix, André. "Note sur la valeur démographique du 'feu' dans l'ancien Dauphiné," in *Revue de géographie alpine*, xi (1923), pp. 635–640.

Arbos, Philippe. "Études sur l'habitat de montagne en Italie," in *Recueil des travaux de l'Institut de géographie alpine*, iv (1916), pp. 259–274.

Blanchard, Raoul. "L'habitation en Queyras," in *La géographie*, xix (1909), pp. 15–44, 97–110. An important article.

Blanchard, Raoul. "Altitudes d'habitat," in *Recueil des travaux de l'Institut de géographie alpine*, vii (1919), pp. 691–702.

Chatelard, Maurice. "Les phénomènes d'habitat dans les Pyrénées Ariégeoises," in *Revue géographique des Pyrénées et du Sud-Ouest*, ii (1931), pp. 448–513. Analytical.

Dellenbach, Marguerite E. "La conquête du Massif alpin et de ses abords par les populations préhistoriques," in *Revue de géographie alpine*, xxiii (1935), pp. 147–416.

Feuerstein, Arnold. "Damüls, die höchste ständige Siedlung im Bregenzerwald," in *Geographischer Jahresbericht aus Österreich*, xiv–xv (1929), pp. 1–28. An excellent local study.

Flückiger, Otto. *Die obere Grenze der menschlichen Siedelungen in der Schweiz*. Bern, 1906. The great study on this subject.

Flückiger, Otto. "Pässe und Grenzen," in *Mitteilungen der Geographisch-Ethnographischen Gesellschaft in Zürich*, xxvii–xxviii (1926–28), pp. 36–65.

Gasperi, G. B. de. "Le casere de Friuli," in *Memorie Geografiche, supplemento alla Rivista Geografica Italiana*, viii (1914), pp. 295–461. Reviewed at length by Arbos, in *Recueil des travaux de l'Institut de géographie alpine*, iv (1916), pp. 267–274.

Knecht, Theodor. *Siedlungsgeographie des Berchtesgadener Landes.* Bad Reichenhall, 1913.

Lehmann, Otto. "Der Begriff der oberen Siedlungsgrenze, seine Herkunft, seine Bestimmungsmethoden und sein geographischer Wert," in *Mitteilungen der Geographischen Gesellschaft in Wien,* lvi (1913), pp. 332–394. An academic discussion reviewing previous literature.

Lehmann, Otto. "Aufruf zur Einsendung von kurzen Mitteilungen über höchste ständige Wohnsitze in den Ostalpen mit Einleitung und Begründung," in *Mitteilungen der Geographischen Gesellschaft in Wien,* lxii (1919), pp. 345–359. Factors in height limits and methods for collecting data.

Lehmann, Otto. "Die Besiedlung und die Verkehrstrassen," in *Die österreichischen Alpen,* ed. by Hans Leitmeier (Leipzig and Vienna, 1928), pp. 256–287.

Lehmann, Otto. "Fortbildung des Begriffes der oberen Grenze der Dauersiedlungen in den Alpen," in *Mitteilungen der Geographischen Gesellschaft in Wien,* lxiii (1920), pp. 153–162.

Löwl, Ferdinand. "Siedlungsarten in den Hochalpen," in *Forschungen zur deutschen Landes- und Volkskunde,* ii (1888), pp. 399–449. Detailed information.

Lugeon, Maurice. "Quelques mots sur le groupement de la population du Valais," in *Étrennes helvétiques pour 1902* (Lausanne, 1902).

Marinelli, Olinto. "I limite altimetrici in Comelico," in *Memorie Geografiche, supplemento alla Rivista Geografica Italiana,* i (1907), pp. 9–99.

Merlini, Giovanni. "I centri abitati della Garfagnana in rapporto al terreno," in *Bollettino della Reale Società Geografica Italiana,* serie vi, vii (1930), pp. 29–49.

Montbas, Hugues. "Le peuplement des Alpes suisses: Sa répartition et ses limites d'altitude," in *Mémoires de la Société fribourgeoise des sciences naturelles,* série géologie et géographie, viii (1919), pp. 155–240. Also printed separately, Fribourg, 1919. In spite of the title this study is confined to areas above 1000 meters. This, with the study by Flückiger, covers the subject.

Österreichische Ingenieur- und Architekten-Verein. *Das Bauernhaus in Österreich-Ungarn und in seinen Grenzegebieten.* Dresden, 1906.

Ott, Adolf. "Die Siedelungs-Verhältnisse beider Appenzell," in *Jahresbericht der Geographisch-Ethnographischen Gesellschaft in Zürich,* xiv–xv (1913–15), pp. 33–163.

Reishauer, Hermann. "Siedlungen der Deutschen und Italiener im Gebiete der Ostalpen," in *Zu Friedrich Ratzels Gedächtnis* (Leipzig, 1904), pp. 289–302.

Rinaldini, Bettina. "Die Obergrenze der Dauersiedlung und die relative Höhe des Siedlungsraumes in Tirol," in *Mitteilungen der Geographischen Gesellschaft in Wien,* lxxii (1929), pp. 23–47.

Sieger, Robert. "Zur Geographie der zeitweise bewohnten Siedlungen in den Alpen," in *Verhandlungen des Sechszehnten Deutschen Geographentages zu Nürnberg* (Berlin, 1907), also in *Geographische Zeitschrift*, xiii (1907), pp. 361–369.

Taylor, Griffith. "Settlement Zones of the Sierra Nevada de Santa Marta, Colombia," in *Geographical Review*, xxi (1931), pp. 539–558.

Wopfner, Hermann. "Die Besiedlung unserer Hochgebirgstäler," in *Zeitschrift des Deutschen und Österreichischen Alpenvereins*, li (1920), pp. 25–86.

Altitude and Health

The many controversial aspects of this subject have brought out a multitude of writings. Many Alpinists have contributed to the subject. Hann, ed. by Knoch, i, pp. 210–227, has numerous references in the footnotes. The *Verhandlungen der Klimatologischen Tagung in Davos*, 1925, contains some forty articles upon the medical character of high altitude climates. Switzerland has led in mountain therapy and in the Davos volume there is perhaps the most important collection of opinions upon such matters that can be found in any single reference.

Bosanquet, R. H. M. "Mountain-Sickness; and Power and Endurance," in *Philosophical Magazine*, 5th series, xxxv (1893), pp. 47–52.

Conway, W. M. *Climbing and Exploration in the Karakorom-Himalayas.* London, 1894.

Dent, Clinton. "Physiological Effects of High Altitudes," in *Geographical Journal*, i (1893), pp. 46–48.

Dorno, Carl. *Studie über Licht und Luft des Hochgebirges.* Braunschweig, 1911. Dorno is here an authority. See his complete bibliography in the *Bulletin of the American Meteorological Society*, xiv (1933), pp. 282–286. See also his "Papers on the Relation of the Atmosphere to Human Comfort," in the *Monthly Weather Review*, liv (1926), pp. 39–43.

Greim, G. "Der Mensch auf den Hochalpen: Nach Mosso," in *Geographische Zeitschrift*, v (1899), pp. 94–104.

Griffith, George. "Mountain Sickness," in *Nature* (London), lii (1895), p. 414.

Hepburn, M. L. "The Influence of High Altitudes in Mountaineering," in *Alpine Journal*, xx (1901), pp. 368–393. A review which is most important.

Jourdanet, Denis. *Influence de la pression de l'air sur la vie de l'homme: Climats d'altitude et climats de montagne.* Paris, 1875. 2 vols.

Kellas, A. M. "A Consideration of the Possibility of Ascending the Loftier Himalaya," in *Geographical Journal*, xlix (1917), pp. 26–48. Physiological considerations. One should follow this with articles in the same journal on the attempts at Mount Everest.

Latham, D. V. "Kilimanjaro and some Observations on the Physiology of High Altitudes in the Tropics," in *Geographical Journal*, lxviii (1926), pp. 492–505.

Longstaff, T. G. *Mountain Sickness and its Probable Causes*. London, 1906.

Mosso, Angelo. *Fisiologia dell' uomo sulle Alpi: Studii fatti sul Monte Rosa*. Milan, 1897.

Mosso, Angelo. *Der Mensch auf den Hochalpen*. Leipzig, 1899. An excellent scientific work.

Whymper, Edward. *Travels amongst the Great Andes of the Equator*. New York, 1892. See pp. 366–384, and the appendix. Whymper was a great Alpinist.

Workman, W. H. "Some Altitude Effects at Camps above Twenty Thousand Feet," in *Appalachia*, xi (1905–08), pp. 350–359.

Zuntz, Nathan; Müller, Franz; Caspari, W. *Höhenklima und Bergwanderungen in ihrer Wirkung auf den Menschen*. Berlin, 1906.

The *Transactions* of the American Climatological and Clinical Association contain much material on this subject.

CHAPTER IX

MATTERS POLITICAL

Mountain States

MOUNTAIN regions and mountain valleys within these re-tions tend to establish, preserve, and increase political independence. The mountain masses or the valleys, where they are sufficiently set off from the surrounding territories, become separate political entities, such as communes, cantons, or independent states. Where independence does not exist there are frequently movements toward separation. Where a degree of independence has been won, the isolation and defensibility of the mountain fastness aid in resisting encroachment or maintaining autonomy. Thus the mountain mass which we know as Grisons was for a long time quite independent of the Swiss Confederation. Was it not the Asturias in the Cantabrian Mountains which alone of the Iberian provinces never bowed to the Moors? The mountain Kurds between Turkey and Persia owe little allegiance to either power, and in the isolated mountains of the Chinese plain there have always been semi-independent peoples.

Tibet is the largest isolated political mountain unit of the world. It rests on the 'roof of the world' at an elevation of some 4600 meters. The great Himalayas lie to the south, and to the north are the formidable Kuen Luen Mountains, where passes leading to Turkestan are seldom less than 5000 meters in altitude. The access from the east has been easier than from the north or south, and hence the cultural and political allegiance has been Chinese. Today, remarkable as it may seem, Tibet is dominated politically by English influence, which has penetrated through the most forbidding range in the world. Actually the life of Tibet flows on with little regard for China or England, and the country will always remain politically aloof.

The Himalayas are of so great a height, the valleys are so deeply inset, and the passes so difficult, that that great range holds other completely defined political entities. Nepal is a native Indian state of which very little is known because of the extreme antipathy of its people toward the foreigner. Nepal is set deep in the Himalayas between Tibet and India. Its area is 50,000 square miles, and it has a population of some five millions. Physical unity has made Nepal a homogeneous state in spite of racial differences. The country has always been hostile to Chinese domination, and Great Britain duly recognizes Nepal's growing military strength, and draws thence many fine soldiers, the Ghurkas. Bhutan also lies between Tibet and British India. It has long persisted as an independent state despite the pressure of the great commercial empire to the south. Kashmir is the best defined of the Indian states. It is in one of the most impressive gorges in the world. No other large valley is flanked by more overpowering mountain walls.

A still more isolated and mountain-guarded political entity, until its conquest by Kashmir in 1834–42, was Ladakh, now a district of Kashmir at the very headwaters of the Indus. It is the highest inhabited country in the world. The peaks that define its territory rise to 5800 meters. Leh, the capital, at 3355 meters, has the highest meteorological observatory in Asia. The failure of so isolated an area to maintain political independence came from the fact that its scant resources and population were insufficient to resist the overwhelming power of Kashmir.

Europe likewise has mountain states. Montenegro in the Balkans, now part of Yugoslavia, proudly maintained its independence until the recent incorporation. Albania, a chaos of mountains and plains, has resisted not only effective political domination but modern culture as well, at least until the infiltration of Italian commerce following the World War. The hill republic of San Marino has been independent since the Middle Ages. More hidden among mountains is Andorra, where independence of her powerful neighbors is taught to the young at every hearthstone of the little country.

The Swiss Confederation is born of the mountains. Even though today most of the Swiss live upon the plain, that plain is marked on the north by the Jura Mountains. But Swiss independence is an outgrowth of her isolated valleys rather than of the mountain mass as a whole. The original Swiss Confederation was cradled in the valleys of four mountain forest cantons in the opposition to the tyranny of the Hapsburgs. The definite physical boundaries of the canton of Grisons nurtured the spirit of freedom which established its federal peasant-republic. Within this little republic there were three distinct leagues set apart by natural barriers. For a time this republican federation of federations was in alliance with the Swiss Confederation; it did not become an integral part of Switzerland until the Treaty of Vienna in 1815. The pastoral republic of Appenzell, independent from about 1400, entered into alliance with the federated Swiss cantons in 1452 and was admitted into the confederation in 1513.

The Austrian mountain provinces differ in culture and play distinct rôles in the nation of today. The Hohe Tauern range separates the provinces of Salzburg and Carinthia. These two provinces, while they can communicate with Tirol, cannot easily communicate with each other on account of their mountain barriers. Since the defeat of Austria in the Great War, there has been a separatist movement in Vorarlberg.

The autonomy of mountain districts is due to physical inaccessibility, differences of climate, and the economic contrasts between plain and mountain. It is, however, to be noted that the meager resources of the mountain as compared with those of the plain have often permitted plains people to rule mountains. Witness the Roman conquest of the Alps in the Augustan Age and the Japanese control of the mountain folk, to cite two examples widely apart in time and space. Nevertheless it has rarely been worth while to subjugate mountains so thoroughly as to extirpate their peculiar spirit and culture.

MOUNTAINS AS BOUNDARIES

The influence of mountains on political history has varied at different times, but, on the whole, it is true to say that next to the sea itself there has been no greater element controlling the settlement and progress of races and the political institutions of mankind. Mountains are a natural element, permanently fixed, and they are at the same time a wall of protection to one people and a barrier of defiance against another. We may read little of the Lazi, warders of the Caucasian Gates against the hordes of the steppes, yet few peoples in ancient history had a more important part to play than they. While, in a way, modern methods of communication and transportation, telephone and tunnel, have pierced the walls of the great mountain masses, we still have important mountain boundaries. We cannot think of Italy without the Alps.

Mountains have to a considerable extent determined the boundaries of European states. Notable among the great mountain boundaries of the world is the wall of the Pyrenees. No less than five states abut upon the Alps alone, while the southern highland frontiers of Germany are formed in turn by the Bavarian Alps, the mountains of the Bohemian Forest, the Erzgebirge, and the Sudeten. The Carpathians bound Poland on the south

FIG. 58. BOUNDARIES OF ANDORRA

The stippled areas are portions of Andorra beyond the true drainage basin of the country.

and Czechoslovakia on the northeast. More often than not mountains are effective and strategic frontiers. The effectiveness of mountain barriers depends upon their height, their lineal extent, their breadth, and particularly upon the accessibility of their passes. No less important has been the character of the relief. A single precipice of no great height may be as effective as the far greater height of the massif. Forested mountains are particularly effective as barriers; witness the low Bohemian Forest.

On the other hand, mountains as barriers to political expansion have in some cases been notably ineffective. An exception to the rule that mountain ranges form boundaries is seen in the Central Andes. It would be thought that so great and decisive a rock wall would everywhere be a political limitation, yet Ecuador, Bolivia, and Peru seem little concerned as to crest line or watershed. The Urals separated Russia from Siberia, yet they presented no effective barrier to Yermak and his Cossacks. Political ambitions or desire for land incite nations to cross even great mountain ranges.

Between Slovenia in Yugoslavia and Carinthia in Austria there is the Karawanken range. This is a formidable Alpine chain with only a single difficult pass. One of the longer tunnels of the world today gives rail connection between the flanking plains. On the north side of the Karawankens is the basin of Klagenfurt. One would expect the basin of Klagenfurt to be ethnically unlike the southern or Slovenian slope. As a matter of fact, the Slovenes occupy the southern part of the basin. Through a plebiscite it was made possible for the voters to set the political boundary either north of the line of the Slovene settlement, or north of the basin, or set it south of the basin. Fortunately the Slovenes of the basin voted in October, 1920, to join with Austria. The expansion of the Slovenes had taken slight notice of the barrier effect of the Karawankens. On the other hand, the Slovenes north of the range have agreed to unite their economic future with that of Austria. Partly this was to avoid the domination of the Serbs in Yugoslavia, but they also recognized the importance of the mountain barrier.

We shall do well to look into the details of boundaries on some of the acknowledged barriers. Is the crest line of the mountain always a boundary? Is the watershed the boundary?

The Pyrenees Mountains are frequently cited as an example of a mountain range whose watershed is a national boundary. In the Pyrenees, however, it is the chief mountain crest which is chosen, and watershed and chief mountain crest do not there always coincide. The exceptions to the coincidence of political boundary and watershed are many. We mention the two best known cases. The upper valley of the Garonne, the Val d'Arán, is Spanish. This valley, belonging to Spain, is reached from the south only by a mountain pass. Communication between the Val d'Arán and France is interrupted only by a senseless custom barrier. The Segre River, a branch of the Spanish Ebro, rises on the plateau of Cerdagne well within France.

Ordinarily one would think of a mountain valley as a single political area. Yet, because of morphological history, mountain rivers may flow through several mountain ranges. Thus the River Inn rises in Switzerland, where its valley is the well defined Engadine. It forms the valley of Central Western Austria. Yet lower in its course it drains part of the Bavarian plain.

The question of the watershed as a political limit came to the front in the boundary dispute between the cantons of Valais and Bern in Switzerland. Bern demanded the fixing of the boundary at the watershed according to an established principle of international law, while Valais took the stand that the limit should extend as far as the property rights of her citizens. Bern objected that such extension of property rights would prejudice her sovereignty. Here there is a conflict of two geographical principles. The first is well substantiated. The water divide between two valley heads is the logical boundary for defense. The second is more economic than political. It involves the right of a people who lack pasture land to balance properly their holdings and so to extend their territory beyond a divide into an area of excess pasture. This type of situation is not uncommon in mountains. Figure 58 illustrates such a case in Andorra.

There is yet another type of exception to the generalization that mountains make good boundaries. Mountains in certain economic matters are an area of transition rather than a sharp boundary. There is an economic interest in the zone along mountain heights which may override the strategic importance of the crest line. In peace economic interests tend to prevail, while in war the question of defense assumes the greater importance. The balance of the two factors determines the location of the boundary. There is no question today of war between Valais and Bern. But in the case of the French-Spanish border or the Austrian-Italian border the case is different. Shall nations recognize the economic needs and claims of high mountain folk, or shall they insist upon the strategic boundary of the crest line?

The case of the mountain folk is worth stating. Those people, whose way of life and economic interests are much the same on both flanks of the crest, have what we shall term 'straddle economies.'

On approaching an alpine, that is, glaciated range, one enters a valley flanked by mountain spurs. There has been no perceptible change in grade on leaving the plain and traversing the valley floor. The people in this valley, though living among the mountains, are hardly mountaineers. The chief agricultural interest is in the valley floor, and secondarily in the mountain spurs. Commercially the towns are marginal to the plains with the mountain back country as a tributary region.

Farther up the valley are communities whose interests are first pastoral and secondarily agricultural. Agriculture is of the kitchen garden type and, in the past, a bread-stuff type. There is no raising of grains in excess of the local demand. Most fields are given over to the raising of hay for winter support of the herds and flocks. Upon the herds and flocks rests the economy of the community. The herds for a considerable part of the year are feeding upon alp meadows above the timber line. The ownership of the upland pasture is vital in the economic program. The men of these high mountain communities then face, economically speaking, up the mountain rather than down the valley. They are, in distinction to the man of the lower valley communities, mountaineers. Moreover, most great Alpine ranges have crystalline cores. Their crests are not always well defined. The upland may be of the dome order. Such mountains have plateaulike surfaces, or, at least, broad, flattish saddles between the peaks.

It is these upland areas, these skyline pastures, that are the physical basis of the political circumstance we are considering. Men of villages of opposing slopes have an equal concern for the pastures. In some cases, because of the asymmetry of the watershed, a village may make use of pastures which are on the far side of the crest line, as in the case of Valais. Villages not uncommonly control pasture lands which are thus without the political domain. The sharing of these upland pastures by men of the opposing mountain slopes binds together the communities of the two slopes. There is an alpine culture, a high level economy, which straddles the mountain range and extends down until, in the valleys, the culture of the plains is met. Such high level cultures common to the opposing upper slopes of a range are 'straddle economies.' Let us call peoples of such economic and political tendencies 'straddle folk.' The recognition of a straddle economy implies a reduction of the significance of mountains as boundaries, and is well illustrated by the Pyrenees.

STRADDLE ECONOMIES OF THE HIGH PYRENEES

The Pyrenees are not so sharp a dividing line between France and Spain as they are generally supposed to be. At places along the summit of the range it is difficult to judge where the water divide may be. In many parts of the Pyrenees the French and Spanish summit pastures are more or less continuous. With pastoral life as a prime element in the existence of both the Spanish and French mountaineers, these pastures are, in summer, the true focus of the local economies. The flocks and herds of the two people here mix. A bond, born of long contact with each other and a common set of economic problems, is established between the people of the two nations. Though more so in the past, even today the Pyrenees are a zone of transition rather than a sharp boundary between governments and cultures. Cultures straddle the range. The Catalans are found in almost equal strengths on the two slopes of the eastern end, as are the Basques at the western. The French Béarnais of the Central Pyrenees speak a dialect intelligible to the Spanish mountaineers.

So differentiated has this transitional zone been from the flanking plains, that the separatist tendency, common to mountain peoples, finds here excellent illustrations. We are reminded of Swiss history when we learn that there was in this range for three centuries a little known federation. The mountaineers, regardless of the national policies of Spain or France, maintained a 'state' possessing frontiers, public law, and a political consciousness. This federation was bound together largely by common interests in the high pasture terrain. Had the range crest to a greater extent been serrated, the state might not have existed. Frequently communes on opposite slopes had more commercial and social relations with each other than with the plains to which they belonged nationally, though not always linguistically. The treaties between such communes, known as *traités de lies et de passeries*, were many, and involved rights to pasture, wood, water, and commerce. Rights to resources and privileges to trade were exchanged without reference to the national governments, and were retained even when the nations to which the communes belonged were at war. Thus Barèges (French) and Bielsa (Spanish) agreed in 1384 to continue friendly relations in case of war between Aragon and England. Ossau, Aspe, and Barétous were neutral during the Hundred Years' War. The residents of the

FIG. 59.   HAY TRANSPORTATION IN THE PYRENEES
Many mountain fields are inaccessible to carts.

FIG. 60.   LOGGERS IN ANDORRA
Breakfast at the edge of the forest zone preparatory to 'snaking' the logs to
the valley.

French valley of Barétous still pay on each July 12 a tribute of three heifers to their Spanish neighbors of the valley of Roncal. The presentation is followed by inspection of their common pastures and a feast. In the War of the Spanish Succession, the transmontane commercial relations were maintained regardless of the will of kings. Indeed, republican tendencies are common enough in these mountains, the natural results of agreements between communes.

The government of Andorra is an example of the same historical movement. Andorra is indeed merely a federation of villages. Its autonomy has arisen out of physical conditions and as an inheritance of feudal rule. Its physical situation in the Pyrenees is such that it is difficult to decide whether it should be Spanish or French. Moreover in feudal days there were frequently interests which traversed the mountains. Foix, Catalonia, and Navarre all held fiefs on the far side of the range. It came about that Andorra was at the same time a fief of the Spanish bishop of Urgel and the French count of Foix. It was thus a *pareage*.[1] That it should have attained this status was partly because its central position gave neither one overlord nor the other the advantage. Its independence today is a direct consequence of the parage, which is, in turn, an outgrowth of its midway position.

An Altitudinal Provincialism: The Tirol

Straddle economies are in a sense altitudinal provincialisms. It is not surprising that they should exist, but rather that they have had so little political recognition, especially in the light of their clearly defined position. Thus in Central Africa, about Kilimanjaro, there are many cattle-breeders on the plains; a little higher on the piedmont there are gardeners with small irrigated tracts; while in the open lands above 1800 meters there are nomads. There is a three-fold cultural stratification of folk in Central Asia. The steppe lands hold a scattered nomadic people. The piedmonts, using mountain streams for irrigation, are more densely populated by tillers of the soil, while occasional cities are to be found, towns of commercial and industrial nature. The high mountain slopes are occupied by the pastoral agriculturalist seeking a meager livelihood.

A simple economic zoning is plainly marked in the case of the

[1] Pareage, a fief held jointly by two overlords.

Tibetans of the western borderlands of Kansu. Below the 3000-meter level most of the inhabitants are farmers, but above that level they are nomads. Because of the changes of natural products with altitude Tibetans do not always take mountain ranges or rivers for their boundaries. Sir Charles Bell describes his experience. When on a tour of exploration through Bhutan to Tibet in 1904, he found that the boundary between these two countries at the point where both meet Sikkim was what the Tibetans called an 'upland-tree lowland-tree' boundary. The pine forests belonged to Tibet and the bamboo forests to Bhutan, which means, in effect, a contour of about 11,500 feet above sea-level. He goes on to say that this was a good practical boundary, for the Tibetans need the higher lands for grazing their yaks and upland sheep, while the Bhutans make great use of the bamboo. This is a boundary not easily recognized by Western people, who look for frontiers along high mountain ranges, which are easily defended and can be delineated on maps.

The Tirol as a political term includes the area between the crest of the Bavarian Alps and the crest of the Austrian-Italian Alps in the region of the Brenner. In reality there are parts of three geographic regions within the Austrian province of Tirol. On the north, in the Bavarian Alps, is a culture which extends to the crests of the precipitous slope which marks the northern wall of the Inn Valley. The Inn Valley is characterized by valley farms, industries, and commerce. The slope south of the Inn has in its deep-set valleys true Tirolean culture. The Zillertal exemplifies this distinctive and true Tirolean manner of life. This culture is marked on the north more or less by elevation contours. Tirolean culture is characteristic of the *high* tributary valleys. Moreover, this culture in the region of the Brenner (Ötztaler and Stubaitaler Alps) extends over the mountains into such deep gorges as Valle Passiria (Passeiertal), where life is as truly Tirolean as the highly characteristic life of the Zillertal. The high pastures of the massif were property of the people on the two flanks, and the relatively low Brenner offers the easiest transmontane communication in the length of the Alps. The Tiroleans on the south flank, that is, of the South Tirol, are pastoral people living distinctly as mountaineers. They are distinct in economy, social habits, and language from the grape-raising Italians. There is, then, on the south as on the north, an altitudinal differentiation.

Failure to recognize the South Tirol as an integral part of Tirol was one of the injustices of the Treaty of St.-Germain. Italy, remembering previous conflicts with Austria, hoped to obtain from the World War a strategic boundary which would exclude Austria from the southern slope of the Alps. President Wilson, seeing that the crest of the Alps was physically the logical boundary for Italy, lent his support to the Italian claim, but later bitterly regretted his action. At the end of the war the South Tirol became the Italian Trentino. This was an injustice in the light of race and culture which, to the Tiroleans, far outweighed the justice of granting Italy the new strategic boundary. The validity of the Italian claims can easily be seen if the point of view of military necessity alone be held. But Italy does not hold the crest line as a boundary against Switzerland. True, the mountain Swiss form a neutral state. Italy does, indeed, hold the crest line along the French border, and thanks to the folly of a French king, extends her boundary across the crest line so as to control strategically a large Provençal valley. The Italians are therefore not without precedent in their claims to the crest line.

The fact remains that the Austrian South Tirol is today the Italian Trentino. German-speaking peoples are compelled by force to adjust themselves to the Italian régime. Tiroleans are serving in an army against which their elder brothers recently fought. It is forbidden in the taverns to sing German songs over the convivial glass.

IMPORTANCE OF THE DALMATIAN ALPS

An excellent example of geographic principles in conflict with each other is exemplified by the problems associated with the Dalmatian Alps. These are a more or less continuous barrier extending from the Istrian Peninsula to the plateau of Montenegro. The mountains are seldom truly alpine in character. They are a limestone upland, presenting an abrupt front to the littoral of the Adriatic and a more gradual slope with extended spurs towards the Yugoslavian interior. Were the plains of the interior more uniform the problem would be simpler. But the approach from the rich valley of the Save towards the alpine barrier is confused.

The Dalmatian range so effectively cuts off the littoral from the interior as to form a coastal province whose people are distinct from the various interior peoples. There is a coastal Dalmatian people in distinction to the Carnilans, Slovenes, and Bosnians of the interior. The Dalmatians have a Venetian element in their historical culture and commonly are able to use Italian as a commercial language.

This littoral is politically and commercially tied to the interior by the formation of Yugoslavia. The people have an intense national spirit which has stamped them as Yugoslavians rather than Italians. A geographic principle has been once again exemplified. A rich interior tends to expand so as to include a sea coast. So strongly has this principle asserted itself that the expansion has surmounted the mountains. Before the war the Save Valley had one communication by rail with the Adriatic. This was at Fiume. Fiume is now Italian and the Slavs are forced to use the suburb of Sušak, unfavorable at best. Now, however, a railroad reaches the sea at Split and another approaches Dubrovnik.

There is a geographic principle of lesser force which asserts itself in this region. An enclosed sea is not unlike a peninsula. It tends to submit politically, commercially, or culturally to a dominant power. Rome early held both shores of the Adriatic under this principle, as did Venice at a later date. Italy has attempted to do likewise and today has several footholds upon the Dalmatian littoral. It holds Fiume, except for inconsequential Sušak, the city of Zara, and certain islands. Farther south it plays the part of protector in Albanian politics and commerce.

Italy holds Fiume and Zara on the basis of the extent of the Italian population there. If there were no Dalmatian Alps, if the plain of the Save merged with the littoral of the Adriatic, this aggression into Balkan territory would not have taken place. The principle of the expansion of an interior to include a littoral is ordinarily stronger than the principle of the unity of an enclosed sea. What has shifted the balance here is the barrier effect of the Dalmatian Alps.

The barrier which mountains offer to political, cultural, or commercial aggression not only depends upon the physical character of the range but upon the moment in history. Much depends upon the political, cultural, and commercial strengths of the forces on the two slopes at the periods in which the mountains and their human histories are studied.

Political Philosophies of Mountaineers

Perhaps no side of the political geography of mountains has been more discussed than the political attitude of mountain folk. Many of the statements are broad generalities which cannot be substantiated. Yet there are political attributes of mountaineers, which, if imponderable, nevertheless deserve discussion. Ratzel, Miss Semple, Vallaux, and others have insisted upon a relationship between the state and the soil. In mountains, the size of the terrain and the character of the topography, as well as the degree of relief, have been little short of deterministic in matters economic and political. But have the inherent characteristics of the mountains affected the political theories of mountaineers? We appreciate the fact that soil, area, and climate have stamped upon Denmark's government the character of a coöperative dairying association. In the Middle Ages the same factors, plus a few others, made Denmark a headquarters of pirates. The strength of mercantilism in England is a function of insularity, over-population, and lack of agricultural back country. Do mountains suggest distinctive elements of political philosophy?

The very difficulties and hardships incident to mountain life are a challenge to man's energies. Therefore, we find in the population of mountain regions a large measure of self-reliance and resourcefulness, together with a rugged hardihood. Mountains impose their character, as it were, upon the inhabitants whom they train. There is the fatigue of ascents and descents, the simple food, the constant struggle for existence: these have given the mountaineer a character all his own. He has usually been rewarded with liberty and other blessings that go with non-interference. In Switzerland we find not only political and religious liberty, but the inevitable traits of character that develop from these privileges. Every man, peasant or workman, stands on his own feet. He is trained to respect leadership, but to despise and reject coercion. He is taught to believe that rights also involve duties in the exercise of citizenship. But if mountain peoples possess a commendable individualism and courage, as well as frugality, they must at the same time pay the penalties for their isolation. For the isolation of mountain regions not only prevents expansion and invasion, but also makes progress in ideas and inventions more difficult.

That the mountaineer by the nature of his homeland is an individualist has long been a popular theme. It is not without a certain justification. The unbending individualism of the feud-waging mountaineer of the Southern Appalachians would support the contention. Clans are confined to valleys. The valleys force upon their people an inbreeding, and thus it is the separated valley spaces rather than blood relationships which in the last analysis are the basis of the feuds. No organization yet developed has broken down the social isolation of the mountain folk of the Balkans. The Balkans, the Scottish Highlands, and the Appalachian mountain areas are uplands maturely dissected. The social response to the character of dissection is in each case the same. Maturely dissected uplands are notorious for the feuds they engender. Their topography prevents progressive culture or social and political unification.

On the other hand, the freedom of the mountaineer in alpine mountains is characteristic of the group rather than the individual. In reality, the corridor character of great glaciated valleys, the communal character of the exploitation of alp pastures, the common danger from catastrophe, and the altitudinal distribution of property rights force upon the people of a single valley a coöperation which creates a syndicate with republican and socialistic aspects. People form a closely knit social group. Alp lands are owned in common because of their indivisible nature. Forested slopes are of public interest. Avalanches are to be prevented by community effort, by planting, or the construction of walls. Public routes of communication are rendered useless by floods, deposits, and avalanches, and must be restored by common effort. Mountain terracing means detailed regulations controlling rights of access, erosion, and soil replacement. Irrigation on these terraces means the construction of a trunk canal and public regulation of the distribution of water. The sending of the cattle, sheep, and goats up to common pastures under a herdsman or group of herdsmen increases the group coöperation. The summer cheese industry means a proportional sharing of profits.

In short, there is here a group organization, political and social, based upon a common interest in the combat against catastrophes and in the use of resources. Nature forces upon the commune a group interest in resources and in the exploitation of those resources. The economic 'folk unity' is the basis of the political division. It has been asserted that from a sociological point of view there is no political boundary, but rather there is a

FIG. 61. MOUNTING TO POTATO FIELDS, SPANISH SIERRA NEVADA

The up journey takes four hours. Note the fuel — the men will remain over night in their fields, which are above the tree line.

FIG. 62. BRINGING RYE TO THE VILLAGE, FRENCH PYRENEES

shifting frontier. Such a statement has an element of truth for areas of the plains, but it has much less application to the mountain-rimmed area.

Each area which has physical definition is found to support, to a greater or less degree, a group consciousness, a cultural provincialism.

There is, however, in mountains, an individualism of one valley as against another. How then is a confederation, such as Switzerland, formed from individualistic communes and cantons? This is the more difficult to comprehend when one remembers that the valleys are radial and open upon the plains of several countries. The element of unity arises not so much from mutual commerce and interchange of resources and productions as from the common economic problems. A government of mountain valleys having the same economic and political problems is more rational than the government of mountain valleys by unsympathetic plains people. In their external relationships mountain groups have all the independence that writers have ascribed to the individual mountaineer. The confederation of valleys into a state is a matter of singleness of economic purpose and the need for protection. It is worthy of note that in Switzerland the communes are older than the cantons and the cantons existed before the confederation. The confederation was created, indeed, as a defense of communal and cantonal autonomy.

The lack of continuity of level inhabitable land has played a rôle in political theory. This breaking up of men into small groups accounts for the fact that strong centralization of authority is not easily understood by the mountaineer. Mountains have, therefore, an essential suggestion of republicanism. The separate units in such a republic have their cultural and political views colored by the plains area in the direction in which their valley tends, and a mountain mass with radial valleys has a strong tendency towards decentralization of authority. Mountain areas may teach plains areas much in theories of liberty, but they will never be dynamic forces among nations because of their centrifugal interests.

BIBLIOGRAPHICAL NOTES

The Political Geography of Mountains

This list does not include treatises from the point of view of the political scientist, but rather works by geographers.

Allen, W. E. D. "New Political Boundaries in the Caucasus," in *Geographical Journal*, lxix (1927), pp. 430–441.

Barnes, J. S. "The Future of the Albanian State," in *Geographical Journal*, lii (1918), pp. 12–30.

Bell, Sir Charles. *Tibet, Past and Present*. Oxford, 1924.

Bishop, C. W. "The Geographical Factor in the Development of Chinese Civilization," in *Geographical Review*, xii (1922), pp. 19–41.

Bowman, Isaiah. *The Andes of Southern Peru*. New York, 1916.

Bowman, Isaiah. *The New World*. Yonkers, 1921. The great book in English on after-war political geography.

Brigham, A. P. *Geographical Influences in American History*. Boston, 1903.

Brigham, A. P. "Principles in the Determination of Boundaries," in *Geographical Review*, vii (1919), pp. 201–219.

Brooks, R. C. *Government and Politics of Switzerland*. Yonkers, 1918.

Brunhes, Jean. *Human Geography*, tr. by I. C. Le Compte. Chicago, 1920.

Bryce, James. *Modern Democracies*. London, 1921. 2 vols.

Cole, D. H. *Elementary Imperial Military Geography*. London, 1924.

Coolidge, W. A. B. *The Alps in Nature and History*. New York, 1908.

Corey, Herbert. "A Unique Republic, where Smuggling is an Industry," in *National Geographic Magazine*, xxxiii (1918), pp. 279–299.

Cowan, A. R. *Master-Clues in World-History*. London, 1914. Chap. viii.

Ehringhaus, Friedrich. *Kleine Staatsbürgerkunde*, 4. Aufl. Göttingen, 1925.

Fairgrieve, James. *Geography and World Power*. London, 1915.

Fawcett, C. B. *Frontiers*. Oxford, 1921.

Flückiger, Otto. "Pässe und Grenzen," in *Mitteilungen der Geographisch-Ethnographischen Gesellschaft in Zürich*, xxvii–xxviii (1926–28), pp. 36–65.

Freeman, E. A. *The Historical Geography of Europe*. London, 1881. 2 vols.

George, H. B. *The Relations of Geography and History*, 4th ed. Oxford, 1910.

Hauser, Henri. "La position géographique de la Suisse: Étude de géographie politique," in *Annales de géographie*, xxv (1916), pp. 413–428.

Haushofer, Albrecht. *Pass-Staaten in den Alpen*. Berlin, 1928.

Hettner, Alfred. *Grundzüge der Länderkunde*. Leipzig, 1907–25. 2 vols.

Hogarth, D. G. *The Nearer East*. London, 1902.

Holdich, Sir Thomas. "Political Boundaries," in *Scottish Geographical Magazine*, xxxii (1916), pp. 497–507.

Huntington, Ellsworth. "The Vale of Kashmir," in *Bulletin of the American Geographical Society*, xxxviii (1906), pp. 657–682.

Keller, A. G. *Colonization*. Boston, 1908.

Little, A. J. *The Far East*. Oxford, 1905.

Lyde, L. W. *The Continent of Europe*, 2d ed. London, 1924.

Machatschek, Fritz. "Zur politischen Geographie der Schweiz," in *Geographischer Jahresbericht aus Österreich*, xiv–xv (1929), pp. 115–135.

Maull, Otto. *Die bayerische Alpengrenze*. Marburg, 1910. This, like the article by Penck, is detailed physical description of the character of the boundary. Maull's article is of little value to the theorist.

Newbigin, Marion Isabel. *Geographical Aspects of Balkan Problems*. London, 1915.

Newbigin, Marion Isabel. *The Mediterranean Lands*. London, 1924.

Newbigin, Marion Isabel. *Southern Europe*. London, 1932. Excellent.

Ogilvie, A. G. *Geography of the Central Andes*. New York, 1922.

Partsch, Josef. *Central Europe*. London, 1903. Important.

Peattie, Roderick. *New College Geography*. Boston, 1932.

Penck, Albrecht. "Die österreichische Alpengrenze," in *Zeitschrift der Gesellschaft für Erdkunde zu Berlin*, 1915, pp. 329–368.

"The Political Significance of Abyssinia," in *Geographical Review*, xiv (1924), pp. 147–148. An editorial note.

Ratzel, Friedrich. *Politische Geographie*, 3. Aufl. Munich, 1923.

Reclus, Élisée. *The History of a Mountain*, tr. from the French by Bertha Ness and John Lillie. London, 1881.

Ripley, W. Z. *The Races of Europe*. New York, 1899.

Rohe, Alice. "Our Littlest Ally," in *National Geographic Magazine*, xxxiv (1918), pp. 139–163.

Semple, Ellen Churchill. *The Geography of the Mediterranean Region*. New York, 1931.

Semple, Ellen Churchill. *Influences of Geographical Environment*. New York, 1911. Much information.

Sölch, Johann. "Die Ostalpen als geographischer Nachbar," in *Zeitschrift für Geopolitik*, viii (1931), pp. 287–295.

Tamaro, Attilio. *La Vénétie Julienne et la Dalmatie: Histoire de la nation Italienne sur ses frontières orientales*. Rome, 1918–19. 3 vols.

Tower, W. S. "The Andes as a Factor in South American Geography," in *Journal of Geography*, xv (1916), pp. 1–8.

Visher, S. S. "What Sort of International Boundary Is Best?" in *Journal of Geography*, xxxi (1932), pp. 288–296.

White, J. C. "Castles in the Air: Experiences and Journeys in Unknown Bhutan," in *National Geographic Magazine*, xxv (1914), pp. 365–455.

White, J. C. "Nepal: A Little-Known Kingdom," in *National Geographic Magazine*, xxxviii (1920), pp. 245–283.

Political Geography of the Pyrenees

Baring-Gould, Sabine. *A Book of the Pyrenees*. London, 1907.

Brutails, J. A. *La Coutume d'Andorre*. Paris, 1904. The monumental book on Andorra.

Carrier, Elsé Haydon. *Water and Grass*. London, 1932. Chap. xviii.

Cavaillès, Henri. "L'association pastorale dans les Pyrénées," in *Le musee social*, 1910, Mémoires et documents, pp. 45–80.

Cavaillès, Henri. "Une fédération pyrénéene sous l'ancien régime: Les traités de lies et de passeries," in *Revue historique*, cv (1910), pp. 1–34, 241–276.

Cavaillès, Henri. "Notes sur les syndicats de communes dans les vallées pyrénéennes," in *Bulletin du Comité des travaux historiques et scientifiques*, section des sciences économiques et sociales, Congrès des sociétés savantes de 1908, pp. 193–201.

Evans, E. E. "The Pyrenees: A Geographical Interpretation of their Rôle in Human Times," in *Studies in Regional Consciousness and Environment presented to H. J. Fleure*, ed. by I. C. Peate (Oxford, 1930), pp. 45–68.

Rios Urruti, Fernando de los. *Vida e Instituciones del Pueblo de Andorra: Una Supervivencia Señorial*. Madrid, 1920. An excellent book.

Whittlesey, Derwent. "Trans-Pyrenean Spain: The Vall d'Arán," in *Scottish Geographical Magazine*, xlix (1933), pp. 217–228.

South Tirol

The question of South Tirol, or Trentino, is one of such importance that this brief bibliography is here given. It was prepared by Dr. Benno Graf of Munich from the Volksbund für das Deutschtum im Ausland in a somewhat more complete form.

Dörrenhaus, Fritz. *Das deutsche Land an der Etsch*. 1933.

Fink, Hans. *Die Kirchenpatrozinien Tirols*. Passau, 1928.

Haspinger. *Wie Deutsch-Südtirol von den Italienern behandelt wird*. 1924.

Hennersdorf, F. K. *Südtirol unter italienischer Herrschaft*. Charlottenburg, 1928.

Mannhardt, J. W. *Südtirol: Ein Kampf um deutsche Volkheit*. Jena, 1928. Political.

Reut-Nicolussi, Eduard. *Tirol unterm Beil*. Munich, 1928. Political.

Rohmeder, Wilhelm. *Das Deutschtum in Südtirol*. Berlin, 1919 and 1932.

Stolz, Otto. *Die Ausbreitung des Deutschtums in Südtirol im Lichte der Urkunden*. Munich, 1927–34. 4 vols.

CHAPTER X

THE CHARACTER OF MOUNTAIN LIFE

MOUNTAINS are found in all latitudes and all climates, set down amidst civilizations ranging from the most primitive to the most advanced. It is therefore impossible to write in general terms upon the social qualities of mountaineers. And yet in order to complete this volume it would seem necessary to describe some types of social problems peculiar to the men of the mountains. Briefly, the social traits which may be ascribed to mountaineers the world over are perhaps three: conservatism, arising from provincialism, frugality accompanied by low standards of living, and an industry undaunted by an almost overwhelming load of toil.

MOUNTAIN CONSERVATISM: APPALACHIA

There is a biological law which points out that any life form, isolated and not fed by new environmental influences and not stimulated by breeding from life forms outside the province, will not alter to the same degree as similar life forms subjected to changing environments and breeding with new varieties. Likewise, customs and social attitudes in isolated mountain provinces with meager resources and few outside stimuli tend to crystallize. Mountain life is conservative. The Pyrenees, the Alps, and the Massif Central of France have contributed little directly to French civilization. The Appalachians, the Ozarks, and the Western Cordillera in the United States have made no progressive cultural contributions to American life. We find in the mountains of India the conservative temper in the most extreme form dominating the whole social structure. In Kashmir, in spite of its incorporation in the British empire, old ideas prevail to an extent which excludes new forms to a remarkable degree. Stein, an authority on the history of Kashmir, says the character of the masses of the people has changed but little for thirteen centuries. If this is true of the people of a great region like Kashmir, we may expect to find smaller and more isolated communities bound by tradition to a yet further extent.

Until the opening of the present century the mountain folk of the secluded valleys of the Pyrenees were traditionalists and hostile to innovations. This is less true of the valleys of the Alps, because they have been traversed by so many pilgrims and travelers passing between the northern countries and the Mediterranean world. But even within the Alps, out of the main lines of travel, certain separate valleys have maintained their conservative ways of life. The Val d'Anniviers, high in the Valais, and the Engadine, remote and mountain-rimmed, are examples to prove the point. Physical isolation and meager resources have kept certain valleys almost medieval in character. It is difficult to conceive of greater mountain isolation than is found in valleys tributary to the River Var in Provence. Three branches of this river are from basins isolated from the outside world by almost impassable gorges. Hence each valley has maintained a distinct social life. The Vésubie tributary valley is well enclosed, and is made terrible by overhanging cliffs, earthquakes, and landslides. So forbidding is the valley that it is much shunned. There are reports of wandering evil spirits who are reincarnated Moors. At intervals the valley has been purified by a sprinkling of holy water.

The difficulty of transportation in mountains isolates valleys from the stream of progress. This is true, likewise, of whole mountain masses in distinction to surrounding plains. Mountain masses are conservative to a degree of intensity directly proportional to the difficulties of inner transportation. The Aures Massif of Algeria is physically set off from the surrounding country and has primitive facilities for transportation. The native customs are peculiarly local. This is shown by the construction of houses, the methods of irrigation, and the games, these last being a relic of the worship of Athena. The Jurdes are a people living in a group of low mountains in Central Spain. Surrounded by progressive folk, the Jurdes are literally savages. This small enclave of barbarism amidst civilization is a startling example of unprogressiveness.

An American example of a mountain folk who suffer from isolation has been analyzed by John Wesley Coulter. The Santa Lucia Mountains lie along the coast of California south of Monterey. The mountaineers there are retarded economically by the ruggedness of the topography, the steep slopes, and the thin soils. Communication with the outside world has been limited. To reach markets with produce was almost prohibitively costly, and even where there was money the procuring of supplies was troublesome.

This mountain range is in line with the north-south communication through California, yet it has had no improved transportation. One town, Lucia, was 25 miles (40 kilometers) by difficult mountain trails from a road on the north and an equal distance to a roadway on the south. The railroad station for the district is 40 miles (64 kilometers) away. This mountain group has many peaks more than 900 meters high. One peak attains an elevation of 1782 meters. The difficulty of transportation lies in the narrow and steep-sided valleys and the poverty of passes. Lucia is indeed on the sea, but without adequate harbor.

The result is that stock raising is prevalent because the beasts can walk to market. The journey from the Lucia region to rails ordinarily takes four days. The meager forage and the rough terrain produce an inferior cattle. A recent development has been the raising of swine. The hogs are transported by boat. The loading is done by means of an aërial cable. So difficult are the trails leading to the sea that a drove of hogs will make no more than a mile an hour.

Supplies are brought to the region by launches that land on the beach. A trip to 'town' once a year is an event. An important occasion of a girl's life is that when she marries she is taken out of the mountains and given a ride in a wheeled vehicle. The coming of the mail carrier has more than usual interest. Education, religious development, and social intercourse correspond to the difficulty of transportation. A state highway is now being constructed along the mountain-sides bordering the coast. The cost of such a road in ten-mile sections varies from $21,400 to $86,200 a mile, but single miles in the worst locations may cost double the higher figure.

Conservatism and the crystallization of culture are nowhere more easily observed than in the little world of the Appalachians. The Appalachian mountains and plateaus were barriers to the expansion of the English colonists of the thirteen colonies. Gradually the tidewater zone and then the piedmont became populated. People began pushing through the mountain ranges. Some sought the mountain valleys by choice, while others, fatigued in their journey towards the Kentucky meadows, pushed no farther than the confused valleys of the plateau. Those who

went on and settled in the Blue Grass were distinguished in no
way from the men who remained in the valleys except in per-
severance and courage. Of those groups that cleared mountain
farms by choice some were Scotch-Irish from Ulster and some
Germans from the Rhenish Palatinate. Generally the settlers
were of Anglo-Saxon stock. The ways of living introduced at the
period of settlement have been altered by the local environment,
but they have not been affected by stimuli from the progressive
plains that flank the mountains. Nowhere in North America
have communities been left so to themselves. The farmers served
as blacksmith, gunsmith, carpenter, furniture-maker, and miller.
Doctoring was accomplished with local herbs, and dentistry with
a tool from the barn.

At the beginning of the twentieth century the farm had a degree of economic independence which was remarkable. The
cabin was of square hewn logs. The fireplace and chimney were
of stone and clay. Corn meal and home grown vegetables, pork
from the household pig, or squirrels shot in the woods constituted
the food. The furniture was homemade and woolen and cotton
cloth was homespun dyed with hickory. The household and impedimenta were colonial in character. The inhabitants have
been called our 'contemporary ancestors.'

It is in the characteristics of their mental culture that provincialism showed itself most strongly. In matters political the
point of view is always local. A national election arouses them
less than the choice of a local judge or sheriff. They have had no
political alliance with the plains people, and, indeed, during the
Civil War, they were opposed to slavery and secession. They
have been individualists with tendencies towards separation.
This is evidenced by the 'lost' State of Franklin which existed for
a brief interval in Eastern Tennessee.

Speech is the truest measure of the crystallization of culture.
The Appalachian mountaineers speak an Anglo-Saxon which is
as pure as exists today. Words obsolete in American diction are
plentiful. 'Holp' and 'holpen' for 'help' and 'helped' are ancient forms with an ancient ending. 'Poke' for 'bag' and 'buss'
for 'kiss' are seldom found elsewhere in America. Their language is at times almost Shakespearean. In their community
singings they still use old books with a form of musical notation
elsewhere passed into museums. The ballads are those of seven-
teenth-century England. Not so long ago a man was found

hunting rabbits with an old English crossbow. This ingrowing of culture is paralleled by the physical inbreeding. In a stretch of forty miles along the Kentucky River every family has the same surname.

Underlying the crystallization of culture, the individualism, and the almost complete isolation of these people is the mountainous terrain, the confusion of mature dissection of the plateau area, the lack of level land, the corridor valleys and passes, and the meager resources.

PHYSICAL FACTORS IN STANDARDS OF LIVING

Since we have made so many generalizations involving altitude, we might add yet one more. In this case the object is to demonstrate the second social trait of mountain life, frugality accompanied by low standards of living. Generally speaking, it is true that, in mountains of the temperate zones, the greater the altitude the lower the standard of living. This, of course, would not hold for elevations in the tropics. There has, indeed, been a serious suggestion that in Switzerland, in order that every one might have a proper minimum standard of living, those who live above a certain contour line have a subsidy, and that the subsidy be increased with altitude. This suggestion certainly supports the rather broad generalization which we have made.

Altitude decreases the materials of life. High villages, unless mining camps or tourist centers, are universally poor and primitive. The rude climate precludes gainful agriculture. The altitude implies expensive transportation. Within sight of plains civilizations are villages of meager and almost medieval culture. The mountain masses about the university towns of Grenoble hold wretched folk struggling almost with their bare hands against the catastrophic forces of nature. The shepherd in the Tirolean Alps, sleeping in a hut that is merely a crude pile of stones, looks down on the brilliantly lit towns of the Inn Valley. Families in the Swiss Alps may winter in the same room as the beasts, dependent upon them for warmth, and yet in the darkness of the brutish cave hear the shrill whistle of the Simplon Express rushing between Paris and Milan. Let us remember that Switzerland is the country of highly cultivated Geneva, Bern, and Zurich. Nowhere on the plains is there discoverable so rapid a gradient of culture.

The difficulty of transportation is, of course, a chief factor in the retarding of the upward advance of civilization. Literally thousands of towns in the mountains of Europe have not yet roadways. Twelve villages in Andorra are connected with the outside world, the doctor, and educational systems, by a single path. Even in the enlightened Swiss Alps people live part of the year in alp villages that are not always easily accessible, while the 'permanent' villages may be cut off by snows and avalanches in the winter. We have told elsewhere how the telephone and telegraph are the first means of communication to go out with the coming of winter, how the sick lack physicians and the dead are unburied.

The isolation is not merely a question of the difficulty of transportation. If the resources of the region are sufficiently great, a roadway or a railroad is built. Even regions of meager economy, as the remote and elevated high villages of the Oisans, are rapidly being reached by fine roads through the enlightened policy of the national governments. The nations which surround the Alps are projecting roads in the face of great difficulties, reaching the most remote communities with telegraph and postal systems, and sending out school teachers as missionaries. Nevertheless, the task is far from complete and the degree of success will always be relative. (Figures 64 and 65.)

Even roads, therefore, are not sufficient to bring in civilization if the resources are slight. A study was made by the writer of two neighboring villages in the Mediterranean Pyrenees of France. One, the village of Py, is connected with the outside world by a road. The elevation of the village is not great, 1000 meters, and the distance from the railway about 20 kilometers. The settlement has 1000 inhabitants. The other village is Mantet, reached best from Py by the Col de Mantet, 1765 meters. Py, then, lies in a different valley from Mantet. The latter village has no proper outside communication along its own valley, because the stream has cut so deep a gorge that even trail building is impracticable. There is no road to Mantet, only the rocky trail shown in Figure 63.

The irrigated hay fields of Py are not continuous with those of the lower valley because of a gorge. The village consists of crude unplastered houses. There are a well built school and a tiny town hall, both of modern construction. All other buildings are marked by their lack of mortar and few windows.

FIG. 63. THE ROAD TO MANTET, FRENCH PYRENEES
This is the route by which Mantet maintains communication with the
outside world.

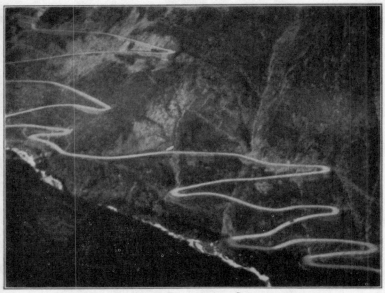

FIG. 64. ROAD ENGINEERING, SWITZERLAND
The modern roadway approaching the St. Gotthard Pass on the Italian side.
(Courtesy of Ginn and Company, *New College Geography*.)

Though the valley bottoms hold the necessary vegetable patches, the better lands are given over to irrigated hay fields. Grain is grown on terraces high on the mountains where the hours of sunlight are longer. The grain is chiefly rye; the people eat black bread. A little wheat is produced, and also maize, which is cut green for fodder. The scarcity of grain means little straw, and the cattle are dirty because of the lack of litter for bedding. The highest wheat field discovered was at 1204 meters, but rye was found at 1700 meters. In the upper levels are straw-thatched barns for the hay and grain harvest. The money crop is meat, produced from beasts that are pastured above the tree zone from June 1 to October 15.

Mantet consists of several score houses, built of rough field stone. The houses are ill kept and everywhere there are signs of decay. Manure piles, of several years' accumulation, lie in the irregular streets. The air during the writer's visit was full of dust from the dirty streets, and most of the people had diseased eyes. A quick survey indicated the majority of the inhabitants to be of subnormal mentality. Imbeciles were not lacking. There was a school, but little evidence of education. The church was in need of repair and without a regular priest. Outside of the church, a forgotten symbol, and the school, there was no apparent social or economic organization to the village: no store, no inn. One girl in the village looked clean and had some bright color to her dress. Was she a visitor? The agriculture was the most primitive that the writer discovered in the Pyrenees. Here altitude, isolation, rocky gorge, and rocky trail had completely defeated progress in human development. It was difficult to conceive of the settlement with its decadent culture as a part of enlightened France.

This brief description of Mantet is an example of low standards of living among mountains. It is not typical. Most mountain villages in Western Europe have the advantages of good roads, fine schools, religious leadership, and an active commercial connection with the main valley or lowland. The amount of electrification in mountain villages is a happy surprise. The Alps, be they French, Italian, Swiss, or Austrian, are provided with inns serving a fastidious tourist trade. The tourist industry has penetrated to many of the more isolated settlements because of the search for solitary beauty and for the quaintness which goes with isolation. Indeed, one's sense of proportion is strained when, as an Alpinist visiting the Alps, one discovers how many peaks may be mounted comfortably in a funicular or cable railway. There is a luxurious hotel near the summit of the Zugspitze. One can dine well in a modern building at the Jungfraujoch overlooking the source of the Aletsch glacier. St. Moritz, one of the highest inhabited towns of the Alps, is glittering and sophisticated.

The most important breaking down of mountain provincialisms is along pass routes. The great routes through the Alps are modernized to serve the worldly tastes of the travelers. Because the history of travel through passes is the story of plainsmen, it hardly deserves a place in a volume devoted to mountains and mountain folk. Indeed the subject is worthy a volume by itself. A brief bibliography of this interesting subject is given at the end of the chapter.

Seasons in the Alps

The third social trait of mountaineers is, in the case of truly alpine mountains, industry in conflict with almost overwhelming toil. Part of the excessive labor is a consequence of the meager resources, but some of it arises from the nomadic movements, in part pastoral and in part agricultural, which carry the weary population up and down the slopes. We can best approach a conception of labor in mountains by considering seasonal work in the Alps. We do this in spite of the fact that one has little right to make a general description of life in so long and varied a mountain range. Many purely local cultures are found there, differentiated by topography, climate, and custom.

At the southern end, in the Alpes-Maritimes of Provence and Nice, we have the home of the goatherd. The town of his origin is a fortified village, perched on the rocks, still with legends of Saracen raids. With his goats the herder spends the day among the thyme moorlands, returning at night to the village, where each beast is milked in the stable of the owner. At the Tirolean end of the Alps there is an idyllic picture, now all but gone. This is of the girl who watches the cattle on a lonely but serene alpland, above the village and above the tree line. For weeks she is alone with her beasts, the flowers of the meadows, and the circle of clear-cut peaks, alone except for Sunday visits of her lover.

For a typical dairy scene let us return to a more central location, Switzerland. The scene, a busy one, is of some five or more men engaged with the cattle. The leader of the group is a cheese maker, upon whose skill much of the reputation of the valley rests. He will be assisted by several herders and milkers. There is one man whose task it is to supply wood for the boiling of the milk, and another worker may care for the alp itself, clearing it of obnoxious weeds and building barriers in the gullies to prevent erosion. If there is a wagon or sled road leading to the valley, the animals may be corraled at night and the manure thus collected for transportation to the fields. In any case, by trail or road, supplies must be taken up to the men, and the cheeses carried valley-ward. There is a variety of wood or wicker burden frames which are attached to the backs of the men who perform this transport duty.

The alp pastures are reached in early spring. Here it is that the herdsmen's life begins in earnest. A cluster of small stone huts marks the first stage of the nomadism. The most commodious one is selected by the chief herdsman and his helpers. The others are shelters for the cattle and perhaps a special hut for the calving cow. The chief hut usually has one living room and a milk room. At one side of the living quarters hay is spread upon the floor for a couch. The herdsmen arise shortly after dawn. As the distant church bells ring, they say a short morning prayer upon their rosaries. The cows are allowed to graze in the early morning while the herdsmen proceed to the cheese making. The best cheese is made from milk fresh from the cow.

The cattle may be taken back into the stables when the heat from the midday sun becomes too strong. The herdsmen eat their dinner and lie down for a rest. Towards evening, when the mountain air is again cool, the cattle are released, the wood is collected, the water for the next day is brought, evening prayers are said, and thus another day has passed.

In the meantime the rest of the population is busy about the labor of the valley farm. Mountain labor is hard, and mountain livings are meager. There is little level land, and soil may be thin on slopes. A score of different catastrophes may overtake the crop and even the field. The mountain earth itself, as a land-slip or a torrent, may overwhelm the crop, road, or village. Mountain weather in its extremes is destructive. Peasants have been known to keep the grain of a successful harvest for four or five years for fear of starvation. The higher the village the more work necessary to maintain life, for communications are maintained with difficulty, travel is arduous, freightage is expensive, the winter period is longer, the fields small, and on precarious slopes catastrophes are frequent. It is the burden of labor in the mountain village which explains why so many avail themselves of the first opportunity of emigration to the plains.

The communication trails between the high regions and the valley village are by their necessary and frequent repairs a considerable burden upon the commune. But the true labor of the trails is the frequent passage, the back-breaking trips up the mountain and the tedious descents. The high field may be one and two hours' climb from the village. Up this slope, men, women, and children toil with deep manure baskets on their backs. Down the trail the rye is carried in sheaves upon the head (Figures 62). The potato fields of the Spanish Sierra Nevada are three and four hours up the trail from the villages (Figure 61), and the chestnut zone an hour's climb. Peasants in the Pyrenees climb three hours to reach alps (*jasses*) where they find a plant good for salads. The weekly journey of a purveyor from village to summer alp is not infrequently an all-day trip.

Perhaps no form of agriculture is more laborious than terrace tillage (Figure 49). The building of the terraces and their repair, the control of rainwater and irrigation, the fertilizing of the fields and the harvest, call for labor which may leave the peasant with a damaged heart and certainly a bent back. Terraces lose soil by washing. This dirt must be carried back 'up the steps.'

The higher the village the more desperate the agriculture, and the greater the attention and area given to hay. In these high altitudes crops will not mature. This is true especially on shady slopes. But in many easily accessible valleys there may be, and often are, areas so isolated as not only to be prohibitive to tillage, but impossible to be reached by beasts without travel on dangerous trails. Thus the village of Saint-Martin-de-la-Porte (Maurienne), at 820 meters, has hay meadows in the Col des Encombres at 2300 meters. The difference in elevation is 1680 meters or 5600 feet. Down steep mountain trails perhaps but one load of 100 kilograms represents a day's work, and it is good fortune if one is not caught on the way by a thunder-shower. Between Châteauroux in Embrunais and certain hay fields mules will make two trips a day, bringing 50 to 60 kilograms a trip. The day starts at midnight and ends at 8 in the evening. Many

Fig. 65. Transportation in the Albula Pass Region, Switzerland

The electric train is shown entering a tunnel. Open fence construction protects the railway from snow. A slide is shown by which avalanches are carried over the track. A highway has been constructed with difficulty, as also two wire lines. (Courtesy of the Rhaetischebahn.)

hay fields are perched so dangerously that there are communal regulations to guard the lives of hay gatherers.

The bringing of the hay to the valley stable presents a problem (Figure 62). Remarkable loads are carried down the slopes on frames set on men's backs. Another worker helps the burden bearer stagger to his feet with the excessive load. The bearer then clambers down a half hour's descent to the village. A horse may bear a load on a frame, the hay all but hiding the beast. Aërial cables are used in many places. Some in the valley of Naves are described in an earlier chapter. In the villages above Chur, in the Grisons, sleds bring hay in autumn down slopes impassable for carts. In the Val d'Anniviers, as elsewhere, sleds bring hay down in winter. Haying occupies most of the summer.

In September the herdsmen begin their descent from the alp pastures with their herds. The people in the valleys ascend the mountains to the village on the *mayen* alp at the same time. When the entire village is again united there is a joyful celebration marked by dancing, drinking, and feasting. A hay crop is harvested from fields about the 'temporary' village, as are also the vegetables that were planted when the alp-drive started in May. The work here completed, the entire group move downward to spend the winter in the valley.

With the coming of the heavy snows, the cattle are put in the barns and not taken out again until spring. The cold is so intense that the houses and barns are almost hermetically sealed. Because of this enforced imprisonment, fuel and food must be stored in sufficient quantities in the autumn to last through the winter. It is this period of confinement that creates the lace-making, wood-carving, watch-making industries of some parts of the Alps. Not everywhere, however, is the confinement of the same degree. In the Fore-Alps winter does not preclude out-of-door work. There is hay to be transported, manure to be spread upon the fields, and wood to cut. The women will wash clothes by a hole in the ice at sub-zero temperatures. The higher the village the longer the duration of the snow. In turn, then, the longer the period of stable feeding and the greater the area of mown grass. The higher the village, the greater the number of hay barns, and the steeper the pitch of the roof in order to be rid of snow.

The confinement of winter is oppressive in a degree to be measured by the joy expressed by the spring liberation. The high insolation and the warmth, once the snow has left and no longer chills the air, are particularly delightful. The valley town may be in the shadow of the mountain so that the south-facing alp first loses its snow cover. Eager flowers literally push up through the snow. Schools are dismissed so that the children may play among the spring flowers. The first influx of visitors begins, coming to look upon the fields of narcissus. Soon the surge of life is felt throughout the valley. The mountainward migration is about to begin. Though today much of the picturesqueness has given way to the modern spirit, the customs of the past are still found in certain isolated villages. The herds are assembled in a large procession, each one preceded by a herdsman and a flock of goats. The herdsman may wear a white shirt with sleeves rolled to the elbows, a pair of broad leather suspenders decorated with figures of cows and goats shaped from bright metal, a scarlet waistcoat, knee trousers of yellow cloth, white stockings, low shoes, and a round black hat of felt or leather bound with a wreath of artificial roses. The main body of cattle is kept in line by a herdboy. Even the cows, wearing wreaths, are eager to be off. Each file of herds may be followed by a wagon or pack train, containing a great copper cheese-kettle and wooden utensils for milk and butter. The procession moves along the road while great bells clang. At the entrance to every inn, the landlord issues forth with decanter of wine and glasses to serve the herdsmen. Many times the majority of the population of the valley villages accompany the herdsmen and herds to the middle pastures or *mayens*. The first hay crop is gathered. Vegetables are planted in well manured fields. The children play in the warm sunshine. There is much activity; everybody is busy. Soon the cows begin to mount to higher pastures and the sheep leave for the very highest areas. The rhythm of life recommences.

THE TENOR OF ANDORRAN LIFE

Lastly, by way of conclusion, let us consider Andorra as a mountain province, illustrating at once conservatism, low standards of living, and hard labor. Withal we hope to reveal a simplicity of life and a beauty that many a poet has felt the lack of words to express.

Andorra is alternate savage gorge and open valley. It has nothing of the complacency of the *gaves* of the Central Pyrenees.

Its mountains are gaunt things. Talus and glacial chaos impend above the fields and threaten the villages. Nature here is catastrophic. It is a land of sheer cliffs that cast deep blue shadows over cold canyons, while far above, amid pink and purple mountains veiled with the green of conifers, are forested valleys. Here echo cascades of limpid water, ideal haunts for the fisherman. Yet higher are rocky cirques with deep blue lakes, or the dreary moors that pasture sheep.

It is a dramatic little land, romantic and tragic. One feels it in the solemnity of the native. It is a land of toil. The casual traveler sees only the fertile valleys. But high on the mountains are pitiful patches of rye which give but meager returns. Even in the valley bottoms there is scarcely enough sun to cure the hay. Above the zone of desperate agriculture are the desolate pastures, where the life of the shepherd is indescribably lonely.

Villages such as Sant Julia, Andorra la Vieja, and Escaldes are in fine valleys, on a highway, and have a brisk trade. But visit Pal, hours from the road; Arinsal, at the foot of a mountain cirque; and Lo Serrat, most distant of Andorran hamlets. On the plea of thirst I entered one home in Arinsal. The way in was through the pig sty, for the pigs held the ground floor. Above, the long living room was blackened by the pine torches used for lighting. Tiny windows let in such light as the darkling sky gave forth. The floor was littered with bean vines that were to be picked over in the evening. The baby in the cradle cried because of the flies that crawled over its face. The pigs could be seen, heard, and smelled through the wide cracks of the floor. Outside, the stream and canyon wind roared in competition.

But Andorra has likewise its charm. Every turn of the road brings scenes that delight the traveler. The first things that made me feel that I truly had found a national individuality characteristic of the region were the old bridges. Slender, long, graceful arches made of cobbles or split stone, half their charm lies in their lack of symmetry and in their imperfection. The villages of dark-brown cobbles are more charming for the long green and brown streamers of drying tobacco leaves that hang from the windows or that fill the open shed on the house-top. The Andorran loves his balcony, and whether with wooden railing or simple iron work, it is a delight. Commonly the street between the houses is so narrow that a single horse, laden with brushwood from the mountains or with hay from the fields, entirely blocks the passage. The tobacco comes to the shed suspended in hammocks on the sides of a horse, or its green leaves fill a two-wheeled cart drawn by oxen.

Let us attend a fête in the village of Ordino. Picture a village square, the church, the stone steps, the little alleyways leading off between the houses, the garlanded cross, the flowing fountain, and every window and balcony filled with onlookers. On a platform are the six Spanish musicians with horns. All about are the cliffs and dark forest, and above, a deep blue sky. As the music starts each girl walks to the stone bench, where, sitting in a row, the belles are to wait till the swain approaches and nonchalantly beckons one of them. The dance is quite à la mode except that there is a leaning towards the polka. Alas, the days have passed when a gallant wore knee-breeches and a scarlet *fache* and *béret*, and the lady had a lace head-dress, a low bodice, and a flowing skirt short enough to show her fine petticoat. Now the dance is modern enough, though done quite solemnly.

Let me paint as best I can an evening in a little *fonda* far from the highway.[1] Picture yourself sitting before a hearth which is overhung by its great mantel, blackened with smoke. On a crane over the fire hangs the pot in which our supper, a rabbit, is boiling. A man tired with the mountain trail is sleeping, his head in his arms upon the table. Other men drop in for a bit of cheer. Outside, the mountain reflects the last rays of the sun. Finally darkness. Within we have our fire and the light reflected from the copper pots that hang in a row on the wall.

From a vantage on a mountain spur the canyon-like valley could be surveyed. I saw a bent man following the plow slowly dragged by oxen. The field in the valley, chilled by drainage of cold air and refrigerated by an icy stream, required thirteen months to produce a rye crop. This was an October evening and the field was being plowed for an autumnal sowing. The shadow of the mountain came down over field and farmer. The valley became deep purple in color, and cold. In the dim light, the man, crippled by labor in these mountains which impended above him, followed the plow. Valleys literally hide their inhabitants. Mountain shadows chill the hearth stone.

I think my favorite spot in Andorra is in the village of Engordany. The houses of the village cluster on a hillside at the end of a valley. And though I know and love the spot at all hours of the

---

[1] The reader will kindly permit the first person for the sake of directness.

day, it is at dusk that I love it best. Then the rush of the waters in the stream seems most lovely. Then the valley lands are deepest green. The jagged Sierra d'Enclar is a deep purple against a fading sky. One single light shows the location of Andorra la Vieja at the foot of its mountain. Far down the valley, just over the Sierra de Leix, rises a star. The peasants pass before me, saluting me with Catalan salutations or with the deep-toned *Buenas tardes*. Here comes the bulk of a donkey all but buried in the hay it carries, the haying party shuffling along behind. From the other direction comes a little herd of sheep following the shepherd, who whistles encouragingly to them. Then the priest passes. A girl comes along with her pigs from their day's grubbing on the mountain. All of the little world passes before me in the growing darkness. Twilight has gone. Night has arrived. In the heavens the lesser stars are come forth. One then takes the road that passes the stone bridge to the cheer of the inn.

Man has modified the face of the mountains by stupendous labor, but the great earth masses that all but blot out the stars of night, and by day limit the sunshine which may penetrate to the fields in the canyons, condition, and always will condition, man's activities.

BIBLIOGRAPHICAL NOTES

The Appalachian Mountaineers

Brigham, A. P. "The Appalachian Valley," in *Scottish Geographical Magazine*, xl (1924), pp. 218–230.

Campbell, J. C. *The Southern Highlander and his Homeland*. New York, 1921.

Davis, D. H. "The Changing Role of the Kentucky Mountains and the Passing of the Kentucky Mountaineer," in *Journal of Geography*, xxiv (1925), pp. 41–52.

Davis, D. H. *The Geography of the Mountains of Eastern Kentucky*. Frankfort, Ky., 1924. (Kentucky Geological Survey, *Geologic Reports*, series vi, xviii.)

Davis, D. H. "A Study of the Succession of Human Activities in the Kentucky Mountains," in *Journal of Geography*, xxix (1930), pp. 85–100.

Hollander, A. N. J. den. "Über die Bevölkerung der Appalachen," in *Zeitschrift der Gesellschaft für Erdkunde zu Berlin*, 1934, Heft 7–8, pp. 241–255. With a bibliography.

Kephart, Horace. *Our Southern Highlanders.* New York, 1913. An authority.

Mason, R. L. *The Lure of the Great Smokies.* Boston, 1927.

McClarty, Julia. "Economic Opportunities in the Southern Appalachians," in *Journal of Geography,* xx (1921), pp. 96–104.

Morley, Margaret Warner. *The Carolina Mountains.* Boston, 1913.

Schockel, B. H. "Changing Conditions in the Kentucky Mountains," in *Scientific Monthly,* iii (1916), pp. 105–131.

Semple, Ellen Churchill. "The Anglo-Saxons of the Kentucky Mountains," in *Bulletin of the American Geographical Society,* xlii (1910), pp. 561–594.

Spaulding, A. W. *The Men of the Mountains.* Nashville, 1915.

Mountain Passes: Together with Characteristic References on Mountain Railway Construction

The subject of mountain passes is an interesting one which is connected with that of mountain isolation. However, passes are more important to extramontane areas than to the mountain regions which they traverse. The Brenner, St. Gotthard, and Mt. Cenis passes have been more significant to Venice, Milan, and Genoa, to Lyons, Augsburg, and Innsbruck, than to the mountain regions. Only occasionally has a mountain city like Chur (Coire) been greatly influenced by travel across the passes. In this volume, which is devoted to the mountain areas rather than to the influence of mountains on remote areas, the subject can be given little place. A bibliography is here given for those who wish to pursue the subject.

Allix, André. "Le trafic en Dauphiné à la fin du Moyen-Âge," in *Revue de géographie alpine,* xi (1923), pp. 373–420.

Arbos, Philippe. "Les communications dans les Alpes françaises," in *Annales de géographie,* xxviii (1919), pp. 161–176.

Blanchard, Marcel. *Les routes des Alpes occidentales a l'époque napoléonienne* (1796–1815). Grenoble, 1920.

Blanchard, Raoul. "Le réseau ferré des Alpes françaises," in *Recueil des travaux offert à M. Jovan Cvijić* (Belgrade, 1924), pp. 233–240. A good example of mountain railway geography.

Blanchard, Raoul. "Les zones d'équidistance des voies ferrées dans les Alpes françaises," in *Revue de géographie alpine,* xii (1924), pp. 79–97.

Bonney, T. G. *The Alpine Regions of Switzerland and the Neighbouring Countries.* Cambridge, England, 1868.

Bonney, T. G. "The Alps from 1856 to 1865," in *Alpine Journal,* xxxi (1917), pp. 16–34.

Chabot, Georges. "Les percées des Vosges," in *Annales de géographie,* xxix (1920), pp. 376–378.

Dainelli, Giotto. "Italia Pass in the Eastern Karakoram," in *Geographi-*

cal Review, xxii (1932), pp. 392–402. No attention in this present volume has been paid to Alpinism. Here is a splendid example which at once describes a high pass and the rigors of mountain climbing.

Featherstone, B. K. *An Unexplored Pass: A Narrative of a Thousand-Mile Journey to the Kara-Koram Himalayas.* London, 1926. Material on heights of habitation and culture of Tibet.

Flückiger, Otto. "Pässe und Grenzen," in *Mitteilungen der Geographisch-Ethnographischen Gesellschaft in Zürich*, xxvii–xxviii (1926–28), pp. 36–65. Very important.

Freshfield, D. W. "The Great Passes of the Western and Central Alps," in *Geographical Journal*, xlix (1917), pp. 2–26.

George, H. B. *The Relations of Geography and History*, 4th ed. Oxford, 1910. Chap. xiv, "The Alpine Passes and their History."

Girardin, Paul. "Les bassins fermés des Alpes suisses," in *Bulletin de la Société Fribourgeoise des sciences naturelles*, xxii (1914), p. 15.

Johnson, D. W. "How Rivers cut Gateways through Mountains," in *Scientific Monthly*, xxxviii (1934), pp. 129–135.

Langwill, Minnie J. "Historic Mountain-Passes of the World," in *Journal of Geography*, xii (1913–14), pp. 193–197.

Montzka, H. "Die Mittenwaldbahn," in *Deutsche Rundschau für Geographie*, xxxiv (1912), pp. 428–434. An example of the difficulty of railway building in mountains.

Onde, H. "La route de Maurienne et du Cenis de la fin du XVIIIᵉ au milieu du XIXᵉ siècle," in *Revue de géographie alpine*, xx (1932), pp. 701–775.

Palmer, A. H. "Snow and Railway Transportation," in *Monthly Weather Review*, xlvii (1917), pp. 698–699.

Preller, C. D. R. "Hannibal's Passage of the Alps," in *Scottish Geographical Magazine*, xlii (1926), pp. 350–359.

Sargent, A. J. "Alpine Railways and International Commerce," in *Geographical Journal*, xxv (1905), pp. 654–658.

Scheffel, P. H. *Verkehrsgeschichte der Alpen.* Berlin, 1908–14. 2 vols. A history of Alpine commerce. There are numerous books and articles on this subject.

Semple, Ellen Churchill. *Influences of Geographic Environment.* New York, 1911. Chap. xv.

Semple, Ellen Churchill. "Mountain Passes: A Study in Anthropogeography," in *Bulletin of the American Geographical Society*, xxxiii (1901), pp. 124–137, 191–203.

Sölch, Johann. *Studien über Gebirgspässe.* Stuttgart, 1908. (*Forschungen zur deutscher Landes- und Volkskunde*, xvii, 2.) The authoritative German work.

Tyler, J. E. *The Alpine Passes: The Middle Ages* (962–1250). Oxford, 1930. An excellent history. Especially recommended.

Ver Steeg, Karl. "Wind Gaps and Water Gaps of the Northern Appalachians," in *Annals of the New York Academy of Sciences*, xxxii (1930), pp. 87–220.

Some References on the Quality of Mountain Life

Baillie-Grohman, W. A. *Tyrol and the Tyrolese*. Leipzig, 1877.

Baud-Bovy, Daniel. *Peasant Art in Switzerland*, tr. by Arthur Palliser. London, 1924. A magnificent book.

Belloc, Hilaire. *The Pyrenees*. London, 1909. A pleasing writer.

Coulter, J. W. "Lucia: An Isolated Mountain District in California," in *Bulletin of the Geographical Society of Philadelphia*, xxix (1931), pp. 183–198. An example of surprising isolation in America.

Cowan, A. R. *Master-Clues in World-History*. London, 1914. Chap. viii.

Demarez, R. "Les modes de vie dans les montagnes de l'Indo-Chine française," in *Recueil des travaux de l'Institut de géographie alpine*, vii (1919), pp. 453–561.

Hilton-Simpson, M. W. "The Influence of its Geography on the People of the Aures Massif, Algeria," in *Geographical Journal*, lix (1922), pp. 19–36.

Lane, Rose Wilder. *The Peaks of Shala*. London, 1922. Isolation in Albania.

Legendre, Maurice. *Las Jurdes*. Bordeaux, etc., 1927. (*Bibliothèque de l'Ecole des hautes études hispaniques*, fasc. xiii.) Reviewed by Raoul Blanchard in *Revue de géographie alpine*, xvi (1928), pp. 545–551. A primitive culture.

Martonne, Emmanuel de. "Quelques données nouvelles sur la jeunesse du relief préglaciaire dans les Alpes," in *Recueil de travaux offert à M. Jovan Cvijić* (Belgrade, 1924), pp. 121–140. Includes physical isolation of valleys of the Var drainage system.

Meylan, René. "La vallée de Joux: Les conditions de vie dans un haut bassin fermé du Jura," in *Bulletin de la Société neuchâteloise de géographie*, xxxviii (1929), pp. 45–179. Social isolation.

Miller, Mrs. Anna C. (Johnson). *The Cottages of the Alps*. New York, 1860. Good.

Oakley, Amy. *Hill-Towns of the Pyrenees*. New York, 1923.

Peattie, Roderick. *New College Geography*. Boston, 1932. Chaps. xxi and xxii.

Peattie, Roderick. "Wanderungen in Andorra," in *Der Erdball*, iv (1930), pp. 287–290.

Peattie, Roderick. "Catalan France and the Canigou," in *Ohio Social Science Journal*, i (1929), pp. 36–43.

Rawnsley, H. D. *Flower-time in the Oberland*. Glasgow, 1904.

Rey, Maurice. "La limite géographique de l'habitat perché dans les

Alpes françaises," in *Revue de géographie alpine*, xvii (1929), pp. 5–39. Relationship between nomadism and the village type.

Robert, Jean. "Un type de cohabitation avec les animaux," in *Revue de géographie alpine*, xxi (1933), pp. 819–829. Primitive pastoral life.

Rock, J. F. "Seeking the Mountains of Mystery," in *National Geographic Magazine*, lvii (1930), pp. 131–185. Remoteness in China.

Semple, Ellen Churchill. *Influences of Geographic Environment*. New York, 1911.

Slovene Studies, by members of the Le Play Society, ed. by L. D. Stamp. London, 1933. Excellent.

Sölch, J. "Raum und Gesellschaft in den Alpen," in *Geographische Zeitschrift*, xxxvii (1931), pp. 143–168. Philosophical.

Stephen, Leslie. *The Playground of Europe*. London, 1871; new ed., 1894. A famous book on Switzerland.

Story, A. T. *Swiss Life in Town and Country*. London, 1902. Informative.

Tissot, Victor. *Unknown Switzerland*, tr. by Mrs. Wilson. New York, 1889.

Webb, Frank. *Switzerland of the Swiss*. London, 1909.

Wilstach, Paul. *Along the Pyrenees*. Indianapolis, 1925.

APPENDICES

APPENDIX A

THE METRIC SYSTEM

WE are not so much inclined to apologize for using the metric system as to regret that we as Americans are not more thoroughly acquainted with it. As most of the material of this study, of an exact sort, comes from French, German, and Italian sources and is in the metric system, it is important that the metric system be here used. To convert these figures into the systems used in America would be to risk accuracy. In some cases, on the other hand, data of the English system are converted to the metric. Where this has not been done, the reasons will be obvious. The conversion of feet to meters has been accomplished by the multiplier 0.305. Miles have been multiplied by 1.6 in the conversion to kilometers. Simple rules for converting meters to feet and kilometers to miles are given. If these are memorized the reader can convert to the English system subconsciously while reading.

For Heights

If meters are divided by 3 and the decimal shifted one point to the right, the height in feet is obtained within a certain limit of error. The exact constant of the error is 1.6 feet too much for every 100 feet. Thus, if an elevation stands at 3048 meters, one divides by 3 and adds a zero, giving 10,160 feet. After applying the correct elevation, it is represented as 10,000 feet. It is not always easy to compute the amount of error. This may be put in a formula: cut off the last three figures, multiply by four, multiply again by four, and subtract from the first rough calculation.

Thus an elevation stands at 2403 meters.

$$3 \mid \underline{2403} \qquad 8 \times 4 \text{ is } 32 \qquad 32 \times 4 \text{ is } 128 \qquad \begin{array}{r} 8010 \\ \underline{128} \\ 7882 \end{array}$$
$$ 801 \text{ (o)}$$

This is within 20 inches of the truth. The exact height of the elevation in English feet is 7883.7624 feet. This is obtained by multiplying 2403 by 3.2808992.

For Distances

One divides kilometers by 8 and multiplies by 5. The result would be correct if the kilometer were equal to 3300 feet. The fact that in reality it is approximately 3281 feet indicates the limits of error.

For Climatic Data

In converting pressure and precipitation data the following formulas are sufficiently accurate:

$$10 \text{ mm.} = 0.394 \text{ inches}$$
$$1 \text{ inch} = 25.40 \text{ mm.}$$

The conversion formula for Centigrade (C) to Fahrenheit (F) is
$$\frac{C}{5} = \frac{F - 32}{9}.$$

In practice the following table has been used:

CONVERSION TABLE FOR TEMPERATURE

°C	°F	°C	°F
−22	−7.60	6	42.80
−21	−5.80	7	44.60
−20	−4.00	8	46.40
−19	−2.20	9	48.20
−18	−0.40	10	50.00
−17	1.40 Plus	11	51.80
−16	3.20	12	53.60
−15	5.00	13	55.40
−14	6.80	14	57.20
−13	8.60	15	59.00
−12	10.40	16	60.80
−11	12.20	17	62.60
−10	14.00	18	64.40
− 9	15.80	19	66.20
− 8	17.60	20	68.00
− 7	19.40	21	69.80
− 6	21.20	22	71.60
− 5	23.00	23	73.40
− 4	24.80	24	75.20
− 3	26.60	25	77.00
− 2	28.40	26	78.80
− 1	30.20	27	80.60
− 0	32.00	28	82.40
+ 1	33.80	29	84.20
2	35.60	30	86.00
3	37.40	31	87.80
4	39.20	32	89.60
5	41.00	33	91.40

APPENDIX B

BIBLIOGRAPHICAL NOTES ON THE GEOMORPHOLOGY OF MOUNTAINS

The Origin of Mountains

The treatises named below are selected as characteristic of this field of knowledge. Some are reviews, while others are recent contributions to theory.

Bonney, T. G. *The Building of the Alps.* London, 1912.

Bonney, T. G. *Volcanoes: Their Structure and Significance.* London, 1899.

Bowie, William. *Isostasy.* New York, 1927. An authority.

Bowie, William. "Proposed Theory in Harmony with Isostasy to Account for Major Changes in the Elevation of the Earth's Crust," in *Beiträge zur Geophysik*, xv (1926), pp. 103–115.

Chamberlin, R. T. "The Building of the Colorado Rockies," in *Journal of Geology*, xxvii (1919), pp. 145–164, 225–251.

Chamberlin, R. T. "On the Crustal Shortening of the Colorado Rockies," in *American Journal of Science*, 5th ser., vi (1923), pp. 215–221.

Chamberlin, R. T. "Vulcanism and Mountain-Making," in *Journal of Geology*, xxix (1921), pp. 166–172.

Collet, L. W. *The Structure of the Alps.* London, 1927.

Daly, R. A. *Our Mobile Earth.* New York, 1926. Excellent.

Dana, J. D. "On the Origin of Mountains," in *American Journal of Science*, 3d ser., v (1873), pp. 347–350.

Geikie, James. "The Architecture and Origin of the Alps," in *Scottish Geographical Magazine*, xxvii (1911), pp. 393–417.

Geikie, James. *Mountains: Their Origin, Growth, and Decay.* Edinburgh, 1913.

Hobbs, W. H. *Earth Features and their Meaning.* 2d ed. New York, 1931. Chap. xxxi.

Joly, John. *The Surface-History of the Earth.* Oxford, 1925. Chap. vii.

Kober, Leopold. *Der Bau der Erde.* Berlin, 1921.

Nevin, Charles M. *Principles of Structural Geology.* New York, 1931. Chap. xi; see also index. Recent and unusually clear.

Reid, H. F. "Isostasy and Mountain Ranges," in *Bulletin of the American Geographical Society*, xliv (1912), pp. 354–360.

Salisbury, R. D. *Physiography*, 3d ed. New York, 1919. Pp. 377–388. A genetic classification.

Shepard, F. P. "Isostasy as a Result of Earth Shrinkage," in *Journal of Geology*, xxxi (1923), pp. 208–216.

Staub, Rudolf. *Der Bewegungsmechanismus de Erde*. Berlin, 1928. Late German philosophy.

Suess, Eduard. *Das Antlitz der Erde*. Prague, etc., 1883–1904. 3 vols. English translation by Hertha B. C. Sollas, *The Face of the Earth*. Oxford, 1904–09, 4 vols. The best review of the mountain systems of the earth.

Swanson, C. O. "Isostasy and Mountain Building," in *Journal of Geology*, xxxvi (1928), pp. 411–433.

Relief Energy

Relief energy represents a new point of view. It deserves further study.

Glock, W. S. "Available Relief as a Factor of Control in the Profile of a Land Form," in *Journal of Geology*, xl (1932), pp. 74–83. Some basic considerations.

Johnson, D. W. "Available Relief and Texture of Topography," in *Journal of Geology*, xli (1933), pp. 293–305. A reply to Glock.

Krebs, Norbert. "Eine Karte der Reliefenergie: Süddeutschlands," in *Petermanns Mitteilungen*, lxviii (1922), pp. 49–53, with map.

Krebs, Norbert. *Die Ostalpen und das heutige Österreich*. Stuttgart, 1928. 2 vols. Vol. i, pp. 44–46, chart opposite p. 40.

Ochocka, Janina. "Krajobruz Polski e Šivretle mapy Wysokości Wzgleclnych" (Map of Relative Relief of Poland), in *Prace Geograficzne wydawane Przez Eugenjusza Romera*, zeszyt xiii (1925). A geographical treatise under the direction of Eugene Romer. A summary in French accompanies the article. It has the most exact form of the cartography of relief.

Partsch, Josef. *Schlesien, eine Landeskunde für das deutsche Volk*. Breslau, 1896–1911. 2 vols. Vol. ii, chart facing p. 586.

Rich, J. L. "A Graphical Method of Determining the Average Inclination of a Land Surface from a Contour Map," in *Transactions of the Illinois State Academy of Science*, ix (1916), pp. 195–199.

Schrepfer, Hans, and Kallner, Horst. "Die maximale Reliefenergie Westdeutschlands," in *Petermanns Mitteilungen*, lxxvi (1930), pp. 225–227. Has three references not in this list.

Smith, G. H. "The Relative Relief of Ohio," in *Geographical Review*, xxv (1935), pp. 272–284.

Wentworth, C. K. "A Simplified Method of Determining the Average Slope of Land Surfaces," in *American Journal of Science*, 5th ser., xx (1930), pp. 184–194.

The Shapes of Alpine Valleys

With two exceptions the references are in English. They are of the general type. There is abundant material on the subject in French, German, and Italian.

Avebury, Sir John Lubbock, 1st Baron. *The Scenery of Switzerland*, 2d ed. London, 1896.

Davis, W. M. "The Sculpture of Mountains by Glaciers," in *Scottish Geographical Magazine*, xxii (1906), pp. 76–89. A classic.

Davis, W. M. *Geographical Essays*. Boston, 1909. Chap. xxiv, "Glacial Erosion in France, Switzerland, and Norway."

Davis, W. M. *Die erklärende Beschreibung der Landformen* (Leipzig, 1912), pp. 401–462, "Der Glaziale Zyklus."

Fenneman, N. M. "Some Anthropo-Geographic Effects of Glacial Erosion in the Alps," in *Journal of Geography*, vii (1907–08), pp. 169–172.

Gastaldi, B. "On the Effects of Glacier-Erosion in Alpine Valleys," in *Quarterly Journal of the Geological Society*, xxix (1873), pp. 396–401.

Gilbert, G. K. "Systematic Asymmetry of Crest Lines in the High Sierra of California," in *Journal of Geology*, xii (1904), pp. 579–588.

Hobbs, W. H. "The Cycle of Mountain Glaciation," in *Geographical Journal*, xxxv (1910), pp. 268–284.

Hobbs, W. H. "Studies of the Cycle of Glaciation," in *Journal of Geology*, xxix (1921), pp. 370–386.

Johnson, D. W. "Hanging Valleys of the Yosemite," in *Bulletin of the American Geographical Society*, xliii (1911), pp. 826–837, 890–903.

Johnson, G. R. *Peru from the Air*. New York, 1930. (American Geographical Society, Special Publication no. 12.)

Johnson, W. D. "The Profile of Maturity in Alpine Glacial Erosion," in *Journal of Geology*, xii (1904), pp. 569–578.

Johnson, W. D. "The Work of Glaciers in High Mountains," in *Science*, n. s., ix (1899), pp. 112–113. An abstract.

Matthes, F. E. *Geologic History of the Yosemite Valley*. Washington, 1930. Relative importance of glacial and stream erosion.

Mittelholzer, Walter. *Switzerland from the Air*, ed. by Otto Flückiger, trans. by A. W. P. Allan. Zurich, 1926,

Nussbaum, Fritz. *Die Täler der Schweizeralpen*. Bern, 1910. Included because of its general interest.

The Classification of Mountains

Bowman, Isaiah. *Forest Physiography*. New York, 1914.

Cleland, H. F. *Geology, Physical and Historical*. New York, 1916. Pp. 352–358.

Emerson, F. V. *Manual of Physical Geography.* New York, 1909. Pp. 113–358.

Mill, H. R., ed. *The International Geography,* 2d ed. New York, 1901.

Obst, Erich. "Terminologie und Klassifikation der Berge," in *Petermanns Mitteilungen,* lx, 1 (1914), pp. 301–310.

Partsch, Josef. *Central Europe.* London, 1903.

Peattie, Roderick. "A Geographic (Human-Use) Classification of Mountains," in *Journal of Geography,* xxxi (1932), pp. 261–264. Incorporated in substance in this book.

Pirsson, L. V. *Physical Geology,* 2d ed. New York, 1920. Chap. xv. Pirsson's work is issued by the publishers as the first part, or volume, of a two-volume set called *A Text-Book of Geology.*

Reclus, Élisée. *The Earth.* New York, 1871. Pp. 117–161.

Salisbury, R. D. *Physiography,* 3d ed. New York, 1919. Pp. 31–36, 377–380.

Suess, Eduard. *The Face of the Earth,* tr. by Hertha B. C. Sollas. Oxford, 1904–09. 4 vols.

Supan, Alexander. *Grundzüge der Physischen Erdkunde.* Leipzig, 1884; 7. Aufl., Berlin, 1927–30, 2 vols. Excellent morphogenetic classification.

Upham, Warren. "A Classification of Mountain Ranges According to their Structure, Origin, and Age," in *Appalachia,* vi (1891), pp. 191–207.

The Mountain Region

Blanchard, Raoul. "The Natural Regions of the French Alps," in *Geographical Review,* xi (1921), pp. 31–49.

Blanchard, Raoul. "Sur les noms des régions naturelles des Alpes françaises," in *Revue de géographie alpine,* xii (1924), pp. 455–462.

Coolidge, W. A. B. *The Alps in Nature and History.* New York, 1908.

Coolidge, W. A. B. Article "Alps" in *Encyclopaedia Britannica,* 11th and 12th eds.

Fenneman, N. M. *Physiography of the Western United States.* New York, 1931.

Freshfield, D. W. "The Division of the Alps into Regions," in *Geographical Journal,* lxxi (1928), pp. 37–42. Includes a review of the work of the Italian Commission.

Krebs, Norbert. *Länderkunde der Österreichischen Alpen.* 1913. Revised edition, *Die Ostalpen und das heutige Österreich.* Stuttgart, 1928. 2 vols.

Lyde, L. W. *The Continent of Europe,* 2d ed. London, 1924.

Martonne, Emmanuel de. "Les divisions naturelles des Alpes," in *Annales de géographie,* xxxiv (1925), pp. 113–132.

Martonne, Emmanuel de. "The Carpathians: Physiographic Features Controlling Human Geography," in *Geographical Review*, iii (1917), pp. 417–437.

Newbigin, Marion Isabel. *Southern Europe*. London, 1932.

Partsch, Josef. *Central Europe*. London, 1903.

Platt, J. I. Article "Alps" in *Encyclopaedia Britannica*, 14th ed.

Suess, Eduard. *The Face of the Earth*, tr. by Hertha B. C. Sollas. Oxford, 1904–09. 4 vols.

INDEX

INDEX

accessibility, 96, 130–131, 161, 181, 189, 203–205, 221–228.
actionometry, 12, 14.
adiabatic changes, 15–16, 18, 21–22.
adret, 78, 88, 95–96, 119, 188, 190; bibliography, 105; see insolation, sunlight.
adret, secondary, 90, 188.
agriculture, importance of type, 85, 87–88, 159 f.
alb, 129.
Albania, 147, 204.
Aletsch glacier, 48.
alm, 129.
alp, definition, 125–130; terms, 127–128; economy, 130–134.
Alp de Loma, 181.
alp huts, 93–94.
alps, physical factors, 127; economy, 130–134; bibliography, 148–151; ownership, 131–132, 167, 209, 228–229; see nomadism.
Alps, the, 5, 26, 73, 86–87, 114, 120, 181; sones in, 79; treeline, 113–114; seasons in, 228–232.
Alps, French, 13, 15, 16, 24–25, 40–41, 42–43, 64, 115, 136, 144–145, 159, 160–161, 176, 178.
altitude, 9, 11, 14–18, 28, 36, 85, 116, 155, 191–197, 225; bibliography, 32–34; see zones.
Andes, 50, 114.
Andorra, 134, 204, 206, 210; zones, 81; bibliography, 105–106; study field limits, 95–96; study relief, 165–169; social life, 232–235.
Appalachia, social study, 223–225.
Appalachian Mountaineers, bibliography, 235–236.
Apennines, 119.
Ariège, 188.
Arizona, 120.
Arosa, 181, 190.
atmosphere, absorbent qualities, 12, 15, 16.
avalanches, 48, 50, 56; track, 114; see snow slides.
Aures Massif, 222.

Austria, 93, 108, 113, 114, 153, 190, 204; soil temperatures, 29.

Bagnères-de-Bigorre, 29, 67.
balds, 110–111.
Balkans, transhumance, 146–148.
Barcelonnette, 25, 90.
barometer, 10.
Bavaria, 44.
beauty and health, 196.
Belledonne Range, 135, 184.
Bern, 208.
Bolivia, 179, 180, 181, 193.
Bora, 70–71.
boundaries, 205–209.
Bourdillon, 7.
Bourg-Saint-Maurice, 137.
Bronze Age, 119.

Carnic Alps, 94.
Carpathian Mountains, 19, 107, 114, 182.
carraïres, 145.
catastrophies, 49, 58–59, 159, 191, 216, 229; see avalanches, floods, snow slides, erosion.
Caucasus Mountains, 175.
Ceillac, 138.
Cerro de Pasco, 179–180, 191.
Chamonix, 27.
Champagny, 137.
Chandolin, 141, 181.
Chartreuse, 127, 135.
Chaudun, 186.
China, sacred peaks, 4.
Chinook wind, 76.
classification of mountains, bibliography, 247–248.
climate, general references on mountain, bibliography, 30–31.
climatic snow line, 45–50.
cloud pennants, 67–68.
cloud zones, 42.
clouds, 9, 65–66; bibliography, 77–78.
Colorado, growing season, 23–24; zones, 79.
Columbia, 19.
coma, 166.